Charles Winick, Professor in the Department of Sociology and Anthropology at the City College of the City University of New York, has taught at the University of Rochester, Columbia University, Massachusetts Institute of Technology, and the Postgraduate Center for Mental Health. He has been research director of the New York State Joint Legislative Commission on Narcotics and consultant to the United States Senate Subcommittee on Juvenile Delinquency and a wide range of agencies dealing with the impact of society on the individual.

Among the contemporary concerns which Dr. Winick explored in many previous publications are prostitution, work satisfaction, effects of mass media and group functioning. He is the author of *The Dictionary of Anthropology* (Ames: Littlefield, Adams, 1960) and the co-author of *For the Young Viewer* (New York: McGraw Hill, 1962) and *A Practicum of Group Psychotherapy* (New York: Harper & Row, 1963).

Charles Winick

THE new PEOPLE

desexualization
in american life

PEGASUS
new york

THE NEW PEOPLE

contents

preface

Archeologists are fond of saying that were it not for graves and garbage piles, buried under the ruins of successive societies, we might know relatively little about the character and lives of people in the past. Today, in our economy of abundance and condition of perpetual war, the litter of civilization seems to be more than sufficient for archeologists in years to come. We have produced enough garbage; it has even been transmuted into art and political rhetoric. Yet it is doubtful that the leftovers of our lives will tell enough. If we succeed in completing the nihilistic formula for self-destruction that has made it possible for the nightmares of Leonardo and St. John to come true, the radioactive garbage will be too hot to handle and the graves will be made of whole continents.

After World War II, the tide of human consciousness and its social expression began to move in a radically different direction in the United States. As a new generation grew up in the midst of this transformation, it was difficult for their parents to appreciate either the meaning or magnitude of the change. While we continued to display the relics of western tradition, we largely ignored the arrival of the New People, the troops of an invading army. Their advent went virtually unnoticed and they quietly took over while we were out fighting the cold war.

They set up camps and fought the battle of the cool war, which led to substantial changes in personality and social life. Many of the changes are not reflected in the palpable material objects of our society that would primarily concern the archeologist. The troop movements slipped by with the invisibility of gradual social change, under the cover of darkness which clouded what was to be later seen as a massive shift of human consciousness and its social expression.

Social change is almost invisible to those inside it. But the cumulative impact of the transformation of our lives is all too apparent in the 1960's. The New People have taken over; they are the authorities when it comes to setting the tone of our living together. When we recognize them at all, it is as figures from some elaborate entertainment which has little to do with sensible, everyday life. We hardly notice the invasion because it has been so widespread and successful.

Our infinitely manipulatable, no-deposit, no-return world reflects the compact which man has made with machines, particularly the machinery of his own destruction. It is such a truism, so much an everyday fact of life, that we have almost become comfortable in our plastic wilderness. The New People dress in clothes that make the Martians and the Space Maiden look conservative. They accept and participate in the destruction of obsolete concepts of identity, sexuality, and ways of living. We have failed to recognize them; they are, in fact, invisible. They are ourselves.

Archeologists of the future may regard a radical dislocation of sexual identity as the single most important event of our time. Ethology, the science concerned with animal behavior and interaction with environment, has repeatedly hinted in recent years that radical changes in sex roles may lead to extermination of whole species. This does not mean that we, the New People, will fail to survive or that we are unable to create a viable substitute for rejected life-styles. It does suggest that the new tone of life, a bitter, metallic existence, may simply not be worth the price of enduring it.

The change could be related to our downgrading of two radical but unrelated developments which entered the western world at about the same time: gunpowder and romantic love. Gunpowder was introduced to the west during the late medieval period, just about when the troubadours were creating what we have since come to know as romantic love, with its lack of fulfillment and idealization of the beloved beyond mere sensual love. The atom bomb has made gunpowder less significant, and many forces, in our day of disposable sex, make romantic love a less meaningful ideal. The bomb is a model of the new technology that is profoundly affecting every aspect of social and sex roles. The decline of romantic love reflects and reinforces other changes that are modifying expressions of the most basic difference in any society—the difference between its men and women.

The hostess at a dinner party attended by Albert Einstein, according to one of the many charming stories told about him, observed the scientist walking on her terrace and looking at the stars. She identified herself as an amateur astronomer and pointed upward: "Every night I come out here and study Venus with my telescope." Einstein followed her suggestion to look through the telescope and said, "Your hobby is very interesting. But, I believe, that planet is Jupiter." The woman was very impressed: "You certainly are brilliant to be able to tell the sex of a planet at such a great distance." It is increasingly difficult to tell the sex of many things, at almost any distance, in America today. As masculinity and femininity show less polarization and fewer differences, extremes of other kinds are becoming blurred into a neuter. This modification of the American way of life could be the most significant change of our time and be intimately related to our society's ability to survive.

The chapters which follow set forth some of the changes that have occurred in our life-style, many of which are usually attributed to a mass society's general leveling effect. Other shifts have been hailed as examples of an increase in American sophistication, or explained in terms of growing social and cultural complexity and a tendency to abstraction. This book examines the changes in a spirit of approximation that raises some questions about our possibilities for the future. To range over so many areas of American life is presumptuous, but we have an obligation to conjecture about them in order to help prepare ourselves for the choices that may present themselves.

CHARLES E. WINICK
New York, N.Y.

THE new PEOPLE

1

arts and the man

Practically every evening, a number of men and women wait outside Arthur, a discotheque on East Fifty-fourth Street in New York City. Most are attractive and well-dressed and acne is conspicuously absent from the faces of the younger adults. At regular intervals, the doorman permits some of the happy few to enter. Ginza, Ondine, L'Entredit, Shepheard's, and Cheetah are among the many other New York discotheques whose success led to an explosion of similar places across the country. A new environment has been created to suit the demands of an originally underground life-style which is now highly commercialized and available in a variety of bright, shiny packages. Each of the arts has been responding, in its own way, to the social forces that led to the multiple fission of discotheques.

Movers and Shakers

The new dances have been hailed as expressions of a new mood of more liberal and permissive sexuality; they also signal a revolution in the way we deal with the social and external environment. The dances are a gigantic

15

screen on which we can throw public projections of our private fantasies. The new freedom that is expressed by the dances calls for a new cast of characters. In the process of defining how we shall live together in years to come, we have accepted a radical alteration of sexual identity.

It is easier to see the larger patterns of meaning of the new developments in a "second-generation" discotheque like Cheetah, a true cathedral of pop culture where an almost total environment has been created: for the visitor who wants to get switched-on and become a true believer, Cheetah provides vestments (it has *boutiques* for men and women), instant food minus flourishes or gourmet distractions, and a visual feast, a psychedelic experience, by bombarding the dancers with films, abstract slides, and color patterns projected at random on walls, floor, ceiling, and dancers. In Andy Warhol's chillingly prophetic words, The Plastic Inevitable.

To paraphrase Yeats, these days it is difficult to tell the dancer from the dance. Our new dances are reasonably clear diagrams of new social patterns, new ways of relating self to others and the external environment. The discotheques are equalizers that attract a broad range of age and economic groups.

One reason for the great, recent success of pop culture is the speed with which rituals and artifacts have been taken out of the possession of the outsiders and priced at what the market will bear. The outsider culture serves an unanticipated function in providing our luxury and leisure market with new games and toys. Once they get into the mainstream, the outsider tastemakers move on to find new ways of affirming their alienation from the respectable world. The dances which they helped shape carry an invisible extra value for the consumer—a new, not terribly systematic style of living. While those who shop in the pop supermarket buy a fairly diluted version of this life-style, they may be accepting more values and attitudes than they suspect.

This is particularly true of the dances and their settings. Whether it's a small, exclusive place like L'Intrigue in Washington or a department store like Cheetah, the atmosphere encourages participation in the action. The twist and the frug have been supplanted by spinoff dances that also involve shaking the body rather than executing steps: Bird, Surf, Swim, Jerk, Bougalou, Popeye, Skate, Hitchhike, Monkey are some of the more formal variations. The partners do not touch but each shimmies around the axis of his own body. Lost in himself and in the music, the dancer shakes his pelvic area and moves his arms. He responds to his own sensations and largely ignores the partner. The dance offers all the motions of sex with a completely paradoxical lack of physical contact, in a charade of non-communication.

In the now quite conventional frug, the two partners face one another and engage in independent free-form vibrations without touching. One way of describing the frugger's movements is to compare them with those of a monkey who alternates masturbating with climbing an invisible tree. While one dancer is shaking and sweating it out, his partner may be in idling gear.

The non-contact aspect is even more obvious in the Itch, which stems from a Calypso tune. While doing a variation of twist or frug, one partner will pick up a "bug." He will touch the "bug" as "it" moves to various parts of his body. Once he finds "it," he can then throw "it" at his partner. She catches "it" and picks the "bug" off her body for perhaps two minutes, while the man continues to shake. She then throws "it" at somebody else. Everybody in the room ultimately gets the "bug," creating a perfect circle of non-communication and hostility.

So numerous are the variations on the twist and frug

that it is hopeless to attempt any systematic classification. The ideal progression is in the direction of improvisation and participation in an exhibitionistic happening. The mechanism for acceptance of these new rituals has been in high gear ever since the twist made its initial appearance in 1961 in a Philadelphia slum. After the first short period of outrage ("the animals have been let out of the cage"), celebrities waiting to twist were standing in line outside New York's Peppermint Lounge. Soon fruggers could be seen in the White House and the shakes moved into school lunchrooms and church socials. A few surly clergy-men, professionally aware of the importance of social ritu-als, thundered against the twist. They saw it as an obvious sexual symbol but what seemed to disturb other critics was something vaguely unnatural.

Havelock Ellis' beautiful metaphor of "the dance of life" reminds us that the dance once symbolized man-woman interaction, leading to the core of life and human society itself. But our new dances are openly anti-life, and symbolize a massive dislocation of sex roles. Rather than allowing for any definite leader and follower, as in the tra-ditional courtship type of dance, the new style calls for autistic, self-absorbed actors. The essentially protective, defensive attitude of the urban man or woman taking care of himself or herself first in a hard-edged, independent way is built right into the dance.[1]

Every ritual calls for an appropriate costume as well as setting. Both men and women in a discotheque are likely to be wearing an expression of blankness or glazed *insouciance* along with clothing that often suggests a new kind of human being. A man might be wearing black boots, red bell-bottomed slacks, a floppy flower-print shirt, and a white plastic tie. His partner could be modishly turned out in white boots, nubby silver-stippled white stockings, and a very short vinyl or aluminum foil dress. Her makeup could be a strange sort of harlequin mask—

white lipstick, gilded cheekbones, green eye-shadow, and sweeping false eyelashes. Both man and woman are likely to have collar-length hair. In some cases, the costume, say a pants suit, could easily do for both.

The action calls for their dancing *at* but seldom looking toward one another; each does a mirror-image series of variations which may be refined into an elaborate, delicate, and slow movement of arms and body in a pantomime of disinterested, autonomous motion. The dancers are cooled out to a condition that borders on a narcotic or psychedelic high and their similarly isolationist, sexless, and non-involved states are anything but coincidental.

The era of ballroom dancing, and the big bands that went with it, are irrevocably past. The popular dances faithfully mirrored courtship and social relationships in the case of the slow and sentimental dances of the 1930's and '40's. Just before the United States entered World War II, Tommy Dorsey's "Gettin' Sentimental over You," Margaret Whiting's "I've Got a Crush on You," Glenn Miller's "Moonlight Serenade," Artie Shaw's "Frenesi," and "Stardust" were favorites of the many people who enjoyed romantic dancing. At a party, the person changing records often played a fast, non-romantic tune when he noticed a friend dancing with a "dog." The stag line, a man's ability to cut in on a dancing couple, and his leading reinforced his masculinity. The woman's role as follower was uncontested, but a very popular girl could change partners often in the course of one evening and even one dance.

The discotheque sound, loud enough for the dancer to feel inside the music itself, is canned or recorded. Even though live groups have somewhat supplanted the earlier reliance on records, the sound is produced and amplified electronically in great measure and this, combined with a super-frenetic beat, reinforces the quasi-automatic quality of the music and dancing. Most discotheques avoid slow music, even as a means of breaking up every fourth or fifth set to make room for some fast conversation and break up the tension built up by the beat. Slow music is actually resented by dancers. One New York discotheque owner complained that "My customers frug during the slow set that I originally introduced to provide an opportunity to carry out the wounded."

The antiseptic, cold quality of the discotheque is reinforced by the bodies vibrating inside, the space age packages in which those bodies are wrapped, and the glass isolation rooms or raised platforms, usually several feet above the dance floor, in which a go-go girl vibrates to the music, without paying any attention to the audience. Here the exhibitionistic moment is at its highest peak—the dancer is on display and no interaction with the audience is allowed. The sign says, "Look but do not touch." The disc jockey may be shaking away in his own private universe, generally out of sight of the dance floor. While one can still find ballroom dancing and some large but aging dancehalls and ballrooms, the greater part of what remains probably exists in a closed-off, isolated universe of couples sitting in the gray light of a television set and listening to Lawrence Welk. Perhaps, in the privacy of the night, they dance wordlessly to the more decorous strains of their youth.

The change seems to have set in with the Latin dances; the rhumba was a choreographed coitus, danced to a surging rhythm with the pelvis of each partner jammed up against the other's. The partners would smile at each other, as if enjoying the afterglow of intercourse, with the woman circling the man as he engaged in a vertical pumping motion. There could be no doubt of who was who.

In the late 1940's, the angular mambo began to replace the curvaceous rhumba in this country, perhaps because it

was the first Latin dance in which sex roles were not reciprocal. The man is entirely self-stimulating in the mambo, with the woman practically an exhibitionistic stage
prop.[2] The man took over so much of the woman's role
that he danced with a handkerchief in his hand, in contrast to the rhumba in which a woman pulled a shawl
across her buttocks as though stimulating and warming
herself up for the man.

The handkerchief may not only have transvestite significance, but could also symbolically represent insulation
against the female genitals, a place to deposit semen from
masturbation, and the man's lack of interest in getting
into a sweat over sex. When the man launches a violent
kick at her genitals in the course of the dance, it is a kick
at the whole idea of sexual intercourse. The mambo's ferocity helped to pave the way for non-contact in later Latin dances, like La Bamba, in which the dancers do not
touch one another, start, or even finish together. Its self-
centered and auto-erotic aspects were a firm step away
from the romantic and sexual meanings of earlier Latin
dances.

Yet the big bands did not really start to fade away, the
ballroom had not been delivered into the hands of Lester
Lanin, until well into the 1950's. At the same time, the
Latin dances started to fade in popularity—with the
young adult population. Yesterday's teenie-boppers had
gone through jitterbugging and jive but finally found
their own music in rock-and-roll. The gestures of teen-age
revolt—and economic assertiveness—were not compatible
with the graceful swoops of ballroom dancing or the elegance of large ballrooms. When the rest of America began
to buy youth, ballroom dancing was only one of many
cultural casualties. While part of western Europe is engaged in a less intense quest for youth, romantic dancing
remains an important ingredient in courtship. A Rome

cafe owner explained why the new dances are not as popular in his country: "With us, dancing is always a means and not an end."[3]

Garcia Lorca said that he could sense the quality of a country by listening to its lullabies and tasting its candy. In the same way, the new dances have significance as a measure of the quality of our present national experience. They have different meanings for teen-agers and adults. The teen-ager can express his loneliness and non-relatedness. His energy and ambivalence about the opposite sex find an outlet in the new styles. The adult can identify with young people and express sex in a narcissistic and completely uninvolving way. For both old and young, hip-swinging is likely to be devoid of real erotic content and is exhibitionistic rather than social, an open admission of profound difficulties in relating to others. When Harold Clurman complained that dancers no longer touched each other, a discotheque owner gently explained, "Harold, contact went out with the 1950's."[4]

While the music sometimes blares out a sensual rhythm, the dancers' auto-erotic movements represent only the secondhand trappings of sexual intercourse. Each dancer achieves satisfaction by himself or herself and one evening is enough to exhaust the dancer. These do-it-yourself qualities have made the dances disappointing for some men. A handsome New York bachelor ruefully observed, "I used to go to the discotheques late at night, hoping to find a girl who had become so excited and worked up that I could snake her away to my place. I expected to watch the girls expose themselves on the dance floor and pick up one who had no inhibitions. But all those I've seen, dance to rock-and-roll till they're ready to drop, like after a workout at a gym. The dancing itself provides enough satisfaction so that they are completely uninterested in me." An older man who had similar sad experiences concluded that "hip movements no longer mean what they did once. Looking at them gives me a 1947 erection, but this is 1967. The girls seem to believe that intercourse may be good but outercourse is a lot better."

The original force of "rock-and-roll" meant sexual entrance and movement.[5] Some favorites contain pleas to "rock around the clock" or "rock me all night" because "you rock me so right." The teen-agers who created the steps seem to be saying to society, "You have surrounded me with sex but I'm not ready for it, so I shall withdraw to an earlier level of satisfaction and commune with myself on the dance floor." In a way, it is a kind of revenge on the parents who so happily dance the new non-steps and are thus forced to engage in the masturbation that they condemn in their children.

Mutual exhibitionism seems to have replaced the contact with the opposite sex that was central to the older dances. Gogi Tchitchinadze, a veteran New York restaurateur, has explained one appeal of the new approach. "It is not dancing, of course. But it is easy to see why it is popular. For the first time the woman is *free!* It has always been, 'Yes, she is a good dancer; she follows well!' What a bore for her! Now she doesn't have to follow the man any more. To hell with that clumsy pest!"[6] One New York woman explained: "I like the frug because I do an individual step and keep men at arm's length. There's no involvement, no touching the man you're dancing with. . . ."

In television shows devoted to teen-age dancing, the dancers' faces are often hard and zombie-like, with little of the joy that music can bring. Such responses are striking because music traditionally enables people to express themselves more directly than is possible in words.[7]

One positive feature of the new dances, in addition to providing self-expression, could be their ability to give alienated people as much contact with a partner as they can stand and a chance to release inner turmoil in a group atmosphere. The dancer doesn't have to talk because the noise level is so high. One veteran drummer sighed, "In the old days, the band would climax the evening with one foot-stomping number. Now, we've got those numbers all night long." Young people no longer worry about learning elaborate steps or need Arthur Murray to teach them dancing in a hurry because their free-form vibrating and shaking are direct expressions of the elaborate life-style that they have already acquired.

Beyond "June-Moon" to "Hound Dog" and "Boots"

The decline of leading and following in the dance is a symptom of romantic love's inability to remain a real choice in our time. Music for dancing can reflect changes so sensitively because its sexual content is usually latent. But the nature of the sexuality in today's popular music hardly requires a Tolstoy to identify it. One great change in popular music has been an increase in women who sing like men and men who sing like women. A growing interest in female singers has paralleled a decline in men, and romantic love is less likely to be a theme of lyrics.

A review of a record by singer Donnie Elbert in *Cash Box* saw a bright future for Miss Elbert ("The gal is a swinging singer . . .").[8] There was considerable chuckling when Donnie Elbert's managers identified "the gal" as a man. Many listeners to the Everly Brothers have assumed them to be women. The husky, smoky voice of Nina Simone has misled many an audience member into thinking that it belonged to a man. Both the Everlys and Miss Simone are very accomplished and gifted performers, but the phenomenon that they represent has not previously been so widespread. The music industry is ignoring the advice of its own Johnny Mercer not to "mess with Mister In-Between."

It was rare for a male vocal group of the 1930's to include a relatively high voice, like Bill Kenny in the Ink Spots, but most male rock-and-roll groups have at least one such member. The Four Seasons boast more hit records than any other group since the beginning of rock-and-roll, and they *all* sing falsetto. Little Anthony and the Imperials are just one of dozens of other high-pitched male quartets that are very successful.

The male falsetto appeals on several levels of musical taste, judging from its success in classical music during the last decade. Russell Oberlin and Alfred Deller, the two most distinguished counter-tenors, are essentially classical male sopranos who sing the sixteenth- and seventeenth-century baroque compositions that once required castrati. The Bach and Purcell pieces that are now sung by the vibratoless high voices of counter-tenors were previously performed by mezzo-sopranos.

During the last fifteen years, women have largely replaced the male pop singers of earlier decades. The leading singers of the 1920's, whose reputations soared with the development of radio, were Gene Austin, Rudy Vallee, and Whispering Jack Smith. During the next decade, Will Osborne, Russ Colombo, and Bing Crosby made the crooner a national hero.

The enormous public response to Frank Sinatra's appoggiaturas began at just about the time that Crosby's appeal was beginning to fade. Billy Eckstine, Frankie Laine, Dick Haymes, Nat "King" Cole, Tony Martin, and Vaughn Monroe dominated record sales in the 1940's. Johnnie Ray and Tony Bennett, who figured prominently on record sales charts of the 1950's, are practically elder statesmen.

The roistering sexuality of male singers once used to excite audiences, but more recently they have turned to soft, bland, relaxed performers (e.g., Perry Como, Johnny Mathis, and Andy Williams).[9] Pat Boone, who has twelve gold records and whose voice's nap is so reminiscent of the

white buck shoes that he still wears, won some unanticipated publicity when he refused to kiss leading lady Shirley
Jones in the movie *April Love,* on the ground that his religion forbade physical contact with anyone other than his
wife. Such singers share a pleasant and respectable style
that fails to communicate masculine excitement. Although Roy Orbison's lyrics are often sexy, his near-falsetto
voice is incongruous with their content. Dean Martin's
heavy-lidded singing style is likely to suggest the soporific
effects of his widely publicized heavy drinking. Paul Anka
and other young singers have a choir-boy quality.

Television's ability to permit an audience to see as well
as hear has helped to increase the popularity of women
singers, who have usually dominated men in media where
they can be seen. The girls from ten to fifteen who are the
most active record buyers began turning away from men
singers and buying records by Annette Funicello, Brenda
Lee, Peggy March, and other teen-agers in the 1950's. The
success possible for a teen favorite can be seen in the forty
million Connie Francis records that were sold in eight years.
Just as she replaced Joni James as the teen queen, Miss
Francis has been supplanted by younger performers. The
thin voice of Mary Wells in rhythm and blues, Dionne War-
wick's sophisticated rock, Janis Ian's sensitive lyrics, Skeeter
Davis' Nashville sound, Lesley Gore's little-girl quality,
"soul queen" Etta James, Bobbie Gentry's Mississippi colors,
Aretha Franklin's "down home" rhythm, the lyricism of Pe-
tula Clark, and the folk-popular style of Gale Garnett have
wildly enthusiastic fans. The Supremes draw standing-
room crowds everywhere and are currently the most successful rock-and-roll group.

A press agent for many teen performers has confided one
of their secrets: "It's Motivation and Identification. You
notice something about the big teen-age girl idols? Most
of them are *ugly*. Ugly-duckling teen-age identification." [10]
"Motivation and Identification" on another level are largely

responsible for the enthusiasm of older fans for Edie Adams, Rosemary Clooney, Eydie Gorme, Lena Horne, Julie London, Giselle MacKenzie, Patti Page, Jo Stafford, Della Reese, Dinah Shore, Kate Smith, and Kay Starr. In jazz, Ella Fitzgerald is still the name of the game, although June Christy, Marilyn Maye, Carmen McRae, Chris Connor, Peggy Lee, Anita O'Day, and Sarah Vaughn command intensely loyal followings and Ethel Ennis is a younger version of Miss Fitzgerald. Nancy Wilson has created her own amalgam of pop and jazz and Ruth Brown and La Vern Baker have succeeded in gaining acceptance for material that might be regarded as too raunchy if sung by men.

The acceptance of such content by record buyers is not surprising because of the pop audience's intense involvement with its performers, most clearly seen in the case of the Beatles. The Beatlemania that swept the country resulted from a combination of the singers' sparse falsetto voices and charming boyishness, coupled with the sexual ambiguity of their wet-mop, Raggedy Andy hair, pretty clothes, and high heels. The Liverpudlians' uncertain sexuality appealed to many American girls between seven and twelve, who could respond to the singers' innocence with relief because our culture has so heavily sexualized these years. Although the Beatles later developed an older and more sophisticated following for their inventive chords and harmonies, daring use of a sitar, and psychedelic lyrics and sound, much of the group's astonishing original impact can probably be traced most directly to its members' sexual ambiguity.

Today's audiences seem far less interested than previous generations in the direct expression of erotic material by men but can accept it in neuters and women. Somewhat similar reasons help to explain the unique status of Elvis Presley, the only superstar among popular singers. Although a bit of a "fancy man," Presley is white and his sensuality has an unreal and non-threatening quality. Among the most brilliant performers of the music that Presley has made popular are Bo Diddley and Ray Charles. American folklore and fantasies about the greater sexuality of the Negro are so deeply rooted that the surging masculinity represented by Diddley and Charles can be troubling, but audiences can accept Presley because he is white. James Brown, who combines the most spectacular features of Presley and Liberace, might be the most successful entertainer in America—if he were white. The orgiastic element in his performances is less acceptable because it taps the stereotypical white fear of Negro sexuality.

The British groups (Beatles, Rolling Stones, Animals, Herman and the Hermits, Chad and Jeremy) that have been most successful in America during the last few years originally combined genderless voice and appearance with a pleasant and non-threatening version of the blues style of a Ray Charles and Memphis Slim. The Merseyites, who once appeared to be copying every phrase and signature of Charles except his grunts, have been infinitely more successful than their mentor. It is ironic that some of the most successful recent white American groups (Paul Revere and the Raiders, Youngbloods, Rascals, Jefferson Airplane) have adapted the British groups' secondhand blues sound rather than go directly to Charles for inspiration.

An occasional success, e.g., the Lovin' Spoonful's "You and Me and the Rain on the Roof," is reminiscent of the romantic melody and lyrics of earlier decades. But the rock-and-roll period has seen the virtual disappearance of idealized romantic love as a guiding principle.[11] "You Were Meant for Me," "My Ideal," "Looking at the World through Rose-Colored Glasses," and "The Little White House at the End of Honeymoon Lane" are typical of the dreamy earlier lyrics, which deal with love and domesticity. Many earlier song writers and their audiences had their roots in a European culture that tended to sentimentalize love. Even Cole Porter and Lorenz Hart, the most sophisticated earlier lyricists, had an upbeat if bittersweet attitude toward romance.

The rock-and-roll music that has largely replaced romantic ballads stresses problems and does not romanticize the love partner. Rock-and-roll represents an amalgam of the country and western style with rhythm and blues, two ethnic specialty styles that were once far less important than the standard 32-bar Tin Pan Alley ballad. Popular for longer than any single style in the history of American popular music, rock-and-roll accounted for over 90 percent of the 130,000,000 single records sold last year.

The frozen faces of discotheque dancers reflect the meanings of many lyrics, which consist of twenty-five or thirty words repeated over and over again. In contrast, the earlier ballads told a story and had a beginning, middle, and an end. Earlier audiences enjoyed humming, singing, and whistling along with the earlier music but such responses are far less likely to the essentially non-verbal and non-melodic content of much rock-and-roll. "June-moon" rhymes have often been replaced by blunt and sometimes bizarre lyrics that may bristle with aggressiveness. One of the most successful phonograph records ever released was "Hound Dog," a paean of hostility and a representative early rock-and-roll number with traditional chord progressions. The Marquis de Sade would have been thrilled by "Boots," a more recent favorite. Nancy Sinatra is sure of a wild surge of applause when she grinds her heels into the stage as she triumphantly exults that her boots will "walk over you."

A symbol of the mood of many young people was suggested in a scene from the film *Blackboard Jungle* (1956). A class of high-school students destroys the record collection of a teacher who had planned to play romantic swing records by Harry James to his class. "Rock Around the

Clock" was played over the film's title and credits and inspired many youngsters to rip up the seats of many a movie house and dance in its aisles.

One reason for the great popularity of rock lyrics with young people is that they can offend and irritate parents, who may also regard the names of some performing groups as a put-on and an affront (e.g., the Fugs, Max Weber and the Charismatics, the Grateful Dead). It is noteworthy that the Beatles became far less popular with young people after they were well received by adults and adopted as a touchstone by the older intelligentsia who praised "Strawberry Fields" as the anthem for the psychedelic generation. Rock-and-roll reinforces the closed nature of the teen society, so that a lonely teen-ager can play the music on his radio and advertise his interest in finding others as lonely as he is. The rhythm of much rock-and-roll mocks the romantic music of the past, while permitting the teen-ager to indulge the sex which society seems to be pushing on him. Many young performers make one kind of response by trying to imitate the spirit of Ray Charles' "I Got a Woman," a major teen-age favorite that contains a very clear but completely narcissistic representation of sexual intercourse. Other performers turn away from such frank sexuality into coolness and still others move into an all-embracing pantheism.

The great success of rock-and-roll has broadened the base of American popular music, given it an unexpectedly eclectic and international quality, and exposed audiences to instruments and styles from other settings. Because so many young people are writing, performing, and even manufacturing records, popular music has become the first mass medium to be dominated by youth. It is making a contribution to better understanding between Negro and white and between rural and urban America. Rock-and-roll has also helped new recording companies, notably Detroit's Motown, to compete with the few New York giants. But its early anti-romanticism indelibly colored the attitudes that many young people have toward the opposite sex, and the popular music that once conveyed the magic and euphoria of love now often communicates stridency and non-relational sex. To paraphrase Kenneth Burke's description of poetry as equipment for living, we could say that much rock-and-roll provided equipment for non-loving.

One Million Guitars

The rock-and-roll beat has, since 1965, been a major component of folk music in the form of folk rock. The guitar is acquiring new followers more rapidly than the piano and the 1.6 million guitars sold annually represent about half the musical instruments purchased in the United States. Folk music's tremendous success among young people is all the more remarkable because of the resounding failure of left-wing groups who used it in the 1930's to attract converts. The city youngsters whose parents ignored the earlier attempt to promote folk music when it employed the soft and mellow sound of the acoustic guitar represent its most enthusiastic audiences now that the electric guitar's hard sound conveys the details of urban life in folk rock.

There are several reasons for the music's new popularity. It resembles rock-and-roll in providing the reassurance of protest as well as membership in an in-group. It gives the security of a commitment while often stressing goals that are as unexceptionable as civil rights and opposition to nuclear war. What appears to make folk music seem daring may represent a non-threatening participation and a safe affirmation.

Youthful new audiences for the millennial themes of

folk music began to emerge during the period of questing that succeeded the McCarthy era and Korean war and as a logical outcome of the interest in ethnic music generated by the calypso revival of the early 1950's. The original and spectacular success of the Kingston Trio and Joan Baez was based on non-ego-involving traditional materials and the decline in folk's popularity began at the same time as the attempt to use song as a weapon and moral force in militant civil-rights activities. In the last few years, themes of "black rain" were replaced by tales of what "they" are doing to "us."

Many students with little money to spend can entertain each other with folk music, and a youngster who learns three chords can play a hundred songs on a guitar. Another reason for young people's interest in folk is its reflection of the female dominance and non-romance of other popular music. Parents can accept the hootenanny format for a child's party because they feel the music is unlikely to foster the sexual activity that popular legend once associated with jazz parties. Another reason for the emergence of many folk fans is the ease with which they can graduate from the insistent beat of rock-and-roll to the electrically amplified rhythms of folk rock. The content of both is often less important than the repetition and action of the singing itself.

Some folk rock lyrics are anti-ideological, like P. F. Sloan's "Eve of Destruction." Others are oblique folk songs of the absurd that capture the generation gap and the bizarre qualities of contemporary life. There are breathtakingly poetic folk lyrics that evaluate the quality of American life with an almost religious fervor. One recent appeal of folk music appears to be its celebration of the sometimes mystical experience that stems from the use of marijuana, LSD, and other drugs ("Eight Miles High," "Rainy Day Women #12 and 35," "Norwegian Wood," "Get Off My Cloud," "Puff the Magic Dragon," "Paint It

Black," "Mother's Little Helper," "5D," "Mr. Tambou-
rine Man"). One best-selling record "blesses . . . pot-sellers
. . . illusion dwellers" and another urges that ". . . everybody *must* get stoned!" The success of such songs suggests
that a good many young folk fans are turning into themselves in what has been hailed as "a positive withdrawal,
a creative apathy."[12]

Some of the most celebrated lyrics that appear to deal
with drugs were written by Bob Dylan, the most successful male folk singer before he sparked folk rock in 1964.
His subsequent rock-and-roll style has most recently become musical black humor and surrealism. Dylan's
"Blowin' in the Wind" probably owes some of its vast appeal to the underlying vagueness of its buckshot lyrics,
which reflect what so many sensitive young people feel
about their world. Dylan originally became the crown
prince of folk because he combined spit-without-polish, an
ambisexual appearance, and social protest in the Woody
Guthrie tradition.

In the last few years, folk music has placed less emphasis on protest themes and become reinvolved with the gritty personal problems that were so important in earlier folk
music: pregnancy before marriage ("Careless Love"), the
departure of a lover ("Good Mornin' Blues"), and reluctance to marry ("Troubled in Mind"). The novelty of
folk's protest themes helped to open the sluices of response
in the early 1960's and made it easier for many young
people to navigate the torrent of musical social comment
that followed.

The depersonalized themes of social protest were ideally
suited for performers whose impersonal style was in sharp
contrast to the sex appeal of their predecessors. Not too
many years ago, folk singers did not hesitate to convey the
sex latent in many songs. The very popular team of Libby
Holman and Josh White exuded sensuousness along with
the mournful happy sound of their urban blues. Miss Hol-

man would sit on a stool, the back of her black crepe, extra-long skirt draped discreetly but interestingly around her head. White's bell-like diction left no doubt about the connotations of "Jelly, Jelly." Poised on a stool, a lit cigarette behind his ear, shirt open at the throat, White conveyed an unmistakable intimacy. Recent folk singers tend to perform in a middle range and are extravagantly praised for being unglamorous, pure, and non–show biz. Boots, blue jeans, and work shirt are standard for men performers.

Joan Baez, who was probably the single performer most responsible for the folk boom and whose praise of Dylan contributed to his reputation, provided a model for other women singers by wearing a sweater and skirt and avoiding makeup. She wears her long hair straight down rather than curled or "done" and is an anti-entertainer whose lack of the usual signs of femininity is hailed as a reinforcement of genuineness and artistic integrity.

Audience enthusiasm for the asexual helped make Peter, Paul, and Mary the single most successful folk group. Mary often stands between Peter and Paul and provides a visual obbligato by shaking her hips in a frug-like motion while the men play their guitars. The group conveys asexual and role-reversed sex from the time they walk onto the stage hand in hand. The trio's thin, tight sound helps to reassure audiences about any sexual connotation of Mary's hip swinging and other mannerisms and the men's identical beards. The beards are trimmed so carefully that, like Mary's helmet-like hair, they look unreal.

The antiseptic quality of Peter, Paul, and Mary differs radically from the warmth of the Weavers and other early mixed groups. Just as new to folk music is its current leadership by women, because men dominated the field up to the 1950's. Cisco Houston's cowboy songs were famous, John Jacob Niles was dean of collector-arrangers, and Richard Dyer-Bennet the leading classicist. The talking blues had been revived by Woody Guthrie, who became "a national possession, like Yellowstone." Josh White's night club and concert appearances attracted new audiences for folk music, and Burl Ives' amiable style pleased two generations. Big Bill Broonzy and Blind Lemon Jefferson helped continue the blues tradition and Leadbelly influenced every phase of folk music.

Susan Reed was the only woman whose popularity before the current folk revival even approached the leading men folk singers. Miss Reed was a charming and musically interesting performer, both feminine and womanly, who communicated warmth and interest in her audiences. In the last few years, Marie Knight, Sister Rosetta Tharpe, Jean Ritchie, Mahalia Jackson, Judy Collins, Peggy Seeger, Buffy Saint-Marie, and Cynthia Gooding have become dominant figures. Odetta and Carolyn Hester have a vocal and subject matter range that is greater than that of any man's.

The changes in folk are similar to the shifts in other popular music and have provided a responsive form of expression for many creative young people. It permits the easy communication of a wide range of feelings, attitudes, and ideas. Sometimes the lyrics directly voice the uncertain sexuality of some of its enthusiasts, and their problems of identity:

> I look like Joan Baez
> I look like Bobby Dylan
> I look like Jesus Christ
> I look like me—maybe.[13]

Pas d'Elégance

The term "choreographer" is only about three decades old. Its relative novelty reminds us how many musicals have followed Rodgers and Hart's *On Your Toes* in integrating ballet into their action. As ballet has become more popular, it has joined the other forms of theatrical dancing in reflecting the changes that have characterized other performing arts. Exhibition, tap, ballet, and modern dance have either become more neuter or declined in lyrical grace.

Angularity has become a major element in exhibition and tap dancing. Fred Astaire's light-boned, long-muscled, and slender physique and curved and asymmetrical movements contributed to his extraordinary elegance and graceful lyricism. In the quarter-century since Astaire's great triumphs, Gene Kelly has been the most successful movie dancer, although his angular and symmetrical movements reflect difficulties in dancing with the torso. Kelly's stockiness and short-muscled body build minimize the potential for fluidity and he gives the impression of moving only his arms and legs and often dances what appears to be a sailor's horn-pipe. Peter Gennaro and other popular television choreographers resemble Kelly in using symmetrical movements that lack lyrical grace and minimize the torso.

A similar metamorphosis has befallen ballet, formerly the quintessence of the romantic, graceful, and delicate. Nijinsky helped to point the way with "Petrouchka," traditionally a pretty puppet part until he infused it with the concept of the people of Russia as puppets. Nijinsky rebelled against classicism with strong and primitive angular movements, daring to dance barefoot and hold and move his arms in a square instead of the traditional circle. Nijinsky's performances of "L'Après-midi d'un Faune" and "Le Sacre du Printemps" were startling enough to provoke riots.

Ballet's revolution against romanticism and delicacy has continued in the half-century since Nijinsky, and American ballet has moved much further away from the graceful in the works of George Balanchine. The large Ford Foundation grant to Mr. Balanchine has, in effect, stated that his technique and style are so superior that they should be developed to the virtual exclusion of other schools of ballet. Although Balanchine is a great and inventive craftsman who has been recognized as a genius in his own lifetime, and in spite of the dazzling variety of his style and range in recent years, he has substantially reinforced the trend away from the graceful and romantic. Much of Balanchine's work is staccato, angular, and lean, often closer to modern dance than ballet in its abandonment of plot and pantomime. Even his costumes and sets may be simple and stark.

"Agon," "Episodes," and "Movements for Piano and Orchestra" are abstract ballets so lacking in feeling and romance that they may not really be ballets in the traditional sense. Their lean complexity and formal architectonics are more likely to provide audiences with a rational exercise than an emotional response. As long ago as 1928, in "Apollo," Balanchine had created the distinctive bare style that is more likely to be remembered as his distinctive contribution than the poetic mood and lovely lyricism of "Liebeslieder Walzer" or the elaborately staged and costumed dramatic pageantry of "Don Quixote."

He has recently used much smaller movements and developed a semi-acrobatic style that involves an emphasis on bursts of pure physical energy. Such explosions, initially so exciting, have eliminated much grace from ballet.[14] Where is the extraordinary and feathery lightness of Markova, the feminine softness of Seymour? Balanchine's approach often negates the difference between the man's leaps and the lighter, faster movements of the woman that are built into ballet and contributed to the charm of the contrast between male and female in grand adagio dancing. Balanchine's abrupt changes lead to more movement per minute than was used in traditional ballet and may be perfect for television, but look robotized on the stage.

The tendency toward the neuter is enhanced by a blur-ring of differences between the training and appearance of men and women ballet dancers. Each sex used to have separate classes and practice, with men concentrating on learning leaps and similar movements, while women worked on steps involving light, quick footwork and lyri-cal movements. In the last two decades, both sexes in-creasingly tend to train together and learn similar posi-tions and steps, with the single exception that a man does not need to learn point technique. They also tend to look alike, as women wear the tutu less and often wear the man's leotard.

Such changes are pointing toward a time when the dancer's sex will be irrelevant. Rudolf Nureyev, who has been hailed by some people as the most exciting ballet star since Nijinsky, has predicted that "the vocabulary of the dance will expand and increase. . . . I think that in the future there will be no importance given to who is man or woman. There will just be the dance, and the sex of the dancer will be just an added extra color."[15] One reason for Nureyev's extraordinary appeal to American audiences could be his ability to reflect the crossing of sex lines that he predicts for the future.

In the first act of "Swan Lake," Nureyev dances an extensive sequence of very feminine slow turns and ara-besques that were not included in the former Royal Ballet version. In other roles, he dances with extreme self-indulgence. This balletic Beatle was not the best dancer of the Russian company from which he came, and it is pos-sible that unisexuality contributed as much to his appeal as the glamor of his defection from Russia. Nureyev's unisexu-ality is probably even more attractive to American audiences than the Oedipal element in his performance of romantic roles opposite Margot Fonteyn, who is a much older woman.

The creators of modern ballet feel that in times like

ours, lovely gestures are not enough. They have changed the content and very meaning of ballet. Some anticipation of the changes could be seen in Degas' many paintings of ballet dancers, slumped and weary, incessantly fatigued, stripped of grace. His dancers could look unglamorous in backstage or rehearsal situations. But on stage, ever since the early nineteenth century when women began to dance on the points of their toes, ballet was the most romantic and fragile of the arts—up to fairly recently.

The revolution in ballet sex roles can be inferred from the opening night riot at "Le Sacre du Printemps," in contrast to extended and respectful applause at the premiere of the same composer's "The Cage," on June 10, 1951, by Balanchine's New York City Ballet. The woman Novice, in this enactment by Jerome Robbins of the courtship of spiders, stabs the first Intruder male with the point of one foot. After piercing him in the chest, she kicks him to one side. The second male, or Suitor, makes love to the Novice, but immediately thereafter she drives her talons into his heart. She straddles the Suitor, grips his head between her knees, and ultimately cracks it. The curtain goes down after the Queen and the Novice do a last triumphant pas de deux. Their final dance marked their pleasure at the death of the two men. It also marked the death of romantic masculine and feminine roles in ballet.

The flattening of sex differences has also left its mark on modern dance, which shares with jazz the distinction of being a unique American contribution to the arts. Merce Cunningham and other modern dancers work on so abstract a level that the dancer's sex is almost completely irrelevant. Now that the abstract is so important that much modern dance can be performed by dancers of either sex, it is only a question of time before women start lifting men.

Young dancers are like young artists in any field and

tend to rebel against established performers. In modern
dance, the most established personality is Martha Graham, who stresses theme and story. Many young dancers
therefore move away from Graham by going toward the
abstract, although their inexperience frequently leads
them to abstract movements no matter what the subject
or approach. A novice might think that his movements
express a theme, although they are really abstract. The
importance of the abstract could be seen in the premiere
program of our first modern dance repertory, the American Dance Theatre, at Lincoln Center in November,
1964. Three of the four works performed were abstract,
and only the 1946 Doris Humphrey "Lament for Ignacio
Sanchez Mejias" contained story content.

"Hot" to "Cool"
and the "New Thing"

Louis Armstrong's strong, full tone and ability to wrap
a melody in a warm overcoat of sound inspired a generation of musicians and attracted a large public. It is a
paradigm of what has happened to jazz that Armstrong's
directness, bark, and deep masculinity have been largely
supplanted by Miles Davis' veiled dry-ice style, often hollow and lacking a center. Davis' sub-tone manner and use
of a mute to cut down volume have been copied by many
trumpeters since his famous 1949–1950 chamber jazz
records.

The other wind instruments have also developed a
sparse and arhythmic sound. Round and mellow, the tone
of Jack Teagarden's slide trombone and his loose-jointed
power provided an ideal counterpoint for Armstrong. But
since the 1950's, the trombone's intrinsically deep sound
has contributed to its declining popularity. The instru-

ment's undisputed current king is J. J. Johnson, who achieves a classical sound that is cold, flat, and smooth.

Unmistakably creamy and plump, Coleman Hawkins' tone would curl sinuously into a room and was *the* tenor saxophone for over two decades. Lester Young, the great poet of jazz, moved away from Hawkins' big tone to a more laconic one, frequently built around a series of evenly placed eighth notes played legato. The Lesterian mode built a bridge to today's cerebral cool tenorists and the delicate, fragile tone of alto saxophonist Paul Desmond and the light, darting style of Gerry Mulligan on baritone saxophone.

When Benny Goodman was King of Swing, the clarinet had undisputed importance. Not only has it declined in significance, but the tone of a Buddy De Franco or Jimmy Giuffre is much thinner and is not as warm as Goodman's tawny feeling, drive, and liquid swooping line. Even today's thin clarinet sound seems too strong for current audiences and it has been partially replaced by the flute's small tone.

The powerful two- and four-bar beat of early jazz has become a historical memory, along with the percussive banjo, rhythm guitar, and stride piano that created the beat. Today's most influential pianists are Thelonious Monk, who has a laconic style, and Bill Evans, who plays ideas rather than rhythm and has a Debussy-esque touch. It is only a short note from their sparse style to total abandonment of the piano by Gerry Mulligan and Ornette Coleman.

Fans used to tap their feet to the steady beat provided by famous drummers Baby Dodds and Jo Jones but their driving pattern has been replaced by the subtleties of Elvin Jones and the polite and restrained brushwork of a Chico Hamilton. Contemporary melodic ideas are less likely to need the 1–2–3–4 rhythm that was once provided by the traditional walking bass. Small wonder that the abbreviated rhythm section of today is unlikely to provide rolling momentum for a jazz band.

Some Reasons and Reactions

The change from strong to soft, heavy to thin, was part of the shift from hot to cool. Although "jazz" derives from the Gullah word for sex, it has lost much of its early gonadic quality. Jazz musicians once worked in New Orleans brothels, where their music was expected to warm up patrons for sex. Louis Armstrong's classic "Mahogany Hall Stomp" derives its title from a well-known New Orleans whorehouse and pianist Tony Jackson's most famous number was "I've Got Elgin Movements in My Hips with Twenty Years' Guarantee."

Jazz musicians, who worked without amplification on riverboats, at carnivals and tent shows, and in marching bands, had to play with tremendous volume. Nightclubs often required their jazz musicians to play loud enough to be heard by passersby. In order to come to the attention of people who were outside his New Orleans club, the volume of Buddy Bolden's trumpet was so great that he was said to be "calling his children back home." Another reason for strong rhythm and full sound in early jazz was the need of bands to make themselves heard above noisy audiences' conversation and the shuffle of dancing feet. Precool jazz represented a form of entertainment but in the last twenty years, jazz has become accepted as a serious art form that is presented to attentive concert audiences.

One musical reason for the shift from heavy to light sound was the great popularity in the late 1930's of the Schillinger music analysis system, which was used in composing and arranging. The famous up-tempo ending of Glenn Miller's "In the Mood" was typical of the many hits developed by the Schillinger method, which eased the way for chromaticism in jazz and helped arrangers to learn how one chord could go to another without necessarily following the cycle of fifths. Schillinger helped to modify traditional harmonic patterns and acted as a transition from the disciplined fire of a Jimmy Lunceford and the tempestuousness of a Count Basie to the crisper, cool music of the next decade.

Other technical changes in the 1930's contributed to a more subdued sound. Raymond Scott's records achieved great success with mixing procedures that balanced the sound of instruments playing together. Other advances in recording techniques made it easier for bands and musicians to play softly.

A cause as well as result of the change is that instrumentalists now use less vibrato than their predecessors. The lower a sound, the more vibrato it can take, so that the deep tones of the earlier instruments were able to give much vibrato. Charlie Parker on the alto saxophone, Davis on the trumpet, and Johnson on the trombone have a vibratoless hard sound with little edge or overtone and sacrifice vibrato timbre for pure straight tones.

One reason for the loss of warm vocalized vibrato was the scorn of many jazz artists of the 1940's for the "Mickey Mouse" or "ricky tick" sound of the very vibratory arrangements of Guy Lombardo or Jan Garber. More recently, the decline of romantic tunes has led to fast, chopped-up melodies that are not very amenable to vibrato. Also, younger musicians entering jazz tend to have more training than their predecessors and are less likely to constrict the throat and squeeze air in a manner that leads to vibrato.

Similar considerations also apply to vocalists. To compare the vibrato of Louis Armstrong's "Do You Know What It Means to Miss New Orleans?" with almost any

popular current vocalist is to hear the difference. Billie Holiday, Lee Wiley, and even small-voiced Mildred Bailey
sang with exquisite vibrato, but most contemporary vocalists have minimal vibrato.

One unplanned effect of the civil-rights movement has
been to make many younger Negro musicians contemptuous of pre-World War II jazz, because they feel
that the heavy rhythms of early jazz are as much a form
of Uncle Tom as teeth-flashing smiles and visual comedy.
Strong vibrato, a fat tone, heavy volume, loud drumming,
and the Dixieland style have become symbols of the Negro's loss of dignity and inferior status. A counter-movement
of the last ten years has been the attempt of Nat and
Cannonball Adderley and other musicians to restore
the blues feeling to jazz in what later became known as
"funk." Another broad-based attempt to restore masculinity to jazz was "hard bop," which represented a combination of nostalgia with a turning away from the thin texture of modern jazz.

However, the two most influential recent tenorists, Sonny
Rollins and the late John Coltrane, play free-form music
that is arhythmic and semi-abstract. The most original
new alto saxophonist, Ornette Coleman, phrases asymmet-
rically, avoids conventional rhythmic coordination, and
told one drummer who played with a strong beat that "I
don't like anyone walking behind me." Such attitudes and
the jagged music of the "new thing," which often sounds
like two oscilloscopes talking to each other, require a vocabulary of sound that differs from the past. What is
being performed has changed consistently enough for us
to suspect that jazz is responding to the same forces as
other arts, in addition to unique, technical, racial, and audience factors. The mellow and assertive masculinity of
earlier jazz will soon be as outmoded as the 78 r.p.m.
"Seventy-eights?" mused one veteran jazz trombonist.
"Those are the things they used to call records."

After
Scarlett O'Hara

The same year in which the King of England abdicated
for love of an American woman also witnessed the publication of *Gone with the Wind*. It became not only the most
widely read book of the time but also the first major
American novel with a woman as hero rather than heroine. The demonstrations by Mrs. Wallis Simpson and
Scarlett O'Hara of a woman's power occurred just before
the novel's traditional male hero began to disappear.

Women were, of course, major characters in American
fiction long before *Gone with the Wind*. Dreiser's *Sister Carrie*
and *Jennie Gerhardt* were forthright women who actively
pursued the good things of life. *Maggie, a Girl of the Streets*
was a prostitute. Other important women characters of
previous American novels tended to be downtrodden or
were heroines, as in popular successes like *Cimarron* or
Main Street. Scarlett O'Hara was so different from earlier
fictional women that *Gone with the Wind* may ultimately
prove more influential than *Vanity Fair* had been almost a
century earlier.

Miss Mitchell's novel was so attractive to readers in
1936 that they bought 50,000 copies on the very first day
of publication and helped the book to cut through previous best-seller records like a laser beam. Scarlett O'Hara
destroyed several men, survived the siege of Atlanta, and
rebuilt a ruined plantation while her society was collaps-
ing. She was *la belle dame sans merci* who was the first
American character with the power, cleverness, and courage that had characterized Ibsen's women.[16] Max
Nordau, who regarded Ibsen as a degenerate for attrib-
uting such qualities to women, would have run out of verbal ammunition in describing the post-Scarlett women
heroes of many modern novels.[17]

Virginia Woolf's metaphor for the transformation of English literature was *Orlando*, a man until he became a woman at thirty. The related change in American novels is exemplified by Allison, the female hero of Grace Metalious' *Peyton Place*, which has sold over eleven million copies and led to a very popular movie and a widely imitated television series. Pre-Scarlett historical "bust sellers" had previously been built around one male hero, like *Anthony Adverse*, who swaggered through adventures and women.[18]

The revolution sparked by Margaret Mitchell has added another dimension of activism in Ayn Rand, the only American novelist of either sex who has generated a social movement and a continuing discussion of her ideas through a newsletter, meetings, and lectures. Miss Rand probably receives more mail from readers than any American novelist. Her Nietzschean characters represent a non-human exaggeration of reality. Just as her politics are reminiscent of D'Annunzio, she directs the Objectivist movement in the same way that he led his cabal.

Miss Rand's fame and the enormous public interest in presumably autobiographical novels by Grace Metalious, Rona Jaffe, and Jacqueline Susann suggest how substantially we have changed our attitudes toward women writers of fiction. Aurore Dupin wrote as George Sand and Marian Evans became George Eliot because a nineteenth-century woman writer would not have been taken seriously. But times have changed, and fiction by women is now so prestigious that prominent men writers adopt female pseudonyms. Patrick Dennis has written three novels as Virginia Rowans, Warren Miller became Amanda Vail for two books, and it has been reported that Roger Longrigg is the Rosalind Erskine who wrote the *Passion Flower* novels. Probably the most energetic writer of novels under a woman's name is Michael Avallone, who has been Dorothea Nile *(Mistress of Farrondale)*, Priscilla Dalton *(Darkening Willows)*, and Edwina Noone *(Dark Cypress)*.

Women writers of mystery and detective novels are in a class by themselves and have been assuming dominance of the form as society became more willing to accept their fantasies about the violence and hostility that represent the core of many plots. It is always hazardous to mistake the genetics of an art form's creators with the genre, but Agatha Christie, Margery Allingham, Josephine Tey, and Ngaio Marsh have towered over detective fiction during the last several decades. Dorothy Sayers is second only to Agatha Christie in range and productivity. In America, Mary Roberts Rinehart, Mignon Eberhart, Leslie Ford, Helen Reilly, and Margaret Millar have enormous followings.

English women writers have a remarkable ability to convey cultural history and the texture and details of a way of life. Dorothy Sayers communicates a feeling for the setting within which a woman don lives, just as Agatha Christie provides extensive documentation on the landed gentry. The reader almost becomes more interested in the details of what is happening than in who did it, because of the women writers' talent for sustaining suspense and creating plausible characters. National characteristics may figure in British women writers' handling of meticulous plots in the same way their countrymen weed gardens, so that bad characters are effectively eliminated and the action is organized as carefully as a vicar's rose garden.

Once women began writing mystery novels, it was inevitable that many of their heroes would be wearing skirts. Mary Roberts Rinehart's Nurse Pinkerton is comfortably middle-aged and as nice a person as Mignon Eberhart's Nurse Sarah Keate. Patricia Wentworth's Maude Silver is a retired teacher who knits and wears Queen Mary hats. Hildegarde Withers is another former teacher who paces a series of novels and is astute enough to let policeman Oscar Piper think that he is solving the crime. Agatha Christie's knowledgeable Jane Marple has deceptively soft and

innocent blue eyes in a crinkled pink face that is framed
by snow-white hair. Leslie Ford's Grace Latham is an attractive widow living near Washington who manages to
combine detective work with considerable social activity.
The woman detective tends to work alone and flourishes
in spite of, or perhaps because of, her lack of a husband.

A resolute young woman who finds her way into a bizarre situation has been celebrated by Mary Stewart and
Victoria Holt, who helped to create the modern neo-
Gothic novel. Its hero is a girl, often described on dust
jackets as having been "caught in an unholy web of evil,"
who stumbles into eerie situations in sinister old houses on
strange islands but cleverly solves the mystery.

As women characters have become more potent in mystery and other novels, there has been a parallel decline in
fictional males' ability to handle their environment.[19] The
progression is illustrated in Thomas Wolfe, whose Eugene
Gant and George Webber roared through his first three
novels, gargantuan and greedy, confident and headstrong.
By the time of *You Can't Go Home Again,* Wolfe's protagonist was more detached and beginning to learn to accept
his limitations. The drive and dominance of Theodore
Dreiser's creative financier Frank Cowperwood metamorphosed to gray anxiety in J. P. Marquand's middle-class
bank employees.

One reason that Ernest Hemingway was the most
influential novelist of the 1930's and early 1940's was that
he wrote of a time and place in which a hero could still
be a romantic individualist. A severe bullet wound would
not prevent him from fighting to the end although, as in
For Whom the Bell Tolls, it was obvious that his cause was
doomed. *For Whom the Bell Tolls* probably represented the
American novel's last major romantic gesture, buried
along with the bugles and banners and fine phrases that
Hemingway despised.

Hemingway's heroes and near-hysterical masculinity

appealed to the public at about the same time that *Little Caesar* and other individualistic gangsters attracted many readers. Fictional gangsters were rugged individualists whom the reader could easily identify with the likes of John Dillinger and Al Capone. By the 1940's, such men gave way to less visible and more anonymous criminal groups, but Frank Costello and other syndicate leaders never fascinated the public in the same way the earlier gangsters did.

The proud and strong hero began to disappear from fiction at just about the time that he departed from the conduct of war, another arena in which he had once conspicuously figured. In World War II, George S. Patton and Douglas MacArthur emerged as our leading bravura generals, with arrogance and a flair for showmanship. But Dwight Eisenhower, a consensus General, rebuked Patton and President Truman removed MacArthur. General Cummings in *The Naked and the Dead,* the most influential novel about World War II, is neurotic and the island that is central to the book's action is captured not by him but by inept Major Dalleson.

As the public seems to have lost interest in both real and fictional aggressive leaders, it has become less responsive to novels with traditional heroes. Mary McCarthy has quite flatly stated that "I haven't got any heroes in my novels."[20] Miniaturization of masculine characteristics may be a special case of the disappearance of characters as well as heroes and could have been anticipated by Kafka's substitution of initials for names.

Although Joyce was as concerned as Kafka with the effects of modern life, sexual intercourse represented a consummation for Joyce. All of life swirled through the flux of Molly Bloom's reverie. But the modern novelist who crosses his t's with sex tends to describe it in terms of technical mastery or comfort. In Norman Mailer and other novelists of the "new apocalypse," Joyce's passion has

become transformed into onanism.[21] Mailer's tedious cat-
aloguing of sexual conquests is an unending masturbation
fantasy, in which the hip male character is forever assur-
ing himself of his potency.

Holden Caulfield is another hipster with misgivings
about his manhood. He not only fails to have intercourse
with a prostitute but is physically assaulted by her pimp
and courted by a man. Holden's ineptitude and inability
to make the "phony" adult world have undoubtedly increased his appeal for many young readers. *Catcher in the
Rye* ends with its non-hero retreating into illness, an appropriate finale for the most influential novel of the
1950's.

Even the older non-hero of current fiction is likely to be
as apprehensive as Holden about his ability to function in
a sexual situation. The depression experienced by near-
hermaphrodite Moses Herzog is partially a reflection of
his impotence, just as his unmailed and frequently
unfinished letters convey sterility and his fantasy about
women embodies passivity. It is ironic that Bellow has
complained that impotence has received too much attention from modern novelists, because it is so clearly a re-
curring theme of his own fiction and especially of *Herzog*.
A similar lack of feeling and inability to relate sexually
characterize the major characters of *The Group*. One reason for both novels' great success may be the timeliness of
their theme of the near-impossibility of relating sexually
to another person.

Ever since *Lucky Jim*, picaresque black satirists like Joseph Heller, Terry Southern, John Barth, and Thomas
Pynchon have squashed traditional categories of the heroic and masculinity-femininity. The appearance of their
work in national picture magazines and the importance of
Catch-22 and *Candy* in the current scene suggest how
difficult it is becoming for the American public to respond
to traditional concepts of masculine and feminine charac-

ter. Some novels that have reached the best-seller lists could almost be described as book-length suicide notes.

Romantic fantasies about the hero of a novel are less likely to flourish under such circumstances. Now that subject matter is so often less important than technique, many readers find it difficult to get emotionally involved with the methodological complexities of novels, in contrast to the simpler style and more evocative action of earlier fiction. As the novel has ceased to be the major medium of sensibility, fiction has lost much of its ability to arouse us to social action. Perhaps the last book that did so was *The Grapes of Wrath.* Such a Big Novel could probably not be written today and would have much less capacity than non-fiction, television, and movies to provoke community and legislative response. A treatise on the dangers of pesticides may generate more reader interest than a superlative novel concerned with a social problem.

It is no longer possible for a novel to bring about major changes in the way that Upton Sinclair's *The Jungle* led to the 1906 meat inspection law. Sinclair and Steinbeck criticized society because they had a vision of a better world in the future, but today's writers do not share Tolstoy's confidence in his ability to prescribe for society. Even those who believe that the wine has turned to vinegar seldom know what to do about it. Many novelists would modify Yossarian's statement in *Catch-22:* "The country's not in danger any more, but I am . . ." to "The country is in grave danger and so am I, but there is nothing that anybody can do about it." Many readers of *Catch-22* who might once have become novelists are too busy experiencing life to want to write about it.

Tastes in fiction are related to preferences in biography, so that we could expect a new kind of non-hero in autobiography. In contrast to the life stories of heroic doctors, dashing foreign correspondents, brave adventurers, masterful statesmen, witty designers, and intrepid athletes, a major genus of recent popular literature has been the autobiography of the sufferer or deviant. A reformed alcoholic (Lillian Roth's *I'll Cry Tomorrow*), ex-addict (Alexander King's *Mine Enemy Grows Older*), convict (Harry Williamson's *Hustler: The Autobiography of a Thief*), former madam (Polly Adler's *A House Is Not a Home*), former prostitute (Virginia McManus' *Not for Love*), victim (Diana Barrymore's *Too Much, Too Soon*), confidence man (J. R. Weil, *Yellow Kid-Weil: The Autobiography of America's Master Swindler*), bank robber *(I, Willie Sutton)*, loser (Mickey Rooney's *I.E., An Autobiography*), masochist (Joyce MacIver's *The Frog Pond*), and former delinquent (Claude Brown, *Manchild in the Promised Land*) have published bestselling autobiographies in recent years. Jean Genet and William Burroughs have received great acclaim for fiction that is a very thinly disguised autobiography of profound pathology.

The popularity of such books of "sick characteristics in search of an author" suggests that many readers can easily identify with non-achievement in non-fiction as well as fiction.[22] The non-fulfillment celebrated by recent novels and autobiographies suggests that the theme of many books has changed from "will she or won't she?" to "can he or can't he?" The next decade's theme could well be an explanation of why it is better that he can't.

Art and Artist

There are differences in how men and women perceive painting and sculpture in our society; many women favor personal, intimate, and sensuous content and men tend to prefer the impersonal, grand, and abstract.[23] Women often enjoy the less powerful and the more controlled form and their tone and color preferences include the soft and modulated.

A shape or object may suggest masculinity or femininity on the basis of cultural connotations, but psychoanalytic theory suggests that the gender of a shape is also determined by its resemblance to the sexual organs. The psychoanalytic theory would regard a baseball as feminine because it was round but a culturally determined association would make a baseball masculine because it is used by men.[24] Psychoanalytic symbolism connects femininity with round, hollow, concave, and enclosing shapes and masculinity with elongated, convex, sharp, and penetrating forms.

The timelessness of femininity may explain the appeal of probably the oldest extant representation of a human being, the 20,000-year-old sculpture of Venus of Willendorf. This early instance of cave art shows a heavy pregnant woman with large breasts and thighs and without much of a face. The sculpture reminds us that the buxom woman has long been an ideal and that direct expressions of women's reproductive function were central in primitive art.[25]

Femininity or masculinity, however, are almost independent of art's subject and a woman may be presented in an extremely masculine style. DeKooning's "Woman One," the most frequently reproduced painting of the 1950's, is very strong and coarse and ferocity distinguishes the banal all-American smile of his "Woman II." Although Renoir celebrated the female body, he did so with a passionately masculine palette.

Painting styles were once distinctively feminine or masculine. At the turn of the century, Mary Cassatt's distinctive manner and colors were beautifully feminine and ideally suited for her impressionist style. More recently, Georgia O'Keeffe uses monochromatic and feminine to-

nalities in a very narrow range: white, pink, blue, and
gray.[26] Grace and delicacy distinguish her depth and
sensuous curves, which seem to have a growing life of
their own. "Ritz Tower" is a typical O'Keeffe painting
which contains vulval clouds and a vaginally shaped
street lamp. In the filminess and delicate gray of "In Passing" and the soft blues, wispy faces, and circles of "Neon
City," Loren MacIver has sustained the feminine tradition. Nell Blaine's landscapes and interiors have a very
personal womanly quality. Such exceptions aside, the
work of most women artists now shows little that is feminine in themes, colors, or techniques. Other than the masculine movement of Jackson Pollock's bold and affirmative
colors and forms and Franz Kline's punch-in-the-face
pictures that throw themselves at the beholder, few recent
men painters have a distinctively masculine style.

It is not necessary for an artist to be a man to paint in a
masculine manner any more than it is important to be a
woman in order to paint like one. Odilon Redon's mystery and symbolism tended to be gentle and fragile and
communicated a feminine poetry. Rosa Bonheur's
painting style was hardly feminine and the horse was her
major subject. Robert and Sonia Delaunay suggest how
femininity and masculinity can be independent of the
artist's sex: both painters were fascinated by concentric
circles but Mrs. Delaunay's work looks more masculine.
Her colors are darker and stronger and the shapes she uses
are less fluid than her husband's.[27]

Sometimes a work of art is memorable because it conveys both masculinity and femininity. Redon's "Silence"
frames a person of indeterminate sex and a major attraction of the picture is its sexual ambiguity. The spell of
Carl Milles' sculpture, "Monument to Genius," lies in
tension and contrast between the legs' masculine strength
and muscles and a uterine quality in the body's upper
part.

One artist may exhibit both sexual modalities.[28] From 1909 through 1914, in paintings like "The Red Studio," "Goldfish," "The Moroccans," and "The Painter and His Model," Matisse exhibited austere color, hard form, straight lines, sharp angles, and jerky and syncopated rhythms. By the early 1920's, Matisse had shifted to more feminine colors, flowing lines, decorative flower effects, and his many versions of "Odalisque" suggest a feminine sensibility. The painter began to combine the two approaches in the late 1920's and by "Decorative Figure on an Ornamental Background" (1928), severe straight lines met at right angles and broke into short segments, with decorative sumptuousness and supple arabesques from a rich palette. Matisse's genius probably reached its peak only after he synthesized the two complementary dimensions. In contrast, Picasso seems to have achieved his most authentic expression in the strong, masculine forms that followed the vagueness and femininity of his blue period.

Sculpture does not necessarily express masculinity, even though its creation involves considerable energy and force. Constantine Brancusi has created many feminine forms and women make massive pieces. Sculpting with hammer and chisel is no longer a man's art, and it would be difficult to identify a woman as the sculptor of Barbara Hepworth's 21-foot and five-ton bronze memorial to Dag Hammarskjöld at the United Nations, "Single Form." The massive size of Miss Hepworth's sculptures negates the femininity of their many apertures. The esthetic appeal of combining masculine and feminine in sculpture is suggested by Michelangelo, who blended Hercules and Christ in powerful yet tender sculpture that demonstrated how strength must be delicate or it may be brutal.

Modern non-sexualized art began when the cubists broke with the past by translating the visible world into geometric forms. Once a painting became a work of architecture and the painter's goal was to take apart and reassemble objects without regard to the traditional central subject, criteria like masculinity and femininity became less relevant. Abstraction brought pure design without cultural or literary connotations and led to acceptance of an artistic beauty that was non-imitative of life.

Abstract painting uses dissociative symbols to separate the self from things that are relational. Paul Klee acutely observed that the more horrible the world, the more abstract our art.[29] Abstract art results from anguish and bewilderment in a complex world, an attempt to leave the capriciousness of the living for dependability and regularity in a world of inert forms.[30] Such painting need have no precedent in nature, or any reference to masculine or feminine. Abstract expressionists paint painting rather than pictures, so that we are less involved with the subject, if there is one, than with the manner in which it is presented.[31] The attempt of California's Bay Area Figurative painters to apply abstract expressionist techniques to figures and other realistic subject matter has had little effect.

What Other Trends Seem Likely?

Andrew Wyeth, who has commanded higher prices than any other living American painter, and whose "Christina's World" is the most popular painting in the Museum of Modern Art, may be one bellwether of the future. His naturalistic composition and literal technique are reminiscent of North German and Flemish pen and ink drawings. He prefers desolate landscapes and low-keyed themes of loneliness. Wyeth's precisionist dry-brush water colors employ a simple hue scale, with a fairly narrow range of greens and browns, and less importance for red, orange, yellow, purple. Dramatic colors or contrasts are less important than the barren and neuter.

As life in America becomes more neuter, painters may express more of the aridity and desensualized color of a

Wyeth. Pop art shares with Wyeth a representational approach and relationship to magazine art. Pop is a market- and media-oriented response that lacks the irony, wit, and social protest of the original Dadaists. In Jasper Johns and Robert Rauschenberg, there has been legitimization of the manipulation of things from the environment into a construction or other work of art. Environmental artists' upgrading of non-human objects and effluvia of our civilization may ultimately make easel painting anachronistic and escalate the process of dehumanization and submission to technology.

Art today, with its succession of trivia and novelties, is an artichoke that has too many leaves and not enough heart. The enthusiasm of the New People for happenings, auto-destructive art, and the total interiorization represented by psychedelic art is rapidly making traditional painting almost historical. In the new nihilism of a Larry Poons, a non-statement or non-revelation becomes the non-picture.[32]

Now that painting and sculpture are in considerable danger of being absorbed into a giant cultural homogenization, masculinity and femininity are almost irrelevant. Even in contemporary attempts to deal directly with sexual material, as in the Erotic Art and Big Nudes shows in New York in the fall of 1966, most of the works were not erotic or sexy or even sniggering. They were bored—and boring.

2

the hero unhorsed

A Greek proverb warns that "when you attack the King, you must kill him." The hero in the major performing arts has been mauled so vigorously over the last few decades that he has been wounded grievously, possibly mortally. The hero has become less traditional, romantic, and heroic as he has yielded center stage to a woman.

The hero's change from strut to limp has led to a chain reaction, because of the trickle effect that operates in popular arts. His departure from one performing art made it easier for him to disappear from others. Today's play becomes tomorrow's musical or movie and a television program spins off a play or movie. Stage directors work in opera and actors who develop reputations in one medium are in demand in others. The hero's exit has surely affected the fantasies and models for behavior provided the New People by opera, theatre, musical theatre, movies, and television.

Brünnhilde without Siegfried

At a Metropolitan Opera performance in 1959 in which Birgit Nilsson sang Isolde, three different tenors were re-

quired to sing Tristan. The incident occurred because the
tenor scheduled for the role had lost his voice and the
Metropolitan did not wish to cancel the performance. But
it provided a spectacularly literal illustration of today's
one-act tenor, who can barely survive a single act of a
Wagnerian opera. Although such tenors do not usually
reach the Metropolitan, the situation dramatized the decline of male voices, especially tenors, that is the most significant recent change in opera.

The men who dominated opera's Golden Age, from
1890 to Caruso's retirement in 1920, and who were the
first matinee idols of the mass communications era, have
been replaced by women in popular appeal. No tenor
since Caruso has approached him in overall quality, lyrical feeling, and the dramatic impact of his way with even
simple music. Gigli's admirers feel their hero surpassed
Caruso in role interpretation and voice nap, and Nicolai
Gedda may be as versatile, but Caruso's extraordinary
eminence has never been equaled. Although his records
cost at least one dollar more than others and some one-
sided discs sold for seven dollars, they far outsold any
competitors. Caruso's 1907 "Vesti la giubba" and his 1908
"La donna e mobile" sold over a million copies each, at a
time when relatively few phonographs were in use.

Jean de Reszke and Leo Slezak were contemporary tenors with large followings and Antonio Scotti was the
reigning baritone. Chaliapin, usually considered a star of
the Golden Age although his greatest success was in the
1920's, was a most consummate artist. More than a craftsman, he projected feeling as it naturally arose from a situation. The men of the Golden Age had voices of pure gold
even on records made under primitive conditions. In those
days an assistant would push a singer away from the mi-
crophone for a high note and toward it for a low note.

The Golden Age was the time of the public's first widespread interest in opera stars' personal lives. People who

never actually heard opera avidly followed the singers' careers and private lives and the first organized fan clubs sprang into life early in this century to honor opera performers. Antonio Scotti's successive engagements to a number of divas provided opportunities for the first extensive newspaper and magazine coverage of an entertainer's romances.

Some prima donnas of the Golden Age had substantial followings. Nellie Melba gave her name to a peach dessert, a soufflé, and toast. Geraldine Farrar's "Gerry Flapper" fan clubs covered the country and Mary Garden became a legend in her own lifetime. Men singers may have received disproportionate attention because Caruso's unique genius probably made it easier for some stardust to rub off on his male colleagues. Even if this was so, the recent loss of interest in male opera singers represents a combination of a falling off in the availability of male talent and the public's attitudes toward men singers.

The new era can almost be said to have begun in the year after Caruso's retirement, with Maria Jeritza's arrival from Vienna in 1921. Her big voice, beauty, and presence gave new life to the Metropolitan and began a momentum that has been accelerated by other women singers. The voices of Helen Traubel, Kirsten Flagstad, Renata Tebaldi, Joan Sutherland, Birgit Nilsson, Maria Callas, and Leontyne Price are diamonds on velvet.

A Wagnerian soprano needs a voice with enough size and range to handle Isolde's low A as well as her high C. Traubel was a glorious singer. Flagstad's powerful but beautiful voice, bell-like in all registers, thrilled audiences at the Metropolitan from the time of her debut as Sieglinde in 1935.

Tebaldi's ability to produce melting tones that sound as if they were floating on air has never been equaled. Even though *pianissimo* sounds are very soft and low, hers can be heard in the gallery. The plush warmth and richness of

Tebaldi's voice and her majestic bearing and special personal charm are unique.

Sutherland's mastery of the scale's upper reaches and her voice's flexibility, size, brilliance, and technique are extraordinary. Its unmatched pure legato and coloratura brilliance enable her effortlessly to sing a *Lucia di Lammermoor*. Nilsson's versatility enables her to perform concert songs beautifully, Verdi with warmth, Mozart with clarity, and bring power, brilliance, and command to Wagner. She is beautifully accurate and musical and conveys exciting warmth in presence and singing. Callas brings extraordinary temperament, intensity, musicality, imagination, and dramatic comprehension to her roles. Her voice, especially lovely in its middle range, is so highly dramatic that its occasional curdle in the upper register is less disturbing than it might be in almost any other singer. She is the absolute soprano of our time. Leontyne Price's fabulous voice has so many colors that it can truly be described as voluptuous.

Such divas overshadow bass Jerome Hines, baritone Robert Merrill, or bass baritone George London. One reason that such men lack the tenor's popular appeal is that the male romantic lead so often is a tenor. *Don Giovanni, Rigoletto,* and *The Marriage of Figaro* are among the very few operas in which a baritone shares the spotlight with a soprano. When non-tenors had enormous audiences, Chaliapin in *Boris Godunov* represented the operatic event of the month, but today's audiences will not get excited about an opera that features a man even if it has the beautiful music, exciting story, and choral dramatics of *Boris Godunov*. Audiences were far readier to cheer Chaliapin than recent fans have been to applaud an Ezio Pinza or a Boris Christoff.

Even Richard Tucker and other very estimable tenors in Dallas, Chicago, and San Francisco have failed to ig-

nite audiences. The post-Lauritz Melchior decline in heroic tenors is one reason that Metropolitan Opera audiences
have heard far less Wagner since 1950.[1] *Lohengrin* slipped
from second most frequently performed opera to twenty-
seventh; *Tristan* from sixth to twenty-third place;
Tannhäuser from eighth to forty-fourth; and *Die Walküre*
from seventh to thirty-fourth.

One additional result of the lack of appropriate male
voices is that many non-Wagnerian operas have disappeared from the standard repertory and others are performed very seldom. *Otello* was absent from the Metropolitan's repertory for a quarter-century after Slezak left. The
tenor in *Barber of Seville* who sings coloratura is typical of
other opera parts that are no longer sung because of lack
of adequate male voices.

Some composers, like Meyerbeer, have fallen into
eclipse because they wrote for male voices that no longer
exist. Although Meyerbeer used considerable meretricious
stage business and indulged in some excesses, he is the
only musically interesting composer of world rank who
has not been revived. There are no men in even the best
American opera companies capable of performing *The
Huguenots* and it is not possible to assemble seven male
singers with matched voices in order to record it.

A few operas that make bel canto demands (e.g., *The
Barber of Seville*) are popular, but others have been difficult
to revive because of a paucity of appropriate male voices.
Only years of training can provide the unbroken flow,
long legato phrases, and pure natural placement of the bel
canto voice. Bellini, Donizetti, and Rossini wrote for tenors who matured over an extensive period. Their runs,
with phrases that touch high D and high F, were not
meant to be sung with the chest alone. Bellini even requires a bass to sing coloratura. Contemporary difficulties
with bel canto roles can be heard on the recordings of

simplified versions of *I Puritani*, featuring Callas (1954) and Sutherland (1964), in which the baritone and tenor do not even approach the divas' agility.

There has been a decline of new operas that enter the standard repertory. *Der Rosenkavalier*, first performed in 1911, was the last work to enter the standard repertory of major companies. The relatively few contemporary operas to be performed reflect their composers' assessment of available voices by usually providing better parts for women than men. It was altogether fitting that the work selected to open the new Metropolitan Opera House in 1966 was *Antony and Cleopatra*, which Samuel Barber wrote specifically for Leontyne Price.

In standard operas, the music may be modified to facilitate a tenor's ability to cope with his part. In a recording of *La Bohème*, Richard Tucker or the conductor appear to have transposed the aria "Che gelida manina" down a half-tone.[2] The aria's highest note is a C but as sung by Tucker, it is a B. Although Tucker's voice has considerable beauty and natural placement, his apparent inability to sustain the higher note seems to have made it necessary to change the key of the whole aria. It is inconceivable that a contemporary soprano would transpose down an important aria like *Aïda*'s Act III "O patria mia" in order to avoid its famous high C.

Why has there been such a decline in men opera singers' voices? Inadequacy of training, attractions of non-operatic singing, overexploitation, acceleration of voice development, and changes in underlying attitudes toward men and women singers are some of the reasons. A student in the Golden Age would practice scales for years before a teacher would permit him to proceed to arias. The qualities expected in teachers of an earlier era are implied in Beethoven's famous remark that Rossini would have been a great composer if only his teacher had beaten him oftener.

Success may come too easily for some tenors who sing professionally before they are really ready. Franco Corelli, for example, had only six months of formal vocal training. Voice quality takes time to develop and many a young male singer who felt that time is money did not want to squander time by extensive preparation. Few young tenors heed the example of Flagstad, a late bloomer whose career only entered its major phase in her late thirties.

A young man who prepared his voice systematically was once able to anticipate an opera career spanning thirty or forty years. The contemporary artist who rushes into roles may never get such ripening, gives a secondary priority to operatic performances, and becomes involved in nonoperatic appearances. The earlier performers had a greater commitment to opera than their successors display, so that a Caruso refused to endorse any commercial product. When the Metropolitan permitted him to name any fee, he set $2,500. At least three artists—later, if not better—have demanded and received more money per performance. Although Scotti was flamboyant, he sang at the Metropolitan for thirty-four years because of his complete identification with opera.

Some male singers' managers may be eager to place their clients in movies, television, whirlwind nightclub tours, and musical comedy. Such opportunities were less available during the Golden Age and may seem more attractive than years of training to an operatic tenor. He is called on to sing in a less natural manner than any other voice and requires more training than a soprano who sings the same pitches one octave higher. Actually, the soprano typically sings at an earlier age and with more facility than the tenor. Even a tenor with a well-placed voice who can support it without tightening his voice box is unlikely to have it placed in the upper register, especially high A or above, without extensive training.

One reason for the importance of training is the number of great tenors who began as baritones, whose potential only emerged slowly and was nurtured by intensive supervision and practice. Caruso's early timbre was so baritonish that for some of the records he made with Scotti, the manufacturer issued a guide to identify who was singing which part. A baritone who manifests the pingy or more brilliant sound often associated with a tenor, especially around F sharp or G, might be a potential tenor. But a baritone who once might have explored his tenor potential through additional training, may today be content to continue as a baritone. The dedicated teachers who helped Jean de Reszke, Melchior, and Set Svanholm move from baritone to tenor seem less available.

The problem may lie less in the disappearance of devoted teachers than in a lack of singers who want to become tenors, since a number of men have succeeded in moving to another voice. Leonard Warren's full baritone was once tenor and Giorgio Tozzi shifted from baritone to bass. But there is no recent change from baritone to tenor, although that voice is more likely than any other to lead to recognition.

Rodin has reminded us that "slowness is beauty." A beautiful voice cannot be created in a hurry and most tenors are products of extensive schooling. In his early twenties, Caruso's voice was quite small and cracked so frequently on high notes that he was called "the cracking tenor" (il tenore dalle stecche).[3]

Another problem is that many a young tenor is engaged in an athletic contest with his voice, a struggle from which the voice can only come out second best. Singers who have sped through training tend to plow their way through a song, an aria, or a role, overburdening the voice without getting maximum results. They often convey the impression that singing is hard labor and must be accompanied by a red neck and strained face.[4] The well-trained singer, in contrast, glides or skates on the tonal line.

Paradoxically, the scarcity of exciting tenors itself contributes to the non-development of new singers. A tenor who is pushed forward so rapidly that he skips necessary training can become anxious, in view of the high stakes. The resulting tension could mar his singing. Since many tenors are married, they are often under great economic pressure to make their reputations as soon as possible, in contrast to women singers, who can receive support from families or husbands.

Many young men singers stress volume, "guts," and "personality" at the expense of artistry, musical line, and dramatic sense. Others feel that a big tone is necessary in order to be heard over the orchestra in a large auditorium and forget that a small voice may be damaged by being forced to extremes of loudness. Some poorly trained men learn crooning, scooping, breaking of phrases, and other "expressive" vocal habits that can truncate their careers.

The relationship between opera and larger social trends is suggested by a story, told in opera circles since the late 1930's, about a well-known soprano who forced her male co-star to make love just before they went on stage. She expected his voice to suffer so that he could not surpass her when they sang together. Whether the incident actually occurred is less important than the frequency and enthusiasm with which the story has been repeated during the last generation, especially since a delicate coloratura voice would suffer more from the after-effects of sexual intercourse than a deeper male voice. The man's tone might actually have its qualities reinforced by coitus, even if his energy level had declined. The story's persistence in spite of its unreality is symptomatic of the change in opera, which is important not only for opera-goers and the twelve million fans who faithfully tune in the Saturday afternoon Metropolitan broadcasts but also for the millions more who read about opera stars.

Gian-Carlo Menotti has amply demonstrated his sensitivity to what the public wants, and two of his operas suggest some directions for the future. In *The Consul,* the principal parts are a soprano and a contralto and there is no major male singing role. In *The Medium,* the major male character is a mute.

Matinee Idols,
Exeunt Omnes

The matinee idol began to leave the theatre at just about the time that masculine opera singers were retreating to the wings. When Actors Equity celebrated its fiftieth birthday in 1963 with a program of representative scenes, Lillian Gish, Helen Hayes, and Beatrice Lillie were the star performers.[5] Not one man did a major scene in Equity's reenactment of the recent past. Although Western theatre was largely Eveless for its first two thousand years, American actresses of the last two generations have helped to redress this imbalance. The idol's final bow, which occurred during Equity's first decade, is significant far beyond Broadway. It affects movies, television, and other mass media that derive content and personnel from the theatre.

Kings have been waiting in dressing rooms for hundreds of years, and Dr. Johnson stopped going to the theatre because his "amorous propensities" were inflamed by "white bosoms and silk stockings."[6] The close relationship between Eros and the performing arts makes the matinee idol's disappearance a clue to larger changes in the warp and woof of our culture, because only in America have the woman's fluttering eyelashes replaced the man's buskin and sonorous voice.

The matinee idol is a male star who appeals to and meets the fantasy needs of adult women and communicates and sustains magnetism over an extended period. Entertainers who appeal to teen-age girls have a much shorter span of popularity and cannot be regarded as idols. A teen favorite does not need an idol's charisma because many youngsters will reach toward him as a symbol of glamor and achievement, almost regardless of his talent.[7] But the teen-agers' grandmothers who responded to matinee idols had more lasting needs.

Women's responses to idols were extraordinarily intense. A fan might write fifty letters a week to her hero, and wait all day in below-freezing temperature for a glimpse of him. The possessiveness and ferocity of some fans were expressed in the nineteenth-century New York Astor Place riots in which twenty-two people were killed in a dispute between fans of idols Forrest and Macready over who was the better Macbeth. One reason for such loyalty was the idol's strikingly handsome appearance and dashing carriage. He was tall and his memorable face included a generous mouth, deep-set eyes, and distinctive nose. The idol's ringing and mellifluous voice could easily be heard even in the balcony of the ten-twenty-thirty theatres.

Contemporary audiences are less likely to respond to the physical appearance of performers than was Percy Hammond. Dipping his pen in gall, he concluded his review of a musical by noting that the only aspect of the show which he had not knocked was the knees of the chorus, but only because nature had already anticipated him. We are not likely ever again to see the like of the actor, now a mature movie star, who first won attention a generation ago by padding his genital area for a Broadway part. Critics praised his "vibrant presence," "restless virility," and "dynamic masculinity." Since his acting was totally undistinguished, the notice he received can be entirely attributed to his revival of the Elizabethan codpiece.

The audience once enjoyed the charms exhibited by male stars as enthusiastically as it now enjoys the cleavage of some actresses. The ancestors of today's falsies were the celluloid symmetricals which actors wore to make their legs more shapely and eliminate knock-knees and bow-legs. The typical idol wore form-fitting jacket and dashing skin-tight breeches, and enjoyed parts that provided a chance to display his legs and prance about the stage. Idol Henry E. Dixey was so eager to exhibit his finely turned calves that he wriggled into his very tight breeches only with the help of a stepladder.

When idolatry flourished, many of New York's sixty theatres were rented for the whole season or even owned by the idols' companies. An idol often performed several different plays during a repertory season and might do one role at a matinee and a second part the same evening. There was considerable choice for "matinee girls." George Clarke's velvety eyes and languid manner were famous. Edwin Booth had great success with melancholy roles. James O'Neill was associated with roles typified by his famous line in *The Count of Monte Cristo:* "The world is mine!" James K. Hackett's sword-swinging robustness achieved recognition in *The Prisoner of Zenda.* Edwin Forrest was so well known for oratorical tragedies that he was able to commission such plays. Other famous idols were E. H. Sothern, Otis Skinner, Richard Mansfield, Edward J. Morgan, William Faversham, Maurice Barrymore, John Drew, and Henry Miller.

The idol transcended his roles, so that Lester Wallack would wear his famous "Burnsides" whiskers even when playing Charles Surface in *School for Scandal.* The erotic magnetism of a Wallack could not be created artificially. No amount of ballyhoo could make a matinee idol of Francis Lederer, who had been imported from Czechoslovakia by Lee Shubert in the 1930's and was appearing on Broadway in *Autumn Crocus.*[8] Even though his managers arranged for thousands of laudatory letters to be signed with false names and sent to critics and columnists, Lederer simply did not have the idol's special vibrations.

One actor who exuded such vibrations was Joseph Schildkraut, "the handsomest man in Europe," who regularly caused riots among women waiting at the stage door. John Barrymore carried off flamboyant roles in private and public life. Such men were far more potent box office attractions than contemporaries like Maude Adams, Ethel Barrymore, Minnie Maddern Fiske, Julia Marlowe, Florence Reed, Frances Starr, Emily Stevens, Margaret Anglin, or Laurette Taylor.

Why Idolatry Declined

Technical advances, the new importance of playwrights, retirements, and new booking procedures helped to bring about the idols' final bow soon after the end of World War I. More important than such changes in the theatre in making the romantically fluttering or fragile heroine less acceptable on the stage, were some larger readjustments of the American people. The presidential election of 1920 was the first in which women could vote and soon after, their smoking in public and wearing their hair short were taken for granted. Psychoanalytic ideas were very extensively discussed and accelerated the postwar revolution in manners, morals, and clothing.[9]

By 1920, technical changes in lighting, acoustics, and makeup made it less necessary for a leading man to be handsome or have a strong, resonant voice. Up to this time, the play had been far less important than its star. Some famous European actors touring the United States actually performed parts in their native language while other characters spoke English. The great idols were able to attract large audiences almost in spite of the claptrap or heavily rewritten classics in which they appeared.

In the very year in which Caruso's retirement ended op-

era's Golden Age, the modern American theatre was born
with *Beyond the Horizon*. The renaissance in American
playwriting that began with James O'Neill's son resulted
in plays becoming more important than their stars. As audiences shifted interest from player to playwright, the idols
began losing their followings.

The early 1920's witnessed the dissolution of several
famous companies that had toured with the classics, e.g.,
that of Sothern and Marlowe, after their principals retired. Idols William Gillette, John Drew, and Richard
Mansfield also left the stage around the same time. Silent
movies made substantial inroads into the idols' audiences,
and John Barrymore's abandonment of Broadway for
Hollywood after his 1922 *Hamlet* encouraged a whole generation of actors to look westward.

Such developments contributed to the decline of actors
and a corresponding ascendance of actresses in audience
and playwright popularity. A simple exercise can illus-
trate how far the pendulum swung. Almost anybody
could suggest candidates for the title of first lady of the
theatre. Jane Cowl, Ina Claire, Katherine Cornell, Jeanne
Eagels, Ruth Gordon, Helen Hayes, Pauline Lord, Tallu-
lah Bankhead, and Eva Le Gallienne would have been
cited not too long ago. Any theatregoer today could prepare a list of several dominant actresses who project characters with valid juices. But what actor would be nomi-
nated to be first man of the theatre? Alfred Lunt is,
perhaps, the only American actor with a major reputation,
and his fame really grew only after he teamed with Lynn
Fontanne.

No successors to the matinee idols have emerged and
today's actors seem to be marching to the beat of a much
more subdued drum. A very talented young actor who
makes a good impression on Broadway (e.g., Marlon
Brando) usually goes to Hollywood—and stays there. Like
the tenor who can make more money outside the opera

house, the actor can better his Broadway income in movies and television. Even if he wanted to perform the great roles before a live audience, the only place where he could do them would be an occasional summer festival.

Actresses are not only bigger than men at the box office; some are actually taller. It is more than coincidence that Ingrid Bergman was probably the first actress to be taller than her co-star in a major Broadway drama. In *Liliom* (1940), she was taller than Burgess Meredith, playing the part created in New York by Joseph Schildkraut in 1921. When Schildkraut slapped a woman in the play, he was the first American actor to have done so, on any American stage. The women in the audience gasped—and they loved it.

But times have changed, and Thurber women dominate our stage. In Edward Albee's *Ballad of the Sad Café,* the female lead wrestles with a man—and wins. Although women characters once represented the goal of a hero's romantic quest, today we are getting the woman as Brute. One reason for the change is lack of interest in the quest itself. Indeed, the obligatory scene in contemporary plays may be the one in which the leading woman and her companion crawl out of bed and dress themselves.[10]

The quest for the beloved has been replaced by the playwright's concern with Oedipal themes centered around a woman who is either fierce or strong. If there are two women, both are usually strong enough to provide wonderful parts for actresses. William Inge, Arthur Miller, and Tennessee Williams have been preoccupied with various aspects of the Oedipus complex and have created a number of men who were programmed for defeat.

Come Back, Little Sheba is almost a stripped Freudian text. The pivotal scene in *Death of a Salesman* derives its power from an Oedipal confrontation. Willy Loman is fumbling and bumbling, but his wife is a rock. *After the Fall* is a nakedly clinical scrutiny of the Oedipal man's problems and his conviction that women want not merely to break even with men, but must win. Williams' interest in the relationships between wounded men and women is obsessive.

Another reason for the shift from men to women on stage is a substantial change in audiences. The swooning idolators wanted to see their heroes but today's matinee audiences include many women who are almost indifferent to the performers and are attending to help a favorite charity. The increasing proportion of women who work has further limited the number with idle matinees in which to enjoy fantasies about matinee idols.

Off-Broadway is unlikely to feature a romantic hero, except to ridicule him. It does not have weekday or Saturday matinees, which have been replaced by late performances on Friday, Saturday, or Sunday evenings. And the kind of women whose attendance at matinees once helped to support the idols are not likely to attend off-Broadway or off-off-Broadway.

These radical changes in audience composition, themes, and casting have led to a decrease in acting jobs for men and a corresponding increase in opportunities for women. The 1960 census recorded much more attrition among actors than actresses, as one consequence of depletion of the rich ore of heroic parts that had once been mined by the idols. Eight out of ten popular plays lack a male hero. Most contemporary plots involve a woman triumphing over a weak man and the rare actor with a strong role often plays it in a manner that suggests Eugene Field's review of a Lear: "He played the King as if he thought someone else had the ace."

With whom could a sensitive male playgoer identify as he watched *Happy Birthday*, which provided Helen Hayes with her longest Broadway run? Its hero is librarian Addie Bemis, who talks, sings, and dances up a storm as she vanquishes her rival and wins the tight-lipped and not-too-bright bank teller whom she fancies. A woman who has destroyed and stuffed her husband and carries him around as a trophy is the hero of Arthur Kopit's *Oh Dad, Poor Dad, Mother's Hung You in the Closet and I'm Feelin' So Sad.*

The characters in *Who's Afraid of Virginia Woolf?*, the most influential play of the decade, are essentially gender-less. The men could speak most of the women's lines and vice versa, or the couples could be Lesbian or homosexual, and the play would lose little of its high voltage. The role reversal and loss of gender that are implicit in a variety of other successful plays cut uncomfortably close to the bone. *Two for the Seesaw* was a brick that smashed through the window of Broadway tradition in 1955, although it was only the third two-character play to do well since the turn of the century. The play's dialogue and characterization were banal in spite of a surface sophistication and its major appeal to audiences seems to have been Anne Bancroft's persistence in pursuing Henry Fonda. When she decides to go to bed with him as a birthday gift, he flees. Were the actors to switch roles, the audience would not be aware that each was reading the other's lines, and the scene would sound like a trite older play.[11]

Broadway plays of the last several years are veined with the theme of the Man as Boob, whose intelligence and integrity have been pawned and never redeemed. The hero of *Mary, Mary* is the title character, whose husband is an unappealing and inept clod. A young mistress tames her foolish master in *Any Wednesday*. *Barefoot in the Park* deals with a woman who is much more aggressive and interesting than her husband. One reason that such plays are successful is the audience's enthusiasm for the combination of a female hero and a male playing the second sex. Many a male protagonist is an anti-hero who seldom has the capacity to sustain his protest. Jerry in *The Zoo Story,* who commits suicide because it is the only positive act in which he can engage, is typical of our new theatre.

With few parts and even fewer romantic roles for men, there is little likelihood that actors will be displaying their figures in romantic costumes. We have replaced the hero in provocative doublet and hose with the actor masturbating or showing the audience his bare buttocks, as in *Marat/Sade.* During the years in which men's romantic costumes have been moving from theatre wardrobes into museums of theatrical history, actors have actually been becoming less handsome. The change can be traced since 1945 in the annual volumes of Daniel Blum's *Theatre World,* each of which includes photographs of leading characters of the season's plays. "Natural" types like Ben Gazzara have replaced the handsome profile and current procedures for training actors are more likely to concentrate on inner feeling than outer appearance.

Such procedures have received their most widely publicized expression in the Actors Studio and few directors have dared to express lack of enthusiasm for its approach. A Studio member asked George Abbott, who was directing him in a rehearsal, "What is my motivation?" Mr. Abbott answered briefly, if unfashionably: "Your salary." Most young directors would be more likely to follow their own conceptions of the Studio style in imposing what often emerges as tongue-tied emotionalism even on relatively literate plays.

A successful contemporary actor may appear in musicals, motion pictures, drama, television narration, and plays and commercials. Such multiple exposure may blur and confuse the image of a performer. Today's playgoer is less likely to fantasy about her hero than her grandmother was in the days when idol Corse Peyton sat on the stage and poured tea for his fans. Her fantasies about Jason Robards, Jr., may be replaced by embarrassment as she watches him solemnly praising the coffee that his wife serves him in a commercial. Instant, not regular, coffee.

The British Theatre

The English theatre, not many years ago regarded as effete, is bursting with unmistakable vitality. One reason for the assertive masculinity of the new generation of English actors is their classical training. Many famous actors and playwrights first won recognition and received invaluable experience by performing Shakespeare, who is essentially a man's playwright, in the fifty-seven full-time provincial repertory companies. Even the actors who have become great movie successes regularly return to the stage, often in very demanding roles.

Paul Scofield's chasmed voice and power to enlarge a role distinguished his *King Lear*. Albert Finney made a huge success in *Macbeth* and Richard Burton was one of the youngest *Hamlets* to be praised in England. Such strong parts are passed on by each generation to the next. Actors trained in Shakespeare and playwrights who grew up in this tradition, as actors, have helped make English theatre very masculine.

Another reason for its virility is the extraordinary impact in 1956 of *Look Back in Anger*, which spurred the theme of kinetic social protest. Such plays feature men because they deal with the problems of men. Even the English musical theatre has been awash in a flood of protest. Social mobility and class conflict were the themes of *Fings Ain't Wot They Used To Be*, *The World of Paul Slickey*, *Half a Sixpence*, *The Roar of the Greasepaint—The Smell of the Crowd*. *Expresso Bongo* dealt with juvenile delinquency, *King Kong* was concerned with racial problems in South Africa, *Walk a Crooked Mile* meandered through Soho prostitution, *The Lord Chamberlain Regrets* attacked censorship.

With the exception of Shaw, earlier British theatre had seldom dealt frontally with problems of social significance.

Pinero and Galsworthy and the few other major playwrights who handled such themes usually were more solemn
than serious. In *The Notorious Mrs. Ebbsmith,* Pinero has a
woman character throw a Bible into the fire. At every performance, the audience gasped at his courage in writing
such a scene and in the actress' daring. The gasps would
be the actress' cue to rush to the fireplace and remove the
Bible. Such was the level of protest before *Look Back in
Anger.*

Current British drama resembles American theatre during the 1930's, which saw the last significant flourishing of
roles for men in the social protest plays of the Group and
Mercury companies. In its decade of activity, the Group
developed not even one actress to match its eight principal actors. Although Odets did not write vehicles for
specific actors, his plays contained more active and significant parts for men than women.

There is a curious parallel between the characteristics
of several of New York's dominant actresses and England's leading actors. Kim Stanley, Geraldine Page, and
Anne Bancroft would appear on almost any list of today's
most talented and accomplished but relatively young actresses. None is beautiful. Each has a gutsy roughness and
can be overwhelming, as Miss Stanley was in dominating
the opening scene of *Three Sisters* without saying a word.
The neurosis they communicate is exciting and conveys
an electricity of its own. Their turbulence and authority
resembles the power and almost brutal vitality that are
conveyed by Finney, Scofield, and Burton.

Even the second leads in London (e.g., Tom Courtenay,
Ian Bannen) project the intensity of the three older men,
who appear to have influenced the recent *Othello* of Lau-
rence Olivier, the previous generation's finest actor. Olivier's Moor has been his most brutally animal performance,
almost as if a wild beast were striving to get out. It is as
impossible to imagine the younger British actors emulat-

ing Gielgud and performing from the neck up as to think of their doing the Lonsdale and Maugham comedies of the past.

Just as Oedipal concerns have helped lead to strong women and weak men on Broadway, one reason for masculinity in English theatre is the declining appeal of such themes. They did occasionally emerge, as in Maugham's *The Sacred Flame* (1929) and Coward's *The Vortex* (1938), but are less attractive to the many post-1956 writers whose tempers burn on very short fuses and who fulminate against society rather than Mother.

Orpheus among the Maenads

The most obvious reverberations of matinee idolatry's disappearance are in the musical, our most indigenous theatre form. The American musical comedy that was once as perfected and stylized as Italian grand opera now provides a declining market for the smiling and handsome leading man with a good voice. *Do Re Mi, Allegro, Carousel, How To Succeed in Business without Really Trying, What Makes Sammy Run?*, and *I Can Get It for You Wholesale* are some of the many musicals built around a male non-hero or anti-hero or scoundrel, who is a descendant of *Pal Joey*.[12]

Many successful musicals feature men who were cast because they were *not* "the gorgeous hunk of man" of previous decades. Anthony Newley, who is certainly not handsome, played an unattractive character in *Stop the World, I Want To Get Off*. Clive Revill ran a school for thieves in *Oliver*. Aging Walter Pidgeon and tubby Jackie Gleason were major attractions of *Take Me Along*. The longest running musical, *Threepenny Opera*, was built around a master criminal, and *My Fair Lady* had a priggish scholar as male lead.

Just as in the non-musical theatre, some heroes are physically less imposing than their ladies. *How To Succeed in Business without Really Trying* may have been the first musical in which a leading lady (Bonnie Scott) was taller than her male co-star (Robert Morse). Miss Scott's height symbolized the increased size of women's roles in musicals.

Audiences before World War II used to look forward to seeing a Ziegfeld production, a Kern or Gershwin or Berlin or Porter or Rodgers and Hart musical. Most of the standout stars were men. Singers (Dennis King, Al Jolson, Harry Richman, Bert Williams); dancers (Fred Astaire, Ray Bolger, Jack Donahue); comedians (Bobby Clark, W. C. Fields, William Gaxton, Eugene and Willie Howard, Victor Moore, Will Rogers, Ed Wynn); and multiple talents (Leon Errol, Fred Stone, Jack Whiting) were some of the many male audience favorites. The first time that any performer's name was listed before the title of a Ziegfeld *Follies* was in 1927, when Eddie Cantor was starred.

Guys and Dolls in 1950 was a transition musical, with major parts for both men and women. The domestication of Nathan Detroit and Sky Masterson became a precursor of many later musicals. In "Marry the Man Today," Adelaide and Sarah give practical details on how to bait the trap and change a man's ways—once he has been caught.

Since *Guys and Dolls,* men stars have been replaced by women who are larger than life, and not beautiful by conventional standards. Although Beatrice Lillie comes on strong, she does so insidiously. You don't realize that she has knocked you down until she has done it, in contrast to the harder breathing of younger women stars.

Tammy Grimes, Miss Lillie's co-star in *High Spirits,* worked hard to be eccentric. Barbra Streisand's graceful gawkiness dominated *Funny Girl,* Carol Burnett energetically mugged throughout *Fade Out—Fade In,* and the florid sexlessness of the oversized kewpie called Carol Channing carried *Hello, Dolly!* to ten Tony awards. Loud and brassy,

Angela Lansbury's *Mame* was a direct lineal descendant of *Dolly*. Mame is overpowering and totally capable throughout the course of a story that has been described as what could have happened to Oedipus if he had met his aunt before his mother. She dominated men and made them love it. Gwen Verdon's brassiness, aggressively gauche postures, and angular dancing made *Sweet Charity* more animated than bittersweet. Each of these women appears almost outlandishly souped up with propulsive energy and projects great force of personality. Each gave her role not only everything she had, but a great deal more.

It makes an interesting comparison to observe that Barbara Cook and Florence Henderson, who are lovely and have beautiful voices, cannot seem to find their stride on Broadway. Joan Roberts, Jan Clayton, and Martha Wright were earlier examples of attractive feminine women who sang beautifully but were too subdued to cope with today's roles. A feminine and beautiful woman who is gentle and sings well cannot hold a candle to the assertive and almost bizarre fizziness of our musical stage's leading ladies.

Rudolf Schildkraut, Joseph's father, once observed that no matter where on the stage he was placed by the director, ". . . the audience will find me." Today's Maenads could make the same statement. Of the ten or so women whose names above a title would attract audiences to a musical, Julie Andrews is the only one not strident or larger than life. In spite of her success in *The Boy Friend,* Miss Andrews has never carried a major musical by herself and is primarily a movie star.

The last significant romantic male in the musical theatre was Alfred Drake, whose reputed $15,000 a week for *Kismet* in 1953 probably represented the last time that a male musical star could receive such recognition. Drake himself, too young for camp and too old for *Hullabaloo,* no longer seems able to find an audience. It is difficult to recall the leading man in most musicals of the last decade. Fritz Weaver (*Baker Street*) and Sidney Chaplin (*Funny Girl*) were typical and could hardly be called romantic singing types. The problem of getting a leading man has become so acute that producers have cast non-singing movie veterans like Don Ameche (*Silk Stockings*) and Robert Ryan (*Mr. President*).

In *The Music Man*, Robert Preston scored the largest personal triumph of any male musical star in recent years. But even though his part was ideal for Preston's brashness and gumption, its anachronistic success was primarily due to the delightful freshness of the show's talking, singing, rhythmic recitation form.

Robert Goulet, whose almost-too-perfect features, physique, and voice might have made him into a genuine idol, has spent little time in the musical theatre after his extraordinary success with women audiences in *Camelot*. Most other men in contemporary musicals tend either to character parts or blandness. Sammy Davis, Jr., and Zero Mostel are enormously energetic and talented exceptions, but there is reason to suspect that some of the audience appeal of *Golden Boy* and *Fiddler on the Roof* was ethnic. Although not romantic types or primarily singers, each man has a twinkle that eases his communication with an audience. But they probably do not have as strong an ability to attract a following as several of the women who dominate musical theatre.

Ethel Merman, still sounding like a whole parade going by, was the aggressive principal of *Annie, Get Your Gun*. Her crowing that "Anything you can do, I can do better" delighted audiences for 1,147 performances. She was the hero of *Gypsy*, who destroyed everyone close to her and emerged triumphant. She had, in *Girl Crazy*, made history by becoming the first successful belter who sang with a chest rather than an operetta voice. The high C that she held for sixteen bars while the orchestra played the melody of "I Got Rhythm" can still be heard echoing in today's theatres.

The belting woman singer who was a prerequisite for the devouring Medusa of later musicals could have been a model for Al Capp's large women. Gretchen Wyler was a tough man-eater in *Silk Stockings* and Carol Haney dominated every scene in *Pajama Game* in which she appeared. Lucille Ball's stridency kept *Wildcat* going at a rapid pace. Gwen Verdon's assurances that Lola got whatever she wanted paced *Damn Yankees* to 1,022 performances. In *New Girl in Town,* she pursued her boy friend almost desperately and stopped the show with a ballet expressing disgust at men's carnal appetites. In *The Unsinkable Molly Brown,* Tammy Grimes dominated her father and brothers, buffaloed a man into marriage, ruined his home life, and won him back by doubletalk. Girl wants, pursues, and gets boy seems to be a more appropriate musical theme than boy seeks girl.

Many current heroines are so relatively unattractive that it is difficult for an audience to believe that they actually would be pursued. The women of earlier musicals, though seldom able to carry a show, were indisputably in the Gibson Girl tradition of beauty, grace, and dignity. Bitter-sweet Fanny Brice, dimple-kneed Ann Pennington, radiant singer-dancer-impersonator Marilyn Miller, and statuesque Lillian Lorraine exuded femininity. Aileen Stanley, Frances Williams, Julia Sanderson, Marion Harris, Nora Bayes, Irene Bordoni, and Ruth Etting were charming singing stars. Today's female leads are so unattractive that only a rare mother would want her daughter to look like them.

The one actress who probably remains an ideal for today's mother is Mary Martin, whose superstar status results from a unique combination of plainness, femininity,

and spicy aggressiveness. Her plainness is non-threatening
to both men and women. Miss Martin's femininity is
spiced with the aggressive touches that have made her
a supreme professional—goo-goo eyes, fluttering hands,
"ooh" at the end of a dull line. Who else but Miss Martin, as the fun nun in *The Sound of Music,* could kick her
heels in the air, expose her legs, and make the gesture
seem completely natural? Wholesome enough to offend no
one, Miss Martin has been engaging in such high jinks
ever since *Leave It to Me.* Barbara Harris, Broadway's newest star, looks like Miss Martin, and has the same magic
triad of characteristics. Other successful young women
stars have built their stage personalities around the spice
that is only one facet of Miss Martin's appeal.

We have lost interest in beautiful singers and dancers
and the light-hearted and sun-filled musicals that they
brightened. Romance and love songs were basic to the
annual feasts of music and lovely girls served in Ziegfeld's *Follies* (1907–1943), J. J. Shubert's *Passing Shows*
(1912–1924), George White's *Scandals* (1919–1939), Irving
Berlin's *Music Box Revues* (1921–1924), and Earl Carroll's
Vanities (1923–1932). A typical tableau in the first *Music
Box Revue* that presented chorus girls dressed as several
courses of a lavish dinner would be campy to today's the-
atregoers, who no longer can believe that love is sweeping
the country.

Audiences would be similarly unresponsive to the op-
erettas that represented America's other major approach
to musical theatre. Rudolf Friml has accurately described
his favorite form: ". . . a full-blooded libretto with lus-
cious melody, rousing choruses, and romantic passions."
Operetta had ceased to be a meaningful style long before
Sigmund Romberg's death in 1951 but continued to exert
considerable influence via Jerome Kern, Kurt Weill, and
Oscar Hammerstein. Although *Man of La Mancha* took
New York by storm because of its operetta qualities, its

success was a fluke and has led to no imitators, even though a musical success usually breeds several offspring by the very next season.

The era of Americanized operetta and traditional musical comedy closed with the Depression, when a charmingly musical "I love you" became less interesting to audiences. The mocking score of *Strike Up the Band* lampooned Babbittry, war, treaties, and secret diplomacy. Social criticism struck a new note in the political satire in *Of Thee I Sing*, perhaps the first musical to shun boy-meets-girl. Marc Blitzstein's influence on several of his more commercially successful contemporaries was a major force in relating text to music. *Show Boat* was the first musical play and *Pal Joey*'s integration of text with music and lyrics helped pave the way for *The Most Happy Fella*, *My Fair Lady*, and other musical plays that lack traditional singing romantic leads.

A typical musical like *Skyscraper* lacked singing stars and even major characters, since its hero was a small brownstone house that defied a large building being built around it. It is a rare musical today that has even one passable ballad, as the sophisticated social criticism of character songs like "Adelaide's Lament" in *Guys and Dolls* and "Something's Coming" in *West Side Story* have replaced John Steel singing "A Pretty Girl Is Like a Melody" or "Lady of the Evening." Dancing has also declined and *West Side Story* was the last musical to have really exciting dance numbers.

Larking and romantic gaiety have tended to disappear at the same time that the musical theatre has expressed more social awareness. The original opening line of "Ol' Man River" in *Show Boat* referred to "niggers." Although Julie's being part Negro is acceptable to her colleagues and is important to the plot, neither of her songs ("Bill" and "Can't Help Lovin' That Man") alludes to race. By the time of *South Pacific*, Oscar Hammerstein made the romance between Lieutenant Cable and the native Liat a musical plea for tolerance ("You've Got To Be Taught To Hate"). Only a few years earlier, audience disapproval of an interracial romance had been largely responsible for the failure of the splendidly cast, beautifully written, sophisticated, and musically exciting *Beggar's Holiday.*

More recent audiences have repeatedly demonstrated enthusiasm for musically attractive social criticism. The decline in popularity and number of musicals since the 1920's has not been caused by such themes, or by mounting costs and competition from other media. It stems from the simple fact that the early smooth flow of melody from Tin Pan Alley has become an occasional leak from a broken tap. Singers once sent audiences from the theatre humming memorable tunes. Lovely melodies and sprightly lyrics have become historical memories as the prolonged musical and lyrical drought has made it amply clear that there are no successors to Gershwin, Kern, Porter, and Youmans. Our eager embracing of take-charge women stars is only one response to a dearth of other qualities in musicals.

The Celluloid Gender

Women's dominance of opera, drama, and musical theatre in recent decades helped prepare the way for their new imporance in motion pictures, epitomized by Elizabeth Taylor's two-million-dollar fee for *Cleopatra.* Today's female superstars, booted and spurred and ready to ride, have achieved more fame than actresses of the silent era, when men loomed so large on the screen. Although early talkies brought fame to a wide range of indisputably male stars, several transitional actors of the 1940's led to the current crop of bland heroes. Such shifts are important in a country where movies still represent the family's largest single leisure expenditure, a major source of its fantasies, and in which trends can be traced with some confidence because the star plays himself over and over again.

The first men movie stars maintained a hold over their audiences that was almost as intense as that of the matinee idols. Their silence made it easy for fans to project all kinds of qualities onto them. True, admirers of a movie idol could not wait at the stage door or see him strolling along the Avenue. But silent actors were often able to give a woman the feeling that "he's looking directly at me." The darkened theatre's flickering images that were somehow real provided an ideal setting for fantasy.

Maurice Costello was the first silent idol, but he received only a fraction of the torrent of letters sent to Francis X. Bushman, the "handsomest man in the world" and the most flamboyant early movie hero. Bushman needed eighteen secretaries to answer his fan mail and received more than 250,000 letters from women in one week when he offered to rent himself out for a day. Bushman was believed to be a bachelor, until he divorced his wife in order to marry co-star Beverly Bayne. His popularity plummeted with the news of his marriage, because a married man could not properly (at the time) be the recipient of romantic fantasies.

Ramon Novarro recalls how "the leading men of silent films were always Adonises and Apollos. . . . The camera angle had to be just so in each shot and every movement was calculated and precise. . . ."[13] The Adonises and Apollos had the traditional strong features that were the trademark of a matinee idol. The jauntiness of many a silent hero is epitomized in a remark attributed to Douglas Fairbanks. After a tour of the Far West, Doug complained that "the Grand Canyon disappointed me; I couldn't jump it." Handsome Wallace Reid's record of fifty-two consecutive box office successes in seven years has never been equaled.

Rudolph Valentino's death in 1926, after an extraordinary career of only five years, unleashed unparalleled public hysteria. Valentino's mythic appeal could be inferred from the enormous popularity of *The Sheik,* in which he kidnaped a beautiful woman and compelled her to fall in love with him, in a manner reminiscent of the ancient rituals in which a bride was won by feats of daring. The Great Lover was virile enough to feel uninhibited about moving gracefully even off the dance floor. He could play Monsieur Beaucaire in silk stockings, lace handkerchief, and beauty spot without seeming ridiculous.[14]

John Gilbert, Richard Barthelmess, Antonio Moreno, Jack Mulhall, Rod La Rocque, and other silent heroes could convey emotion by a curl of the lip, a flick of the finger, a glance. Primitive technological procedures and lighting required the movie hero to have handsome and interesting features because the talented makeup men, dentists, and cinematographers of later years had not yet been developed. Women's fantasies of sentiment and romance were reinforced by an actor's soft mouth, arresting eyes, and handsome nose.[15]

Idols Who Talked

Talking pictures led to the popularity of actors who represented many different facets of maleness and became the idols of millions of American women. Perhaps the Depression contributed to the preference of audiences for assertive men who accomplished things on a movie screen at a time when it was so difficult to achieve goals in the real world.

Clark Gable was helped to become the King by slapping Norma Shearer in *A Free Soul.* Millions of women thought it would be exciting to be slapped by Gable, whose quizzically cocked eyebrows, amused dimpled grin, and "Come here, baby" helped to convey an arrogant virility. Other actors exuded the toughness of James Cagney, whose simian gait was reinforced by the way in which he carried his hands, palms to the rear. The grapefruit that he pushed in Mae Clarke's face in *Public Enemy* became a symbol of his cockiness and a model for many later scenes. Edward G. Robinson as *Little Caesar* had made it easy for the American public to love to hate a ruthless gangster and Humphrey Bogart continued the tough tradition through the 1930's and '40's and added his unique combination of courage, individualism, and integrity.

John Barrymore moved from *Beau Brummel* and similar silent parts to romantic talkie leads. Leslie Howard, probably the only movie actor who looked luminous, had a special ability to mesmerize women. Tyrone Power's eyelashes blinked semaphores of romance. Charm and restrained sensuousness were hallmarks of Fred Astaire's impeccable dancing sophisticates. Errol Flynn was as handsome as Robert Taylor and, in addition, had bravura and ruggedness.

The disarming candor of Gary Cooper, Henry Fonda, and James Stewart helped endear them to women. Cary Grant threw japes and quips over his shoulder while weaving, bobbing, and attracting women along the boulevard. He continued the bantering and sophisticated tradition established by Ronald Colman, Warner Baxter, Brian Aherne, Herbert Marshall, and William Powell, and later represented by Ray Milland.

Robert Montgomery was both an accomplished comedian and a hesitant lover. Spencer Tracy patented the role of the virtuous man who always came through in a pinch. John Wayne's muscular rectitude was as magnetic as the world-weary but spiritual determination of John Garfield, who played the sensitive and intense young man so incandescently.

The feisty male heroes who dominated when Americans went to the movies once a week represented a combination of the average and unique, exciting as well as ordinary, glamorous but approachable, intriguing yet understandable.[16] Different enough to be interesting, they had enough common clay to be reassuringly familiar.[17]

Gregory Peck, Van Johnson, and William Holden helped to provide a bridge between the varied personalities of the talking era's first fifteen years and today's more thin-lipped, outré-world actors. Peck would give the impression of speaking softly even if he were to shout and paved the way for many later uncertain and indecisive heroes. Underacting would be a polite term for Peck's earnest woodenness, which comes across as an almost schizoid detachedness.

Van Johnson's replacement of warm and ruggedly handsome Lew Ayres as Dr. Kildare was typical of the change in movie heroes during the war years. Johnson's open smile and eager features led to many "boys next door," including Richard Quine, who has since become a director, and Robert Walker, whose great talent enabled him to mature out of such roles. Tom Drake's combination of "boy-next-door" and the man-unsure-of-himself was timely enough so that he should have achieved much greater success.

William Holden was, for many years, a consistently popular leading man. Why? He looks handsome, but is ordinary enough not to rub men the wrong way. Women feel that their response to him is acceptable, because he looks undistinguished and therefore poses no challenge (e.g., "I won't fall for him just because he's so good-looking"). Holden seems about to ask, "Tennis, anyone?"— and mean it. The blank ambience of Rock Hudson and the beach boys is a throwback to Holden.

Peck, Johnson, and Holden were transitional figures en

route to today's younger performers who share an ambiguous masculinity and hollow personality. Their features are so blurred that the camera often seems out of focus and their personalities lack resonance, depth, and edges. Many newer actors are less effeminate than pretty, with a beach-boy sameness of expression. Who can distinguish among George Peppard, Robert Wagner, and George Hamilton? The faces of these George Spelvins are neutral enough to have been made of plastic and rubber.

The search for stars with snap, crackle, and pop may be ushering in a new era of slop, cackle, and pap.[18] The young men with ambiguous first names—Troy, Rory, Tab —look like their names, in contrast to the male sentience of silent stars who had atypical names like Rudolph and Francis. The younger actors often project a powder-puffy and indeterminate sexuality, a quality of not knowing what they want, either of the world or women. Tony Curtis manages to be simultaneously faunlike and neuter and Jack Lemmon is about as sexy as Penrod, and both actors come across as middle-aged boys.

Post–World War II attempts to develop interest in forceful male actors like Darren McGavin have generally failed. One reason that Robert Mitchum could not achieve super-stardom is that audiences could practically hear the orgones popping when Mitchum walked across a screen and exuded his semi-somnolent sexuality. Among younger actors who project masculinity, only Steve McQueen has developed a large following, probably because he softens his controlled ferocity by looking as if he had just inadvertently swallowed an extremely sour pickle. The casual toughness which Lee Marvin conveys is given a relieving grace by his white hair and up-tight roles that put him at a sharp angle to ordinary life. If James Dean had lived, he might have been an excitingly virile actor.

Even Marlon Brando, whose mixture of intensity, violent eruptibility, and tenderness can be so exciting, has never approached the audience appeal of earlier idols. The contrast between his feminine voice and eyes and otherwise strong face may be confusing, and men find it so difficult to identify with Brando that most of his films do badly at the box office. One reason that Paul Newman, who resembles Brando in some ways, is much more successful could be that his unblinking eyes and sculptured face provide no such incongruity. His face's youthful and not-lived-in quality is just right for the non-hero parts that have provided Newman with his greatest recognition. Newman is the only major star of his generation who comes across on the screen as a strong and completely masculine hero.

Survivors of the movies' heroic manhood include John Wayne (born 1907) and Cary Grant (born 1904). Burt Lancaster (born 1913) projects an almost ferocious masculinity but his ability to attract audiences, like that of Kirk Douglas, has been marred by a number of completely inappropriate roles. Most of the other actors successful since World War II have conveyed a subdued manhood that contrasts with the broad-shouldered types who once thronged the screen.

The changing needs of movie audiences can also be seen in differences between actresses who once were popular and current favorites. Joan Crawford dominated the early 1930's and Bette Davis was the favorite during the decade's second half. Not only was each a unique and memorable personality; many of their contemporaries were made of stronger stuff than today's heroines. Carole Lombard brilliantly created the woman playing against the comic image and Kay Kendall later did a thinner version of the same role. Paula Prentiss is a less substantial version of Miss Kendall. Janet Gaynor was quintessentially pure and sweet, but June Allyson displayed a sugary quality in similar parts in the 1940's. Sugar hardened to treacle when similar roles were later played by Debbie Reynolds. It is almost as if there has been a blurring at the center from one decade to the next.

Parallel to the decline of masculinity in actors has been a loss of femininity in actresses. The womanliness so beautifully conveyed by Greta Garbo, in spite of her awkward carriage, and the ladylike qualities of Greer Garson have been replaced by a blatant dishy sexuality that is almost exaggerated enough to be neuter and was anticipated by pneumatic Betty Grable's replacement of sweet Alice Faye in musicals. Acceptance of the sex kitten represented one way in which audiences could respond to the changes in social life required by World War II. The typical pin-up girl had a localized personality: bosom (Lana Turner), legs (Betty Grable), torso (Marie MacDonald), hair (Veronica Lake), voice (Lauren Bacall), and even "oomph" (Ann Sheridan).

Audience preferences for such caricaturish sexuality paved the way for the depersonalized heroines of the last fifteen years. Mannequin stiffness and immobility characterized Grace Kelly and helps to explain why Audrey Hepburn is the only actress whose representation is in demand as a store-window mannequin.[19] The appeal of such qualities can be inferred from the one million dollars that Miss Hepburn received for *My Fair Lady* in contrast to Rex Harrison's mere $350,000.

Although Miss Hepburn has a unique elfin charm and delightful never-never quality, her static faciness, arched neck, and stiff spine give her the appearance of a cute but androgynous adolescent ballet dancer. Her lack of hip and torso movements contributes to mannishness and the coincidental popularity of dresses that avoid the body has provided one way of exploiting limited assets.[20] Miss Hepburn's face forms an inverted triangle and square planes

dominate Miss Kelly's and Shirley MacLaine's. Such
sharp angles are in contrast to the oval faces of Hedy La-
marr and earlier actresses.

In the light of other current preferences, it is less astonishing that Doris Day has remained so durable a box-
office attraction. Part of her unreal and distant appearance derives from use of a scrimlike diffusion filter that
gives Miss Day's face a hazy quality. The haziness seemingly appeals to American audiences, because Miss Day
has received top star billing in all but two of her films
over a period of fifteen years. Miss Day's inability to project womanliness is suggested in Oscar Levant's claim that
he knew Miss Day before she became a virgin.

Doris Day's relatively emotionless face at least conveys
a minimal concern for what is happening. Such interest
has often been lacking in Elizabeth Taylor, who managed
to look bored or expressionless much of the time. Her
flawless performance in *Who's Afraid of Virginia Woolf?*,
however, demonstrated that she can be a superlative actress, given an appropriate script and direction. Miss Taylor's fairly heavy torso and clumsy gait are distinctions
that she shares with Kim Novak. Miss Novak, in addition
to a blank expression, also conveys a satiated and a "no
one can reach me" quality that contrasts with the vulnerability of a Marilyn Monroe. Miss Monroe's ability to
communicate such sensibility may have contributed to the
lack of audience interest in her serious films, just as the
hardness projected by Natalie Wood may be one reason
for Miss Wood's considerable success.

The American audiences who rejected Miss Monroe as
a serious actress only seem willing to accept femininity
when it is personified in European actresses like Jeanne
Moreau, Sophia Loren, or Simone Signoret. Perhaps we
can respond to womanliness in foreign actresses because it
is distant enough to be non-threatening.

Today's actresses tend to be more potent at the box

office than their men co-stars. Fans who once avidly followed actors' amours are today more likely to be titillated by actresses' romances. Americans' enormous interest in Elizabeth Taylor's private life was reminiscent of the earlier preoccupation with Ingrid Bergman's passionate pilgrimage. Both women conducted their amours amid Italy's established romantic connotations, fiddling in Rome while their husbands burned. Miss Bergman, like Miss Taylor, presented the image of a woman who seeks release from tremendous feelings entrapped within her body.[21] Miss Bergman's obvious gentility made it easy for Americans to regard her submission to such feelings as inevitable and genuine, just as the combination of Miss Taylor's illnesses, children, pets, and honesty eased public acceptance of her seeming audacity.[22]

A symbol of current male-female relations in Hollywood was provided by Eddie Fisher, a pawn between aggressively virginal Debbie Reynolds and Miss Taylor. When Miss Taylor wanted Fisher, she took him, although or perhaps because he had been a close friend of former husband Mike Todd. After marriage to Fisher, she became involved with Richard Burton, whose previous marriage was terminated by divorce in a manner reminiscent of Fisher's.

Ingrid Bergman's marriage to a distinguished surgeon had previously been terminated so that she could marry Roberto Rossellini, whom she later divorced before marrying another man. In both cases, the woman appeared to be the aggressor who made key decisions that determined the man's fate. Gertrude Stein might have been describing these romances in her account of the man who "comes with a run" when "I say go and come" and "hears and sees me" when "I say hear and see." Such predatory women have revived the tradition of Mae West, whose wit and directness in going after the men she wanted ("Come up and see me sometime") and explicitness about sex ("I like a man who takes his time") were once revolutionary.

The seeming aggressiveness of such female stars makes it easier for them to play the assertive roles with which audiences are already familiar from drama and musical theatre. In *What a Way To Go*, Shirley MacLaine becomes a multimillionaire by surviving several husbands. Every female emerges unscathed from *It's a Mad, Mad, Mad, Mad World*, but each male ends up with broken arms or legs. Role reversal is so common that traditional categories like a man's picture (e.g., *The Maltese Falcon*) and a woman's picture (e.g., *A Woman's Face*) are no longer relevant.

One very rare exception is *The Sound of Music*, which became the highest grossing film ever released, perhaps because it is a woman's picture that provides a quintessential Oedipal story. It presents the same lodestone theme that made *Jane Eyre* and such later stencils as *Rebecca* and *Mistress of Mellyn* popular with women. The basic story deals with a virginal young woman who marries an older aristocrat but is unable to achieve full happiness because of some shadow from the past that interposes itself between the couple. In the earlier books, a fire provides purgation and in *The Sound of Music*, the Nazis represent the ordeal which, when overcome, will permit the couple to "sin" without guilt. Julie Andrews' awkwardness and healthy, open-faced youth were perfect for the part.

Hollywood's shift from men to women was expedited during World War II. By joining the armed forces, many actors reminded audiences that they were subject to the stresses of ordinary life. As a result of the disappearance of many leading men, it was easier to publicize the actresses who remained and many of them were able to achieve enormous exposure and momentum by 1945.

The actors who did not go to war were deglamorized by their studios in order to avoid invidious comparisons with men who were risking their lives. The resulting loss of tin-

sel and glamor and the war-caused hiatus in habit and
fantasy patterns helped to dim the aura of illusion surrounding male stars.[23] Actors of an earlier period had
looked distinctive and encouraged legends about themselves. When a star wanted to shop, his studio would get
an Isotta-Fraschini or Hispano-Suiza that was upholstered
in leopard skin and rent a leopard to ride around next to
the chauffeur. Nowadays we see stars pushing their own
shopping carts in supermarkets, eager to be just plain
folks.

The fantasy distance between pre-World War II stars
and their fans was relatively short in fantasy, so that a girl
could emulate her favorite by appropriate makeup, dyeing
her hair and buying a bias-cut gown. A boy might imitate
the gait and speech of his hero. But it is less likely that
the New People will seek to imitate the contemporary
stars who have so few distinctive characteristics of appearance, costume, or speech.

Another contributor to the phasing out of the star is the
recent importance of agents in assembling films and
trying to squeeze as much money as possible out of each
one. The end of the era in which a studio selected each
role as part of a developmental plan for its contract players was marked by Sandra Dee's termination of her exclusive contract with Universal in December 1965. The pre-
television seven-year contract had encouraged studios to
invest money in an actor with star potential because there
would be ample time to place him in appropriate parts.
When it seemed desirable to balance the almost overwhelming handsomeness of Robert Taylor and Tyrone
Power, their studios could give them "tougher" parts in
Johnny Eager and *Johnny Apollo*.

During the 1930's, the steel-muscled studio publicity
offices built an elaborate apparatus for sustaining interest
in the stars' daily doings. More recently, the studios' decreasing output of films has led to a slowing down of the

machinery for publicizing new performers. Many veteran stars have moved abroad or to New York and see no need to pretend interest in being interviewed or otherwise co-operating with the media. William Holden, who had not lived in Hollywood for seven years before making *Alvarez Kelly* in 1965, "stared icily" at an interviewer and asked, "Why should I tell anyone what I think about anything?" He complained, "Just because I am a star and supposedly have an image to uphold, why does that mean I . . . give my opinions to reporters? I don't give a damn about my image."[24]

Such surliness will not enhance Holden's popularity, no matter how attractive his clean-cut blankness still may be to audiences. And even cooperative actors are less avail-able for interviews as the studios become television pro-duction centers that make most of their movies overseas. Of forty-five films in production by the seven major American studios in the summer of 1966, only twelve were being made in Hollywood.

Publicity could sustain interest in a star but could not create one. Audiences must respond on a visceral level to stars, just as the "matinee girls" once reacted to the idols. What the star projects may vary from one decade to an-other, but cannot be artificially created. Robert Taylor was probably the only major movie star whose fame was substantially enhanced by a build-up. Other attempts to manufacture stars were unsuccessful, even in the case of talented women like Anna Sten and Simone Simon. Some failed because the stars projected qualities for which the public was not ready. Kay Francis, for example, was an original and interesting actress who never achieved top stardom. Depression audiences were simply not interested in the sophisticated coolness and slim, boyish beauty that subsequently made household names of Grace Kelly and Audrey Hepburn.

Some young actors who might possess a capacity for

stardom may never get the chance because rising costs have made producers cautious about using unknowns. So long as millions of moviegoers retain their enthusiasm for a Cary Grant or John Wayne, who represent such excellent box-office insurance, competitive bidding will drive their fee per picture to seven-figure heights. Producers' conservatism leads them to avoid younger performers who might have become the stars of tomorrow.

In the days when studios turned out products rather than individual films, audiences went to see a favorite performer almost regardless of his vehicle. Films are no longer planned on an assembly-line basis and grapple with themes of race relations, juvenile delinquency, illegitimacy, drug addiction, and even atomic survival.[25] As the scenario becomes more significant, we are less likely to project our fantasies on performers. Today's increasingly serious themes require the actor to adapt his personality to his role, where the star of formula films could express his personal characteristics regardless of the part. Current audiences are also interested in techniques and in the psychological dimensions of character that were less relevant in the days of the male superstar.

The stars could devote themselves to single-minded pursuit of romance when they were working with an average of five character actors, who added a variety of colors and textures to a film. The name and face of a Henry Armetta or Guy Kibbee would telegraph his role to moviegoers. In addition to the pleasure of recognition, fans would enjoy the directorial satisfaction of responding to the variation of his established role in which the picture had placed an actor.[26] But after a number of films (e.g., *It Happened One Night*) successfully presented a romantic hero and heroine acting as their own comic relief, it became more difficult for audiences to accept the pure romantic hero.

In the movie industry's early panic response to television, most of the character actors were dismissed and their functions were absorbed by male and female stars, who were also sometimes required to play non- or anti-heroic parts. The audiences that used to enjoy the charm of a romantic comedy (e.g., *Tom, Dick, and Harry*) in 1941 now applaud leering prurience in a contemporary romantic comedy (e.g., *The Apartment*). Movies have followed the lead of other art forms in expressing themes of alienation, and even black comedy (e.g., *Dr. Strangelove*) has occasionally appealed to moviegoers. Such changes have substantially undercut the believability of traditional romantic roles.[27]

The fantasies of the audience before World War II were reinforced by the rococo movie palaces' plush carpeting, ceiling nymphs and angels, gilded woodwork, glamorous lobbies, and ornate curtains. Such appointments helped audiences to anticipate, enjoy, and afterglow in reverie satisfactions. Fans' involvement with movie stars reached its peak in the Prohibition and Depression periods during which the palaces were built. They provided open spaces in which people felt free to dawdle, chat, study stills, nibble on candy, wait for the picture to begin, and otherwise enjoy the florid surroundings.[28]

The small theatres being built today are likely to have 500 seats and a stripped-down utilitarianism.[29] Confronted by such austerity, patrons tend to hurry in and flit away as rapidly as possible. Perhaps the grim sterility of carefully drab lobbies and interiors is appropriate for the neuter young stars whose images flicker on the screen.

The emotions formerly let loose in temples of the seventh art now find many additional outlets as other art forms and media have become permeated with sex. The granddaughter of a woman who panted for John Barrymore might be riffling through *120 Days of Sodom, The Story of O,* or *Fanny Hill* while lounging at the beach in a bikini and whistling to the rock-and-roll music on her transistor radio.

A woman's fantasies about her tiger lover could flourish

at a time when sex expression was hush-hush but today's frankness makes fantasies about a Valentino or Schild-kraut seem amusing curiosa from the past. The power that such fantasies once generated could be inferred from the comparative attendance at funeral services for Mario Lan-za and Errol Flynn, which were held within a few days of each other in Hollywood. Few came to honor Lanza, a famous artist who had presumably led an exemplary fam-ily life, but throngs came to salute swashbuckler Flynn, whose dash died with his generation.

Liberace:
Television's Matinee Idol

Television programs during prime time have three male stars for every female lead. Although television appears to provide an exception to women's domination of the arts, the quantity of men performers is less significant than the qualities of the only star who had so intense a relationship with women fans that he could be regarded as an idol: the pianist Wladziu Valentino Liberace. From an obscure start on a Denver television station in 1952, Liberace had become the most popular single personality in television three years later, even though his program was not shown over a network.

During 1955, Liberace's picture appeared on the cover of forty-five national magazines. His 113 filmed half-hour television programs were rerun more than thirty times on some of the 225 stations that carried them. Liberace be-came America's biggest concert attraction and was the only musician since Paderewski to fill both Carnegie Hall and Madison Square Garden.[30]

Liberace helped make classical music more popular and popularized classical music. Typical of his fans' loyalty was a woman who wrote that "every day I buy a five-gallon can of the gasoline that sponsors you. Since I have no car, I give the gasoline away to my friends." What inspired such loyalty in the fans who sent an average of eleven thousand letters a week to "Val" or "Lee"? Like the older idols, Liberace projected intimacy between himself and the viewer. His manager observed that "he looked right into the camera, made you feel that he was performing just for you." Each viewer could enjoy an experience rather than a performance.

Liberace showed a childlike delight in applause, continuous laughter, the trappings of a costume. Youthfulness was reinforced by his program's air of the unexpected. His fans often mentioned his "cuteness" and referred to him as a "boy." Liberace's delight in himself ("Look at my leg, isn't it pretty?"), tricks, and winking contributed to his childlike appearance. He combined the attractiveness of a grown man with the genderless and non-threatening charm of a young child, so that a woman's fantasies about him had a built-in safety valve.

Liberace won $22,400 damages in a 1959 London libel suit in which he charged a columnist with calling him a homosexual. There is every reason to believe the verdict was in accordance with British justice. Yet the very existence of allegations of homosexuality indicates the radical changes in fantasy needs of women who respond to idols. Any imputation of homosexuality about an earlier idol would have been unthinkable. That such a charge was made about an American performer suggests how our expectations had changed.

Liberace was like a number of other early television figures who conveyed warmth and self-revelation. They have been succeeded by performers who tend to work from the outside in, but usually stop short of contact. Milton Berle, Sid Caesar, Groucho Marx, and similar strong comedy stars have been replaced by the muted personalities of the Smothers Brothers. Johnny Carson's cool at-

tracts an audience 40 percent larger than the 2,500,000
homes which nightly tuned in the volatility, emotionality,
and enthusiasms of Jack Paar. For similar reasons, Edward R. Murrow's deep sense of commitment has yielded
to the deftly packaged 7 o'clock news. It is altogether
fitting that the only survivor of the medium's youth is Ed
Sullivan, who so perfectly embodies the man without
qualities.

Have Chum,
Will Travel

Older performing arts had reversed the roles of men and
women so completely that it would be logical to expect
our newest medium to reflect the change. One way in which
it has done so is by giving Liberace matinee idol status
and another is a major modification in the content of
western and private detective stories.

Time was when parentheses-legged men won the West
by straight shooting, clean living, and playing a lone hand.
During the period in which Americans were beginning to
enjoy stories about such heroes, readers were savoring the
solo cleverness of private detectives, who coped with
criminals as well as police. Although westerns and detective stories have flourished for over a century, the last
fifteen years have witnessed the single hero in both forms
being replaced by a group. The lone hero is no longer in
business for himself. Like other individual entrepreneurs,
he has been replaced by something resembling a corporation and his clear solo tones have become *pianissimos* from
a chorus. The fission from loner to gaggle can be traced
as detective stories and westerns have moved from novels
to movies and, most recently, into television.

How radically the conference approach to dramatic
problem-solving has changed westerns can be seen in

several television sagebrush sagas that present the hero as a family man, strong on togetherness. Patriarch Lorne Greene, in what has long been the single most popular television program (*Bonanza*), engages in good works with his sons. Not too far from the Ponderosa, Big John Cannon lives on *The High Chaparral* with his brother and son.[31]

Other television cowboys who were not members of the same family often were close enough to one another to be kinfolk.[32] In some television westerns, the work situation was the excuse for doing a double.[33] Of the fifty-five major television westerns, *Have Gun, Will Travel* was the only successful program with a lone hero, and he was a very unusual egghead cowboy who enjoyed chess and cookery and was a walking Great Books Club.[34] Practically every other successful western on television was built around a brace of heroes or a family situation.

The earlier western heroes who once accounted for one-fourth of all movies were easy to accept as masters of their own destiny because they sat firmly in the saddle with authority, cowboys first and actors second. Today's audiences no longer have an opportunity to identify with the rugged individualism of a lone cowboy who handled problems with independence and autonomy. Even appearance differentiates the new from the old, and the suety and well-barbered Cartwrights are in sharp contrast to the hungry look and shaggy mane of earlier movie cowboys. Characters in the traditional western had few relatives and the family groups often consisted of villains, like the James boys or Dalton brothers.

The first multiple hero in a major movie western emerged in *My Darling Clementine* (1946), in which Wyatt Earp agreed to become sheriff of Tombstone on the condition that his two brothers could work with him. The group hero got more exposure with the team of Billy the Kid and Doc Holliday in *The Outlaw* (1947). Released in the same year, *Red River*'s father (John Wayne) and adopted son (Montgomery Clift) did not battle for Joanne Dru, but ended up cooperating with each laughing in the other's arms.[35] The western hero as family man became even more popular in 1952 in *High Noon*, which received enormous attention during television's early days. Not only does hero Gary Cooper get married before the climactic standoff, but his wife (Grace Kelly) coldbloodedly shoots and kills one of the four villains with whom Cooper is fighting. Cooper's inability to win a gun battle without his Quaker bride's help anticipated the group hero.

Gunfight domesticity in *High Noon* was so startling because the loner had dominated the sagebrush ever since William S. Hart built his authentic films around a quiet but effective hero. The cowboy became louder and more dandified in the 1930's, when a number of actors followed the trail of Tom Mix, whose shiny boots, tailored Stetson, embroidered shirt, and fancy buckle and guns contributed to his enormous appeal from 1928 to 1934.

The shy cowboy loped further into the sunset after 1936, when Gene Autry moved to Republic Pictures from the National Barn Dance radio program. Although Ken Maynard was responsible for bringing rhythm to the range, Gene Autry was the first singing cowboy. The final two or three bars of the hero's opening song were punctuated with gunshots, usually from a stagecoach robbery or a villain shooting windows out of a house. The final scene always had a major number sung by a group like the Riders of the Purple Sage or Sons of the Pioneers, who were either deputy sheriffs or ranch hands standing around from a previous scene.

The western melody man ultimately drowned out the stammers of the once shy and scruffy cowboy hero. Roy Rogers, who became the leading western musician when Autry went off to World War II, looked like the victim of an explosion in a paint factory because of his provocative costumes, which usually included Eagle-stitched boots and peach flower embroidery on his shirts.

Such debonair and garrulous guitarists were a far cry from James Fenimore Cooper's Leatherstocking, who went west in order to turn his back on women and civilization. By the mid-nineteenth century, Kit Carson was the reading public's favorite Indian fighter and mesquite hero, whose only companions were a rifle and a horse. Dime novels of the 1870's were built around crack shot Deadwood Dick, and Moccasin Mat singlehandedly fought off groups of cattle rustlers in the next decade's fiction. During the 1890's, Buffalo Bill, famous from the Ned Buntline stories, developed a traveling show that helped to whet public interest in the western tradition.

For some years after 1908, an average of one Bronco Billy movie was made each week. Over the next four decades, the good-guy bad-guy western was perfected by Ken Maynard, Harry Carey, Tim McCoy, Hoot Gibson, and Buck Jones. Its standard ingredients included the stagecoach robbery, stampede, necktie party, barroom brawl, and the hero's long pursuit of the villain. The hero's being alone and unencumbered was as central as the final gun battle. The hero-centaur lived off the land and seldom talked, even to his faithful horse. Fans were sometimes more enthusiastic about horse than master and hoofprints of Buck Jones's Silver King, Ken Maynard's Tarzan, William S. Hart's Fritz, and Tom Mix's Tony were sought almost as actively as their riders' autographs. Any human companion of the cowboy was clearly subservient, e.g., the Long Ranger's Tonto.

Pre-musical and pre-group westerns presented a man standing alone in a world of moral simplicities, exerting his will and achieving mastery over events. In the final gun-fight, a hero's ability to control his world was expressed unequivocally. The new hero is less likely than his

predecessors to kill the villain.[36] He usually wounds the
culprit, reflecting the symbolic decrease in firepower oc-
casioned by his becoming a family man or team player as
well as the cautions of the television code of self-regulation.

Decreased violence and fewer killings in television westerns may ultimately make the form less popular. One of
its original appeals was provision of a legitimized indul-
gence in the kind of violence which is prohibited by our
morality. By localizing the violence, westerns reminded us
of the prohibition's validity while permitting a veiled
expression of instincts which were represented by cultural
norms.[37]

Traditional movie westerns also had the aging villain
who often captured an attractive young woman and a
climactic scene in which the young hero attempted to rescue her. The wicked old man fired his shots off target or
too soon or too late but the young hero was on target with
a minimum number of shots fired from the hip. In addition to such obvious symbolism, another dimension of the
western as moral fable was its taking place in the past and
generally ending and beginning in the dust and heat of
noon on the same street. Moviegoers could feel that the
future would not differ from the past and that they did
not have to do anything to save themselves so long as the
cowboy hero was functioning.

Audiences could identify with the residents of Fricassee
Gorge, whose problems were solved by a single cowboy and
whose guilts and problems could be unloaded on a cowboy-
hero because he was unknown. His anonymity and celibacy
made him a priest who shrived the whole community and
could conveniently disappear after eliminating the villain.
Saddled with chums or family, the new cowboy can less
freely ride away into the hills. He provides a lesser resolution
of problems faced by the town—and audience. It is not too
hard to see today's cowboy as a man hounded by install-
ment collectors and insurance agents. His saddle, spurs,

and gun-butt are often sticky with the flypaper of modern living.[38]

Today's lack of interest in the old-fashioned western hero is underlined by disappearance of the *Lone Ranger*, who had been seen and heard for three decades in radio, motion pictures, and television. *Lone Ranger* re-runs had much larger audiences than Chet Huntley and Leonard Bernstein programs shown at the same hour as recently as 1959, but no new episodes have been produced for some time. In contrast, there have been endless re-runs of episodes from Bill Boyd's *Hopalong Cassidy* movie series, in which the heroic trio includes young Russell Hayden and older Gabby Hayes. It is only a question of time before television discovers other western movie series with a clutch of heroes, like the *Three Mesquiteers*, starring two-gun Ray Corrigan, cowboy Bob Livingstone, and ventriloquist Max Terhune.

Television group heroes attract such huge audiences that the occasional post-*High Noon* movies built around a loner appear almost anachronistic, e.g., *Shane* (1953); *3:10 to Yuma* (1957); *One-Eyed Jacks* (1961); *Nevada Smith* (1966). *A Fistful of Dollars* (1967) was denounced as a "campy fraud" *because* its tall, laconic, and steely-eyed hero is a Man with No Name who blows into an evil frontier town, depopulates San Miguel of its wicked and greedy varmints, and then rides out of town.[39] At a time when there is a lack of major new stars and directors and the classic western is denounced as "campy," it seems unlikely that the form can recover its former vitality.

The Private Detective

Older detective fiction buffs can remember when Nick Carter and The Shadow were solving crimes all by themselves. Charlie Chan was turning in criminals in spite of continuing interference provided by his Number One Son and Number Two Son. But the private detective hero,

like the cowboy, now is a team player. Television private
eyes enjoy being part of a syndicate, live on expensive
houseboats, go to nightclubs, eat in posh restaurants, drive
sleek automobiles, and are beautifully tailored. Poor old
Sam Spade, in contrast, had frayed cuffs, missing buttons,
and ate hamburgers.[40]

Although it is easy to trace the progress of the cowboy
group hero, there are fewer clues to the multiple detective.
Movies and television have long presented policeman
buddies, but private detectives had not worked together
extensively before four Los Angeles private eyes began
blinking at the world from their office at *77 Sunset Strip*.[41]
They were followed by many programs built around
groups of sleuths.[42]

One spy used to do the work of two and often even
served as a double agent, but Robert Culp and Bill Cosby
were necessary to do the work of one in *I Spy* and Agent
99 regularly saves Maxwell Smart from disaster. *Batman*
battened because trusty Robin was at his side. In spite of
his name, Napoleon Solo of *The Man from U.N.C.L.E.*
would not be very effective without his chum Ilya. One
network replaced a clever and effective lone *Secret Agent*
with a whole force of mercenaries in *Mission: Impossible,* for
the key 9 p.m. hour on Saturday.

The lack of success of a program built around a single
sleuth is one measure of evolution from Edgar Allan Poe's
original detective, who was so brilliant that he was set
apart from others. A central satisfaction for the fan has always been his ability to identify with a lone detective who
pits his logic against crime and evil. Sherlock Holmes
added an element of personal danger and the ingenuity
that enabled him to outwit the groupthink represented by
Inspector Lestrade of Scotland Yard. Another widely
copied innovation was sober Dr. Watson, the friend who
chronicled Holmes's adventures and acted as a foil. Other
famous detectives followed Holmes in having a foil: Poirot

(Captain Hastings), Peter Wimsey (Mr. Bunter), Philo
Vance (Van Dine), Ellery Queen (Inspector Queen), Albert Campion (Lugg).

The detectives' foils were not partners but represented
avenues for leaking clues to readers. They also gave readers a feeling of superiority because they were seldom
astute or even very helpful. Nero Wolfe was the only noted investigator who had a helpful associate, in the person
of Archie Goodwin.

Hammer and Bond

Mickey Spillane's Mike Hammer and Ian Fleming's
James Bond became extraordinarily successful at the same
time as the group hero. Spillane had created the character
Mike Danger for comic books. When the industry's uneasiness about censorship led to a decline in comic book
sales, Spillane had little difficulty in adapting his techniques to the Mike Hammer series. Hammer is a killer
who takes the law into his own hands—the first book celebrating his exploits was aptly called *I, The Jury*.

Hammer and James Bond prefer gratuitous killing to
solving cases by using their wits. We have so little confidence in what lone intelligence can accomplish in the
urbanized world that our two most popular detectives
solve cases by the vendetta morality of murder. The Mike
Hammer novels account for seven of the fifteen leading
American best-sellers of all time and Bond, the professional assassin who lacks personal identity and real allegiance,
is an American hero.

If there is an obligatory scene in a Spillane novel, it is
one in which Hammer shoots his girl friend in the stomach. "It was easy," is Hammer's comment after gratu-
itously shooting his nude fiancee in *I, The Jury*.[43] In the
film version of Fleming's *From Russia with Love,* a key scene
shows a man being shot while dangling from the mouth of
Anita Ekberg in a large painting on the side of a building.

The best evidence of the huge audience response to such material is provided by the astonishing $150 million grossed by the first four Bond films and the more than $100 million that Americans spent on "007"-licensed products during 1966.

Sean Connery has almost agreed with Pravda's description of Bond as a "sadistic rapist" in his observation that the series is successful because it is "sadism for the whole family."[44] Like Hammer, Bond has no continuing personal relationships with women but conducts detached adventures. His major thrill seems to come from arousing women and then *not* making love to them, in a kind of sexless sex. In *Goldfinger,* Bond is in bed with a woman, tells his chief on the telephone that "I can't talk to you now, something big's come up"—and then ignores the woman. American audiences reserve their greatest applause for three kinds of situations: non-fulfillment, as in the *Goldfinger* scene; Bond's use of gratuitous violence; and the mechanical devices that are the films' real hero.

Several interview studies have established that the most typical American fans of Bond are men who tend to alienation, impotence, hostility toward women, and passivity, with fantasies of violence. Similar characteristics have been reported in other countries.[45] Small wonder that many Bond fans happily hummed along with the title song of *Thunderball* about a man who knew the secret of success: "His needs are more so he gives less."

Bond's cruelty to women has received recognition in the advertising for the "007" line of men's toiletries. The Colgate-Palmolive Company has been spending $400,000 a week to disseminate slogans like "007 for the license to kill . . . women."[46] Such advertising is primarily directed at young men, whose fantasies about women, once nurtured on romance and soft music, may now be more amenable to brutality.

The Bond novels received considerable impetus from

the enormous publicity afforded the Profumo affair in England. The combination of fast women, peers, weekend country orgies, Soviet espionage, an American procurer who committed suicide, a lying cabinet minister, and a famous actress made life appear to be imitating art in its corroboration of Ian Fleming's vision of reality. There was a sharp increase in the sale of Bond books during and after the Profumo publicity, suggesting that many readers may have regarded Stephen Ward's trial as a confirmation of Fleming's themes.

Bond's great popularity is less surprising in England than the United States, because the English have long enjoyed heroes who murder out of a sense of duty. T. E. Lawrence's legendary status in his own country is partially attributable to his celibacy, but largely to his enthusiasm for dynamiting trains and engaging in other kinds of brutality, while serving the Crown, just as the detailed technology of Bond's murders is presumably part of his patriotic responsibility. One reason that Bond is more of a hero in America than England could be his many resemblances to a Fascist or Nazi officer, which may stir some uncomfortable memories even in a country that shared Lawrence's relish for the minutiae of violence.

Bond is an ideal American hero because he triumphantly represents the new technology. The Bond movies would be ordinary thrillers without the complicated gadgets that make gratuitous murder such fun. When depersonalization and alienation are rife, it is easier for us to respond to Bond's machinery and unbelievable luck than to courage, integrity, and similar old-fashioned virtues.

Bond and Hammer are amoral, sadistic, misogynistic. They could encourage paranoid fantasies because the evil they are fighting can never be vanquished and is always coming up strong for the next encounter. Bond's employer is identified by a code (M.) and has extraordinary potentialities for good and evil.[47] Bond and Hammer are proponents of a lynch or vigilante morality that encourages people to take law into their own hands. Each man implies that extant procedures for establishing order are inadequate and is an extra-legal avenger who typically ends each story by participating in a symbolic lynching. The culprit is killed instead of being turned over to the police in accordance with orderly processes of justice, as Sam Spade would have done. American enthusiasm for Bond and Hammer is especially troubling in the light of our traditional respect for law and law enforcement. No other country has any analogue to our veneration for J. Edgar Hoover and the police and T-men and G-men who have been glorified in American popular culture and are regarded as necessary evils in other countries.[48]

Our preoccupation with vigilantes suggests the possibility that many Americans are losing confidence in the ability of reason and intelligence to solve problems. We have honored reason and intelligence ever since the Areopagus law court in Athens reminded us that public good cannot be advanced by private murders or the vendetta morality of terror. When Orestes killed Aegisthus and Clytemnestra in an act of revenge, Athena was wise enough to refer the case to jurors of the Areopagus.[49] This early example of man's ability to think in terms of abstract Justice contrasts with Bond and Hammer, who represent the barbaric cruelty of the childhood of the human race, the archaic and unintelligible emotions of the Furies who are more interested in the blood on Orestes' hands than in how it got there.

One reason for the almost unbearably intense guilt that Americans experienced after President Kennedy's assassination was our identification with fictional and movie vigilantes who take the law into their own hands. The awful horror of what happened when this was done in Dallas was a sobering reminder of our enthusiasm for vigilante heroes. President Kennedy's widely publicized enthusiasm for the Bond books added an additional poignant note to the events of November 1963. Lee Oswald had read Ian Fleming, according to New Orleans Public Library records. Without adopting any primitive thinking about the effects of mass media, we can consider the possibility, however remote, that James Bond's glorification of violence, marksmanship, and ability to kill without guilt may have been one of the many strands in Oswald's fantasies about using murder in achieving his own goals.

The close relationship between sex and violence in Bond and Hammer reminds us of the reciprocal relationship between sex and violence.[50] Some slang words reflect the connotations of sex as an attack, and "violate" and "violence" come from the same root. A related reason for our interest in violence could be its status as one of the few remaining mysteries, now that sex has become less awesome.

We abhor the violence in which Hammer and Bond engage but are attracted by its provision of a respite from the boredom of everyday life. Their great popularity may reflect our desperate need to reach beyond a world of neuter people and identify with persons who assert themselves in an ultimate manner—by killing. The private detective once asserted himself by integrity and crusading, seeking out and fighting evil—because it existed. Bond and Hammer resemble other recent private detectives who fight crime for pay, in contrast to Spade and Marlowe, who talked tough but were more concerned about helping people than making money.

Gratuitous killing is as new in detective fiction as is the communal approach. The solo-sleuth was once able to outwit his adversary and provide a satisfactory solution to a complex problem, in contrast to many readers' own lives and the inefficiency of hordes of police with elaborate technical facilities. Sam Spade anticipated the comments of many of his successors when he said, "It's a long while since I burst out crying because policemen didn't like me." Philip Marlowe typifies a peculiar loneliness that Raymond Chandler regarded as a necessary lot of the moral man. Only one generation separates Spade and Marlowe and other lonely outsiders from the current wave of collective sleuthing.

Why It Happened

Although groups of two had long been popular in comedy (Amos 'n Andy, Laurel and Hardy) and domestic comedy-cum-sleuth stories (Mr. and Mrs. North, and Mr. and Mrs. Nick Charles), the group hero in western and detective stories came with World War II. One reason for audience acceptance of multiple heroes is the situation in which they are experienced. The detective and western story used to appear in books and magazines that were usually read in privacy and experienced in psychic isolation. A reader could develop a one-to-one identification with the hero of a story. Western and detective television programs, however, are typically seen by the whole family, so that viewers' identification with the screen group is easier.

The large movie screen also made it easier for audiences to accept an outsize hero than does television, which shrinks his dimensions. Other than Liberace, television has not developed a single performer who could sustain a series by himself in the way that a movie star could attract an audience, although it has spawned promising directors and writers.

By using co-heroes, the producer can provide one of his stars with a vacation or temporary subordinate role. When George Maharis turned off *Route 66* because of illness, he was replaced by Glenn Corbett. The series might have lost much of its audience, or even been canceled, if it had had only one hero. Two or more heroes permit a producer to show contrasting personalities, each of whom appeals to different elements in an audience. Dark hair and skin characterized Maharis and Glenn Corbett, but co-hero Martin Milner was taller, blond, and freckled. On another level, the combination of slender David Brinkley's wit and stocky Chet Huntley's seriousness has enabled them consistently to get a larger audience than Walter Cronkite, in communities where the two programs are shown at the same time on opposing channels.[51]

Another aspect of the additional dimension provided by a group of heroes, each of whom has different qualities, can be seen in the White House. Every recent president except Mr. Johnson has had at least one negative alter ego who could be blamed when things went wrong. His lack of such advisers may be one reason for President Johnson's inability to generate the Kennedy magic, part of which resulted from the blamability of his Harvard camarilla, Irish Mafia, and brother Robert, who drained off much criticism that might otherwise have been directed against the President. Sherman Adams deflected fire from Eisenhower, and Truman's cronies put into deep freeze much of the denunciation he would have received. The New Deal professors and Harry Hopkins performed similar functions for Roosevelt. Such a Rasputin would provide Mr. Johnson with the contrast that contributes to the success of multiple heroes on television.

Perhaps one reason for the outcome of the 1964 presidential campaign was that it provided the public with a chance to respond to a symbol of the lone, sun-tanned trouble-shooter who would conquer Communism and unemployment with his six-gun. One element in Goldwater's defeat could have been his inability to realize how out of date such individualism was.[52]

The several institutions that mediate between audience and final production—production company, advertising agency, network—are more important in television than in other popular arts. It is possible that staff members at these institutions may be communicating their own basic attitudes by selecting role-ambiguous and multiple-hero content.

Television's time format has further hastened acceptance of the couple or trio. The medium's segmented schedule makes it difficult to convey evocative exploits in a half hour or even an hour. Fiction may be read over several weeks, during which the reader may nurture fantasies about the hero. The time involved in hearing and reading about a movie and the trip to the theatre permitted a building-up of fantasy expectations. The trip home permitted a simmering down from contact with the solo hero, who might have been on screen for as long as two hours. On television the same movie might be chopped up by commercials, and trips to the refrigerator and bathroom; sipping beer, cooking, checking on the baby, talking, and other home activities further interrupt the viewer's involvement with what is happening on the screen.

The rapid sequence of programs, one after the other, further blocks a viewer's ability to respond emotionally to any one program or hero. When he had fewer heroes, the moviegoer could invest more emotional energy in each one. The dreams once provided by movies have become transferred into a diffuse service on television. Although Clark Gable sustained audience involvement for three decades, he would have become just another casual experience as a performer on a weekly television series.

External and circumstantial factors could not have given birth to the multiple hero without substantial change in audience needs. American audiences after World War II resembled the generation of the 1920's in their response to a decline in moral idealism, the postwar lack of security, disillusionment, and a growing feeling that men were not fully able to cope with or even comprehend the forces they were facing.

Audiences who doubt the ability of any single hero to

cope with today's problems have become more aware of yesterday's difficulties via debunking biographies. Scholars have mortally wounded the myth of Buffalo Bill, "rider of the phony express." Cody, it turned out, bought his colonelcy from the governor of Nebraska, was an office boy at the time of his alleged career with the Pony Express, and never killed an Indian. On the only occasion when he ever shot real bullets, he accidentally shot a boy in the gallery of a Baltimore theatre. As the public learns to be skeptical of such legends, it becomes less likely to believe in the abilities of any one historical or contemporary hero.[53]

Western and detective co-heroes are involved in hazardous work in which life is often at stake. Their comradeship makes heavier demands than characterize the life of a typical viewer and may be reassuring to him. The multi-hero tends to thrive in times of uncertainty or transition and the single hero to flourish when there is greater confidence. The dual hero figured in the very earliest tradition in literature, some five thousand years ago in the Babylonian epic of *Gilgamesh*. The lone hero became firmly established in the person of Odysseus, and continued to dominate world literature through the age of chivalry and the adventures of Roland and King Arthur. The Knight reigned supreme, his squire always a subordinate, until the Renaissance witnessed the co-equal companion's return.

The single hero had reappeared by the mid-nineteenth century, when western and detective fiction were developing audiences. He remained so popular that even the genius of Edgar Wallace could not interest readers in a premature group detective hero. After Wallace published his brilliant account of *The Four Just Men* in 1920, the multiple hero theme was not used for a generation. America's complex and outsize problems since 1945 provided an ideal setting for the let's-share-the-blame syndrome of our group hero. It was inevitable that *The Four Just Men* would become a successful television serial—and it did.

Continued exposure to multiple heroes for twenty years has reinforced some changes in the American character. The hero in many modern movies is more likely to require than be able to give help. Our acceptance of a hero who is decreasingly the master of his fate has been reinforced by psychotic leaders like Hitler, who have made us aware of the enormous harm that could result from a single unchecked leader. The multiple hero provides a compromise by which we can identify with a hero whose potential for good as well as evil is blunted and offers a minimum of individual responsibility as well as blame.

The hero who jumped into the lake to save a damsel in distress has been replaced by a rescue boat loaded with technicians. A decrease in responsibility is also found in other places where individual skill formerly won the laurel. There was a time when each football player used to be a 60-minute man who could do everything, but today's platoon system depends on specialized team members. And it is unlikely that we shall see another Albie Booth or Sid Luckman, now that football coaches use computers. The ingenuity of a Thomas Edison, whose record of over one thousand active patents remains unequaled, has been replaced by a corporate laboratory research team. The solo heroism of Sergeant York is giving way to specialized military technicians and the family doctor is yielding to the specialized panel or group practice of medicine.

A boy could once project fantasies of being a crack shot as a policeman, detective, or cowboy via his egg-crate revolver or broomstick rifle. The most popular recent boy's toy (which sold more pieces in one year [1964] than any toy in history) is the Johnny Seven, a weapon with seven different sub-weapons, that is advertised as a "one-man army." Other manufacturers now make multi-purpose toys with as many as 15 sub-weapons. The enthusiastic acceptance of such toys suggests that many a boy who feels inadequate may seek the support provided by multi-weapon toys. As the single hero has experienced multiple fission, the toy gun has become a multiple weapon.

Many Americans enjoy a relatively good life and high standard of living. It is unpleasant to think that everything may be taken away by someone dropping a bomb or committing a murder. Living with the reality that two-thirds of the crimes known to police and over half the murders committed in American are never solved, we enjoy westerns and detective stories, where evil characters are always stopped. The fantasy satisfactions of the stories may help us feel more secure about the unlikelihood of someone taking away what we have. Like a neurotic with a repetition compulsion, we watch the good triumph over the bad, over and over again.

The mass media have long provided model situations in which anxieties are shown in the process of being controlled.[54] Audiences' fantasies of power and achievement are enhanced by seeing someone successfully coping with fears and problems. The inadequacy of any single member of a group of heroes may lead to fantasy productions that more closely resemble reality, and ultimately make the media less effective means of escape. The new group-ness may also help raise to consciousness repressions that had previously been handled for some people by media in which one hero coped with an anxiety-producing situation.[55]

Although it has been asserted that heroes have the common denominator of expanding the human capability, the modern hero is more likely to contract it. Such a change could only occur because of substantial changes in the supporting players: the audiences. As audiences continue to become even more other-directed, we can expect that our mass media will continue to embrace group-ness. Television has already responded, in detective fiction, to the new roles of women. Their success may have helped to inspire *The Avengers,* in which Honor Blackman played a woman Ph.D. crime fighter and multilingual judo expert who wore leather jerkin and breeches with high black boots. Her favorite throw was hurling evil men through a plate-glass window.

Old-fashioned romantic heroines wrote books on cosmetics, clothing, or cooking, but Honor Blackman represents a new breed and has written a book on judo and karate.[56] The publisher promises that Miss Blackman provides enough information on the "manly arts of self-defense" to "teach any girl how to defend herself from attack." *The Avengers'* appearance on American television in 1966 was one augury of new dimensions of the heroic, and perhaps we shall be replacing the two or three weak men heroes who fumble through a typical detective program with one woman who is strong. Just how strong is suggested in some remarks by Diana Rigg, who replaced Miss Blackman in *The Avengers*: "I never think of myself as sexy. I identify with the new woman in our society . . . fighting is the most obvious quality. I always win my fights and, personally, I enjoy it."[57]

One possible trend is suggested in a television network's announcement that it was considering a series called *My Son, the Detective,* dealing with a mother who works for the Police Athletic League and her policeman son. A mother and son team of private detectives is obviously inevitable. And we can imagine the dialogue between a western hero of the future and his deputy, or deputies if he has a *ménage à trois,* in an epic of the new Mild West that would inevitably be called *Have Chum, Will Travel:*

DEPUTY: Quick-Gun McGraw is down to the OK Corral waitin' on you. He's alone. He says to come a-shootin'.
HERO *(buckling on his gun):* We'll accommodate him. Stop messin' around with that percolator. Go down to the saloon and gather up Allison, Robin, and Jackie . . .

3

fun and games

When *The Father* is placed in a straitjacket by his wife near the climax of Strindberg's play, he shouts: "Omphale, Omphale!" referring to the Queen of Lydia who employed Hercules as a servant, wore the great athlete's lion-skin, and hunted with his club and spear. Today's American women are emulating Omphale although not too long ago embroidery and painting china were almost their only approved leisure pursuits.

Throughout most of the nineteenth century, our prudery and assumption of women's delicacy had made it almost impossible for men and women to participate in outdoor activities together. In the late 1870's, croquet became the first outdoor game in which both sexes could join. Not until the liberalization of bathing costumes during the 1920's was there any substantial acceptance of women's right to enjoy recreation in free association with men and costumed in accordance with the situation.

Annie
Got His Gun

Annie, Get Your Gun was an extraordinary example of art's ability to predict life. So many women followed An-

nie's advice that they now account for 32 percent of our
25,000,000 gun owners. Along with the gun, they took over
as town marshal. A generation after Irving Berlin's prophetic words, the wife was most often the person who made
key family decisions.[1] Such leadership is only one reflection
of her recent dominance of other facets of leisure.

The new look in the sporting life was signaled in 1964
by appointment of a woman to announce the Kansas City
Athletics' games on television. Although the best man
competitor can usually beat the best woman in a sport,
there has been a strong improvement in the quantity and
quality of women's participation in athletics and competitive sports. In the defiantly masculine arena, women's
new role is certainly a sign that they now share some of
the competitiveness that had long been regarded as a
male trait.

Although women have the advantage of a more compact frame than do men, menstrual periods interfere with
their training. Nonetheless, their athletic performance has
been improving continually, as they become heavier and
taller. The average American woman is fourteen pounds
heavier than her counterpart of thirty years ago and the
typical Miss America contestant who stood five feet high
in 1921 was six inches taller by 1962.[2]

In only two generations, the average woman's foot has
jumped from 6 to 8, and sample shoe sizes have increased
from 4–4½ to 5½–6. Feet have become so much wider that
only B and C widths of many popular lines are in stock. A
and AA narrow widths, regularly available as recently as
the 1950's, can be bought only on special order and AAA
is carried by very few shops.[3]

Women's shoulders are becoming broader in relation to
their hips and their physique is otherwise assuming more
masculine proportions. Today's women are also more
muscular and mesomorphic than their ancestors and meso-
morphy is positively correlated with strength and pow-

er.[4] Such changes contribute to the decrease in sexual dimorphism and are occurring even though the decreasing age at menarche provides less time for growth to occur.

Form follows function and the women in earlier societies in which they had dominant roles, like the Germans described by Tacitus or the Congo Andombis, were also characterized by physiques with traditional masculine characteristics. In societies where women take initiative in work and wooing, like the Bosjemans, they are often taller than men.

As American women become increasingly mesomorphic, their personalities could well become more aggressive, self-starting, and dominant than their mothers' or grandmothers'. Such changes in temperament and character and more accepting social attitudes on the part of the community have facilitated women's participation in sports. Although women who seriously engaged in sports a generation ago were rare, many now regularly compete in squash, handball, and other formerly male sports.

Women contenders use sophisticated training procedures and set goals that are progressively more difficult. Wilma Rudolph's preparation for the 1960 Olympic track competition was typical of the thoroughness that has enabled many women to break records more spectacularly than their men counterparts. Another reason could be that men have been competing for so long that they have already approached their potential. Even in medium- and long-distance swimming, where so much depends on the body's upper musculature, women's systematic clipping of Amateur Athletic Union records is superior to men's. By 1962, women had shaved 81.4 seconds from the 1946 400-meter freestyle time of 5' 26.7"; men cut only 37.6 seconds from their 1946 time of 4' 49.8". Women pruned 3' 22.1" from the 1,500-meter freestyle time of 22' 8.1" between 1946 and 1962; men nicked a mere 2' 7.4" from their mark of 19' 23.1".

Our country's swimmers and divers won an unprecedented seven of ten women's events in the 1964 Olympics, and in 1960 Miss Rudolph proved the efficacy of her training by becoming the first American woman to win three Olympic track and field gold medals. The United States' women's showing in their 1964 Los Angeles meet with Russia was especially impressive because of the Russian advantage in size and musculature.

Women are not only competing more actively on the playing field but can increasingly be found in the audiences for baseball, horse racing, and boxing. The sport least comfortable for a spectator is professional football, often played in weather cold enough to require fur coats and mufflers, but women now represent two-fifths of its audience, while more and more men watch football on television. Of the women expressing a preference for attending outdoor events, 42 percent actually attend them as often as they would like, compared with only 33 percent of the men.[5] Women who attend sports events are hardly passive spectators and can ventilate aggression when they boo, cheer, heckle, hiss, jeer, scream, shout, and taunt for victory.[6] It is not surprising that female sports fans are giving less and less time to reports of sewing circles and knitting or flower clubs and teas in the women's pages of newspapers. Sixty-nine percent of American women who look at newspapers open them to the sports pages, where they read about competitors who beat, blast, bomb, boff, bury, clout, flay, paste, jolt, rip, scalp, sink, slug, swamp, tear, trim, and whip one another.[7]

Today's prime suburban blood vendetta may be taking place on tennis courts. Only 30 percent of the 4,100,000 tennis players were women in 1946 but they now account for 45 percent of our 8,500,000 players. Women's tennis has changed from exercise to competition, with tournaments at every age level. Women have become more active in tournament, public court, and club play at the very time that tennis has involved more speed and power. A powerful serve tends to be followed by a rush to the net, putting away an opponent's return before it bounces.

Women adapt to the new game in a variety of ways. Althea Gibson developed a very powerful flat serve with a whipping wrist motion that was very difficult to return. Billie Jean King is preeminent in women's tennis today because of her aggressiveness around the court, rushing net game, and strong ground strokes. Others skillfully serve to corners of the service box so that an opponent must race off the court in order to return the ball. Some serve with slices and twists in which the ball is hit at an angle and bounces high and away. Others who concentrate on their back-court game emulate William Tilden, perhaps the greatest tennis player of all time.

Paddle tennis is one of the few sports in which a woman can do about as well as a man. The game is faster and wilder than tennis and is played with a hard rubber ball on a raised wooden platform that is about half the length and width of a regulation tennis court, sanded and surrounded by a wire fence. Its near-domination by women may be one reason that paddle tennis is an important "social" game.

Women have also taken over the golf course, that traditional male Garden of Eden. They represented ten percent of our 2,450,000 golfers in 1946, but now account for over one-third of the 7,750,000 Americans who tee off regularly. In July 1965, the U.S. Women's Open became the first such event to get network television coverage. Any lack of strength that limits the length of women's wood shots can be largely overcome by their superior manual dexterity and deftness in medium- and even long-iron play. A three-inch putt and a three-hundred-yard drive, after all, each count for one stroke. Women who concentrate on an accurate short game and perfect their chipping and putting can apply their accuracy to best advantage.

Women's great success in tournament golf has demonstrated that power and strength can be less important than grace and rhythm, especially within one hundred twenty-five yards of the cup. Gary Player, who is only 5'7", stands up against much bigger men. Chichi Rodriguez is 5'6" and weighs 126 pounds, but can drive a ball as far as Arnold Palmer.

The first woman to get an athletic scholarship at the University of Kentucky received it for golf prowess. Women now play on other varsity teams, so that a coed may play against a male. A woman has been a member of Stetson University's varsity tennis team and Pam Hayes and Martha Leveritt swam well enough to make the men's squad at Tulane. Women college athletes have so far been confined to golf, tennis, and swimming, but baseball and basketball are obviously next.[8]

Even sports that were once regarded as hazardous seem to hold no terror for many women. In sledding and tobogganning, their participation averages 1.38 times per year in contrast to 2.2 for men. Women represent a growing proportion of the 3,500,000 American skiers, whose number is increasing at the rate of 20 percent each year as the sport becomes an occasion for social activity that cuts across class lines. Any fear of disfigurement that once deterred many women skiers is no longer operative.[9]

Free fall parachuting was formerly considered so risky that only men attempted it less than a decade ago, but the 20,000 women recreational sky jumpers now represent one-fifth of the total. Surfing was also once too dangerous for women, but they now account for one-third of all surfers. Water skiing has more women than men devotees, and all-girl rowing teams compete successfully with men.

The male sanctuary in the wilderness has yielded to women, who have been heeding the call of the wild in such numbers that they now do more camping than men. The fair sex also represents an increasing proportion of

our 42 million boaters, although not too long ago the
sport was a symbol of man's untrammeled spirit and
proud seafaring heritage. Joshua Slocum's bringing the
thirty-seven foot *Spray* into the harbor of Newport, R.I.,
on June 27, 1898, marked the first time a man had sailed
around the world by himself.[10] The seagoing Thoreauism
represented by Captain Slocum has become a historical
memory as women have bent the rigging of men's traditional nautical fantasies into new shapes. Frank Lloyd
Wright's comment that he needed the customer's wife as
an ally has not been lost on builders of yachts and cabin
cruisers. Interior designer Doris Slane, who works exclusively with ship interiors, has asked, "If a man gets what
he wants in a hull, why should a wife be stuck in a little
old dark galley?"[11] In deference to their new first mate,
many vessels now have electric kitchens, and exteriors that
were traditionally white or mahogany come in pastels.
Bunk and cockpit cushions, countertops, cabin curtains,
and even the spinnaker appear in decorator colors.

Another outdoor activity that has attracted many wom-
en is horseback riding, and girls and young women now
engage in more horseback riding than boys and young
men. Seventy percent of the riders under 21 are female
and women in the northeast ride four times as frequently
as men. A former president of the United States Pony
Clubs gave some reasons: "Girls have the temperament to
be patient and persistent. Boys . . . don't like a sport in
which girls can compete on an equal basis with them."[12]
Women used to wear skirts when they rode side-saddle
but changed to divided skirts, culottes, breeches under
skirts, and most recently, men's riding breeches, once they
sat astride the horse. Women's new participation in riding
is important now that horsemanship has become a middle-
class sport and more people ride saddle horses than did
before the automobile. Women have also become much
more active in showing, jumping, and riding at horse

shows. Women outnumber men on the United States' show jumping team, which swept the 1967 European shows.

Participation by women has changed other sports and games. Twenty-five years ago, the tennis racket was unpainted and had a simple wood grip but today it is painted, varnished, multicolored, has a leather grip, and could decorate a boudoir wall. The throat connecting head with shaft is tapered, where it was once straight, and the head has become more shapely. Perhaps the most revolutionary development in tennis equipment during the last half century is the steel racket, which was used by all three American quarter-finalists in the 1967 National Singles Championship. Two slender tubes connect the handle to the head's graceful curve and contribute to the racket's delicate light appearance.

Lack of color once characterized the gut used in high-priced rackets as well as the silk in less expensive models. Today's best gut is likely to be light blue with royal blue striping, and nylon stringing comes in stripes and white, brown, and blue. Racket covers, once black or green, are available in a wide range of colors. The brown or black saxophone-shaped container for tennis gear that was used by many players is being replaced by brightly colored soft plastic cases. Even the gray or black cement or asphalt tennis court is metamorphosing to red or green concrete or composition.

At the same time that women have helped to soften the starkness of tennis courts and equipment, their costumes have become less feminine. The long tennis dress has yielded to the straight shift line and to white shorts and shirts. Husband and wife wear a similar shirt, often the Perry with a tiny green wreath appliqué, or the Lacoste, with a small green alligator appliqué. Both sexes sport identical white sneakers and socks and are likely to wear a similar white cable stitch pullover or cardigan for going to and from the court and warming up. From the late 1940's into the early 1950's, some women followed the lead of Gussie Moran and wore tennis clothes with feminine necks and pleated ruffles. But the sugar-plum-fairy look is as obsolete as a wire-strung racket, Miss Moran's lace-ruffled bloomers have left the courts, and the functional simple look is the overhead smash of the season.[13]

Women are largely responsible for the move away from relatively informal skiing costumes to colors like pink and burgundy for each part of the day, and even skiing techniques show a distaff influence. They began to change after one of the few scientific analyses ever made of a sport's established techniques. For decades, students were taught to make turns by the rotation method, in which shoulders move in the direction of a turn. In the early 1950's, Professor Stefan Kruckenhauser of the Austrian State Ski School analyzed motion pictures of famous races and concluded that champion skiers turned their shoulders in a direction away from the turn.[14] He developed the reverse shoulder method of turning, moving shoulders away from the turn. Experience with the reverse shoulder method eventually gave rise to another innovation in Wedeln, which means to wag, like a dog's tail. This sharp s-turn is a change in direction by swaying the hips from side to side in a rhumba-like motion. Wedeln is more elegant and fluid than longer and more traditional turns like a Stem Christie or Christiana. Some of the American enthusiasm for Wedeln, and its quicker and more graceful version called the Mambo, results from women's realization of the high octane potential of graceful hip movements while going down a ski slope in colorful skin-tight ski pants or jump suits. As the manager of a Grosse Pointe ski shop noted, "A good fit is when you can tell if a coin in the gal's back pocket is heads or tails."[15]

American women's extensive participation has substantially changed the automobile rallye, in which a distance is covered at a prescribed average speed per hour on each section of the course. Participants lose points by going either too fast or too slow, for damages to the car, getting lost, or not having route cards stamped at various checkpoints.

A typical European rallye team consists of two men, but many American rallye teams consist of a man driver and a woman as navigator or co-driver. In Europe, the prescribed rate is difficult to maintain because the course often includes badly rutted or damaged roads, often flooded or covered by ice or snow. Drivers on the 2,712 icy miles of the Monte Carlo rallye pack axes, shovels, and chains. Paddy Hopkirk, the 1964 winner, described the course: "It was marvelous . . . intolerable conditions all the way . . . let's hope next year the weather is worse."

Largely as a result of women's participation, the competition in American rallyes is less grueling and tends to be based on precision rather than speed, endurance, and courage. The course seldom contains roads that are badly damaged or include unexpected hazards. Women navigators often work the computers that determine the accuracy with which speed is being maintained and that were developed because a slide rule was not precise enough.

European rallyes still retain the competition's original character as a test of an automobile's stamina under difficult conditions of everyday use. In the 1965 Monte Carlo competition, only thirty-five of two hundred thirty-seven starters reached the goal within prescribed time limits and the winning car required eight changes of tires to complete the last 378 miles. A car that wins such a rallye uses its victory to convince potential purchasers that it can cope with difficult driving conditions. In America, precision is so important that a manufacturer seldom uses a rallye victory as a significant sales point.

Many American rallye drivers wear straight line suits, ties, and snappy little caps. Dandification has become so important that designer John Weitz has written a book of advice on clothing to wear in different racing situations. "A race driver's clothes . . . can give him confidence . . . full of dash and daring and personal display . . . be sure *not* to wear the scarf Ascot fashion. . . ."[16] In contrast, European drivers are far more likely to wear sweaters or work clothes.

Not unexpectedly, indoor recreational activities reflect much distaff influence. Time was, men would plan an evening with their chums to go bowling. They are less likely to do so without wives or girl friends now that so many of our 25 million bowlers are women. Many bowl while using closed-circuit television to watch their children playing in an adjacent nursery. Soft pastel colors prettify many a bowling alley and balls and carrying cases come in royal blue, Kelly green, and red. A "gutter" is now a "channel."

Women's interest in billiards has enabled the sport to gain new adherents almost as spectacularly as it had previously lost them during the Depression, during the course of which the 40,000 "pool halls" declined by 80 percent. The "pool parlor" has evolved from dinginess and spittoons into the family "billiard center" that services 14 million Americans. Many "centers" have thick carpeting and tables covered in tangerine, rust, coral, and pale blue rather than traditional green. The bright and airy rooms are lavishly appointed and usually have automatic scorekeepers and fluorescent lighting.

A 1961 photograph of Queen Mother Elizabeth lining up a shot helped greatly in making billiards more socially acceptable. Masako Katsura, the first woman to try for the world's three-cushion billiard title, suggested another reason for billiards' appeal: "It is just the right kind of sport for women. You use every part of the body, all the muscles, and it keeps the body beautiful."[17] But a Brooklyn man who is less sympathetic to women's needs complained: "The pool parlor was the only place a fellow could go to relax and get away from women. Now even this refuge is gone. The only place left is the men's room."[18]

Ever since commercial billiard lounges came from behind the eight-ball in 1962, sales of home equipment have increased and more than a quarter-million home tables are sold in a typical year. Most tables are used by the whole family and many come in round or elliptoid shapes that blend with unusually shaped rooms and can be transformed into surfaces for dining or ping pong.

As green billiard tables have been giving way to decorator colors, the proportion of women to men gambling at the green felt crap tables of Las Vegas has doubled over the last ten years. Dice traditionally requires its participants to be aggressive masters of their fate. The dice are thrown forward vigorously and the game's vocabulary is challenging, masculine, profane, and sexualized ("come to me, baby").

Women's increased interest in shooting craps may have a reciprocal relationship to men's growing participation in Las Vegas roulette over the last decade. Roulette has long been regarded as a feminine game because a bettor passively waits for the ball to come to rest in a slot after someone else has spun the wheel. Gambling is thus reflecting crisscrossing of sex roles, if the 12 million visitors who throw three billion dollars across the Las Vegas gambling tables in a year are typical.

One of the few leisure activities resisting ambisexuality is chess, with men representing approximately 99 percent of America's 35 million chess players. One reason could be the game's symbolic attack on the father-king. Men chess players seem to have a combativeness that is less likely to be found in women and even an outstanding woman player like Lisa Lane is no match for a male master.

Poker still remains the most popular man's card game. A poker game is often played in an anti-feminine atmo-

sphere, with queens referred to as "whores."[19] Fumes
from cigars, cigarettes, and the passing of wind seem to be
an acceptable part of the game's anal and scatological
framework. The stag atmosphere is brilliantly evoked in
the opening scene of *The Odd Couple,* in which participants
in a weekly poker game loosen their ties, remove their
jackets, curse, spill their drinks and cigarette butts on the
floor, and otherwise behave in a manner that would not
gladden their wives. George S. Kaufman once wrote a hi-
larious vaudeville skit about how the game would change
if women took it over.

Beyond the
Nineteenth Hole

A New York executive recently decided to turn his back
on a crushing work load and relax for a week by playing
golf at his Westchester country club. On three of the four
mornings on which he wanted to tee off, he learned that
the course had been preempted for women's tournament
activities. Hopefully, the comments that he muttered to
himself helped drain off the tension that had led him to
seek a golfing holiday. His experience constitutes a sharp
reminder of changes in the country club, a stronghold of
male supremacy only a generation ago.

The young caddy in Fitzgerald's short story has "Winter Dreams" about the sexual goings on that pervade the
Sherry Island Golf Club[20] and were identified as the core
of much country-club life by John O'Hara in *Appointment
in Samarra* and many later books. Club snobbishness and
extramarital sex have become a staple of popular humor,
as in a typical 1930's story about three members' wives
who were guests at a social function and found themselves
standing opposite the men's shower room. A man was
drying himself and the shower's swinging door had some-

how opened so that each woman could see him, nude
from the waist down. Jane said, "That's not my husband." Ruth looked and said, "It's nobody I know." Mary
craned her neck and sniffed, "He's not even a member of
the club." The sexual buccaneering implied in the story
is not possible today, when children and wives are
everywhere.

One veteran of country-club dalliances of the 1930's recently reminisced: "I used to meet the wife of one of the
other members at exactly ten minutes after sundown every Thursday for some flagrante delicious in my car. Our
code was the time listed for sunset in the daily paper. She
would look in the paper and know exactly when to meet
me without our ever having to talk with each other during the week. Every Thursday we'd set the location of the
next meeting. It was dark enough for us not to be seen.
There was enough time so that she could be back home
by nine-thirty, since she had told her husband she was
going to shop."

The clubs which many a man had originally joined in
order to avoid the rest of his family were forced to open
their doors to women and children after the Depression
closed every fourth club, income tax deductions were
tightened, and the expanding economy of 1940–1945
made it easy for club employees to find better positions
elsewhere. Family participation has been the only way in
which the tourniquet of rising costs could be loosened in
the years since World War II. Many places that had
proudly identified themselves as "golf clubs" changed
their names to "country clubs" as one way of suggesting
that women and children were welcome.

The typical wife uses her club's golf course 40 percent
more often than does her husband. Women are generally
not permitted to tee off before noon on weekends, but are
very much in evidence on other mornings. Tuesday is usually ladies' day, Wednesday is frequently reserved for

women's tournament activity, and many women also play on Thursdays and Fridays. Most clubs are pleased to have women using the links so often because they provide substantial income. Many clubs have a twilight game for married couples, who tee off between 4 and 5:30 p.m., play nine leisurely holes in mixed doubles, and have a buffet or dinner around seven. The couples are welcome because they usually buy drinks as well as food.

Almost as profound a change has occurred in the city clubs that were once patterned after British men's clubs but have now substantially abandoned their exclusionist attitudes toward women.[21] Even girl friends of a member once felt free to write to his club, knowing that such a letter would be brought to him face side down on a tray so that the employee who handled the letter would not embarrass its recipient. Clubs' historical hostility toward women was expressed in the venerable story about the executive who asked, "Do you believe in clubs for women?" His friend replied, "Certainly, but only after kindness has failed." A similar attitude was expressed in an incident said to have occurred at New York's Union Club. A member's wife managed to get into the club, interrupted her husband's game of whist, and waited impatiently while he calmly finished his hand. They left together and went home—where he committed suicide because of his humiliation at her invasion of the sanctum.

The Union Club was typical in permitting women to visit one evening a week during World War II. They were admitted for another evening each week after the war and were ultimately able to come every weekday for dinner and for lunch on Saturday. There is now a separate ladies' cocktail lounge. Although a plaque identifies the men's grill at the Princeton Club in New York ("Where Women Cease from Troubling and the Wicked Are at Rest"), women roam freely in the rest of the building and wives can stay overnight.

The same economic reasons that led to a feminine beach-head at golf clubs were responsible for changes in city clubs. Men's clubs simply can no longer keep their doors open without the income from wives, who bring guests to dinner and have drinks before and after theatre. The Yale Club in New York has a roof dining room and sleeping accommodations for women. Other formerly restricted New York men's clubs with facilities for women include the Friars, Lambs, Pinnacle, New York Athletic, White-hall, Players, Racquet and Tennis, New York Yacht, and the Metropolitan.[22]

New York's Harvard Club established a ladies' lounge in the early 1940's, at just about the time that other clubs began to consider doing so, as one way of meeting rising wartime costs. Women were not permitted to stay over-night. Today, women and their children can stay for weekends, and on summer evenings they can even breach the previously impregnable fortress of the main dining room. Such coeducation has led to a decrease in the number of the club's traditional large brown leather chairs.

The mystique of the British custom is illustrated in a story told about the Beefsteak, a club at the top of a stair-case off Leicester Square.[23] Police had noticed a number of old men emerging happily every night and assumed the place was a brothel. They raided it one night, found four men sitting around, and asked them to identify them-selves. "I am the Lord Chancellor." "Ah! And you, sir?" "The Archbishop of Canterbury." "Oh, yes. And the next?" "I am the Governor of the Bank of England." "And I suppose," said the policeman to the fourth, "that you're the Prime Minister." "As a matter of fact, I am," said Arthur Balfour. A few British men's clubs have reluc-tantly established a ladies' night and others an annex. More typical is the Savile, which admits them once a year. But there is no place where a woman can sign chits and have the privileges she enjoys at American clubs.

Feminization of clubs has an analogue in changes in voluntary associations, to which so many Americans belonged even in De Tocqueville's day. Many subsequent observers have been struck by our enthusiasm for fraternal, civic, service, cultural, religious, social, and sport groups. The American As Joiner was the smiling hero of many early analyses of American character that cited George Washington's membership in the Masons. Voluntary associations once provided a sanctuary for mutual propitiation at which men could spend regular nights out with the boys. But with the growth of female auxiliaries and of new groups created by and for women, more women (57%) than men (54%) now belong to voluntary organizations.[24] The pace of women's participation in such groups has been increasing and there are now over 18,000 women's clubs. Dominoes and backgammon are representative games that were once largely played in men's clubrooms but are increasingly popular with women's organizations.

Even the business convention, a traditional escape hatch for the American male, is becoming a family affair. Before World War II, less than five percent of convention-goers brought their wives, but two out of five do so today. One wife attending a New York convention firmly noted, "A man nowadays ought to get used to the idea that he just can't go off on a blast and have a good time on his own. Not any more; the old lady and kids are right behind him . . ."

"Beware of the Owner"

Outside his estate at Lake Garda, D'Annunzio used to have a sign reading "Beware of the Owner." Such close identification between a pet and its owner could be intense in a country like ours, where more is spent on pet than baby food, and "pet" is both an affectionate noun and a verb for making love.[25]

The children who are helped to become aware of life processes and to take care of others by feeding and playing with pets, develop specific kinds of relationships with their charges. People who buy a specific pet have fairly explicit expectations about how the pet will relate to them. A change in what their masters seek from pets is probably one major reason that the cat's purr has been replacing the dog's bark in many homes over the last decade. Our twenty-eight million cats and twenty-six million dogs compare with nineteen million cats and twenty-three million dogs a decade ago.[26] The passivity of many cats seems to be more satisfying to many Americans than dogs' more aggressive and forceful activities. And smaller ornamental dogs like the Yorkshire terrier are becoming more popular, now that large dogs enjoy lesser demand.

The wide range of dog personalities includes the relatively aloof basset hound and cuddly lap dog. Two dogs from the same litter may have different personalities. In spite of such differences among dogs, it is possible to make some generalizations about the satisfactions they provide a master. The owner of a dog must relate to it, if only to take his pet outside to relieve itself. The dog's devotion and loyalty figure in the Welsh folktale of Prince Llewellyn, who was shocked to return home one day and find that his dog's mouth was bloodstained. Assuming that the dog had eaten his young son, he killed the dog. When he heard the child singing happily in the next room, a few feet from the mangled body of a wolf, the prince realized that the dog had saved his child's life. The dog as a children's companion has been widely celebrated and its ability to provide and reciprocate emotional support, sociability, and affection has been personified in Rin Tin Tin, Strongheart, and Lassie.

In spite of such enthusiasm, one reason that the cat has recently become our most popular pet could be its passivity.[27] Tabby sets the rules of the game and fixes a steady and baleful gaze on her master in response to his cheerful "hello." Many a cat owner—perhaps a more accurate description than "master"—will try to conceal the claw scratches on his hand as he apologetically assures his visitor that Tobermory "is not himself today."

The cat's disagreeableness is one major reason that it did not become a hero in mass media. Its unattractive folklore connotations emerge in many words and phrases (fat cat, cat's paw, catamite, caterwaul, catcall, cat-o'-nine-tails). Much of the hostility probably reflects a feeling that cats prefer not to be bothered with humans. As William Faulkner described the cat, "he neither toils nor spins, he is a parasite on you, but he does not love you . . ." A related sentiment is Matthew Arnold's description of his Atossa: "Cruel, but composed and bland/Dumb, inscrutable and grand,/So Tiberius might have sat/Had Tiberius been a cat."

The cat can minimize relationships with its owner because, unlike the dog, it uses a box to take care of its needs and need not go outside the house. Francis Galton described the cat as "the only non-gregarious domestic animal" and Henry Morgan has pointed out that cat owners "adore being ignored."[28] The Siamese's independence is probably even more responsible than its appearance for its great popularity. The Lockridges described one of their favorites as displaying a "detached courtesy" and fellow aelurophile Agnes Repplier almost proudly observed that her Agrippina was the "most contemptuous" of cats, "the most contemptuous of creatures." Agrippina was so independent that she did not come when called, and "if I tell

her to go away, she remains where she is; if I try to per-
suade her to show off her one or two little accomplish-
ments, she refuses, with courageous but unswerving
decision."[29]

An increase in such semi-masochistic needs in American
pet owners may be another reason for cats' current popularity. Between Labor Day and December 1, 1963, a book
about cats was published on the average of every eight
days. Cats no longer even perform the utilitarian functions implied in Charles Darwin's advice on how to get a
barren field to bloom. He urged that a group of spinsters
move to the area, with their pet cats. The cats would
eliminate the field mice, which would no longer molest
the beehives. The bees could then be free to pollinate
flowers, which would finally bloom. Cat ownership in this
country, however, is no longer restricted to the maiden
aunts with whom it was traditionally associated in Darwin's day.

The cat's being what G. Stanley Hall called "the least
useful of domestic animals" has not interfered with its
ability to sustain fealty from millions of subjects. Possibly
the first book to carry only negative critical comments on
its dust jacket was William Cole's and Tomi Ungerer's *A
Cat Hater's Handbook,* an analysis and anthology of the
pet's less lovely aspects. Prominent cat lovers were so outraged that they denounced the authors in very vigorous
language and probably contributed to the book's inability
to find an audience.

The dog's yielding in popularity to the cat suggests the
possibility that passivity could be becoming more important to many Americans than aggressiveness and emotional warmth. Similar reasons could help to explain the extraordinary popularity of parrakeets, the favorite of 71
percent of pet bird owners.[30] Although the canary used to
be the most popular pet bird a generation ago, there are
now ten times as many parrakeets as canaries. In 1953,

4.7% of United States families had a parrakeet, 8% had one in 1954, and 15.4% by 1955. The parrakeet's popularity began to level off by the late 1950's, but is still very substantial. Although the canary is sociable and sings without much training, the parrakeet cannot sing and only talks after considerable training. It can only chirp, where a canary could emit schockels, glucks, water rolls, and flutes. Parrakeets' popularity may also be related to husbands' interest in the pet. Many men enjoy feeding parrakeets but few took care of canaries. Perhaps men find it easier to cope with parrakeets' passivity.

The Shape of Things That Go

Luggage preferences have been changing at the same time as pets, although there is no organic connection between the two. It used to be easy to distinguish the gladstone or satchel and other angular and rectangular masculine leather luggage from women's light-colored, slender, rounder, and softer bags. The wide use of lightweight fabrics and rounded edges has made it difficult to tell men's from women's luggage. Colors like blue, black, and plaid designs tend to be used almost interchangeably for both sexes.

The most popular luggage for air travel combines an undercoating of very lightweight metal, usually magnesium, with a plastic or canvas on the outside. Such materials and non-protuberant flush snap locks help reinforce the pieces' neutral quality and make the inadvertent exchange of luggage a daily occurrence at any large airport.

The few airlines that issue luggage to their personnel provide bags of the same size and color to both men and women. Several airline studies have established that men and women travelers average 1.5 items of luggage each.

Wash-and-wear clothing and the relative disappearance of bulky fabrics, seasonal clothing, and wide skirts have made it easier for a woman to use a smaller bag. Luggage will probably become even less distinguishable as leisure and travel become more important.[31]

4

the country of the bland

Spinoza once observed that "it is the part of a wise man to feed himself with moderate food and drink." If "moderate" connotes blandness, many of the New People are making rapid progress toward wisdom, by consuming savorless edibles and potables. Walter de la Mare's rhyme that "Whatever Miss T eats turns into Miss T" expresses the profound relationship between food and personality, which is carried into some of our descriptions of personality characteristics: peppery, sour, sweet, spicy, salty. As alcoholic beverages, usually consumed to bolster a mood or heighten a situation, become even blander, the range of moods or experiences of many Americans may become similarly constricted.

Muted Spirits
and Devitalized Vittles

The White House physician is said to have advised President and Mrs. Johnson to relax over a drink of Scotch with soda before their evening meal. In New York City, the United States' largest liquor market, Scotch is second in popularity only to blended whiskey. Consumers of Scotch are more likely than other drinkers to respond to a brand name because the product goes through complicated processing and represents a very acquired taste.

Most of its current fans prefer a Scotch because of its comparative *lack* of maltiness, smokiness, and body. Sales mount as a brand becomes known for being dry and light. Consumers often assume that a light amber Scotch must "taste" light, few know that the color derives from a dye, and many cannot specify if the lightness they admire refers to weight, aroma, density, or taste. One reason for their reliance on color is the difficulty of being consistent in judging any lightly flavored spirits.

The strong and peaty brands that once dominated the American market became casualties of World War II, when the need for alcohol in munitions manufacture led to its rationing to distilleries. Since four years are minimally required to age Scotch, the product was just beginning to trickle back when the Korean war broke in 1950. Korea looked like the beginning of a major war, so alcohol was once again in short supply. The distilleries belonging to the consortium that dominates the manufacture of Scotch, concerned about their ability to meet the demand, began to ration their American distributors.

As it became increasingly difficult to get the established labels in America, distributors of several light and less popular brands saw an opportunity to expand their share of the market. They assured bars and package stores that their brands were available without rationing or quota. Some of the distributors did not control or own stills, so that the liquor they bought from other distillers necessarily varied in quality and taste. It also included "heads" and "tails." In the run from a still, the first gallons (the "head") are likely to have too many congeners, the substances that provide aroma, flavor, and body. "Center" run has the purest flavor because the distillation and fermentation process favors the core. The last gallons (the "tail") include the mildest liquor. "Heads" and "tails" that had previously been discarded by the major distilleries were purchased and redistilled by several of the brands that have become known since Korea.

The brands that represented a standard product and owned their distilleries began losing sales as many Americans who had originally bought the new brands only because they were available soon became loyal fans of Scotch that was not a full-flavored quaff. When the established consortium labels tried to counter the trend, there were already many customers for "instant Scotch"[1]—a liquor with the same relationship to traditional brands' smoky pungency as instant coffee has to regular coffee, in terms of texture, aroma, flavor, and taste.

The importance of what happened to Scotch is its place on the escalator of liquor taste. The hobo on a park bench nurses cheap sherry in a brown paper bag, beer is the traditional blue-collar drink, a white-collar worker typically favors mixed drinks, and the executive is likely to prefer Scotch and request it by brand name. "Scotch is always in demand," observed the bartender at New York's St. Regis Hotel, which stocks 135 different brands. It is the single most popular drink at the Carnegie Hall bar.

The expensive sherry that enjoys more status than Scotch appeals to a very small minority earning in excess of $25,000 a year. Along the continuum from cheap to expensive sherry, Scotch represents the most attainable goal of social drinkers. The growing social desirability of the newer brands' blandness is largely responsible for America's consumption of over seventy percent of the Scotch produced for export.

Blended whiskey is another product that has acquired many postwar followers because of its comparatively light body. With a substantial content of neutral spirits, it uses relatively little of the aged straight whiskeys that were in short supply during and after World War II. Blended whiskey's comparative lack of bouquet and flavor is probably the chief reason for its now accounting for over two-thirds of all domestic whiskey production.

Such changes in liquor preferences are related to women's new role in liquor purchase and use. As women have been achieving first-class citizenship, they have been doing more drinking. One possible clue to the future of some of the sixty percent of American women who now drink could be detected in the second act of *Happily Never After,* which opened on Broadway in March, 1966: its major drunk scene was played by two women. As the Whiskey Sour and other mixed drinks that were once distinctively feminine have become more popular with men, women who once dawdled over a Pink Lady or Clover Club now order Martinis as dry as their husbands'.

Women's tippling on stage was probably inevitable, once they began appearing in liquor advertising during the 1960's. Women's service magazines had not carried liquor advertising before *Ladies' Home Journal* and *American Home* began doing so during 1962. At the present time, a woman makes every third liquor purchase and every tenth married woman actually buys her own favorite brands and ignores her husband's wishes.[2] As new brands have been created for women, "soft" and "delicate" taste is an increasing theme of liquor advertising.

The dilution of distinguishing characteristics that is represented by "soft" liquor can be seen most dramatically in vodka, which jumped from one percent of the 1952 domestic liquor market to ten percent in 1966. U.S. government regulations specify that it must be "without distinctive character, aroma, or taste" so that its major appeal is a lack of the very qualities that traditionally make liquor attractive. A representative group of San Francisco men preferred vodka *because* it was tasteless and odorless.[3] Such changes are important because of California's role in starting many new trends in drinking (Bloody Mary, Irish Coffee, Gimlet, Margarita). Although some of its fans claim that vodka enables them to drink without exuding an aroma, it actually leaves a slight breath and is usually consumed in social situations as part of a Screwdriver or Bloody Mary. Many first-generation drinkers prefer such comparatively mild combinations as one way of coping with their guilt about alcohol.

Constant attrition in the flavor and taste of beer affects many people because Americans drink more beer than any other beverage except milk and coffee.[4] Ale, porter, stout, and other robust products have declined in popularity as beer has been moving from saloon to salon. In one recent five-year period, American ale production dropped from 894,000 to 529,000 barrels, and porter and stout from 221,000 to 105,000 barrels.[5] Americans whose fathers might have taken their porter and stout straight now dilute them with beer.

The thinner taste of beer can be measured by the diminishing proportion of malt and hops used in its manufacture. In 1934, 38.1 pounds of malt were required to produce an average barrel of beer, but in 1962, 28.2 pounds were used. The 0.70 of a pound of hops in an average barrel in 1934 had declined to 0.31 in 1962.

Modern Americans do not appear to share Shakespeare's dislike of "small beer" that has a thin taste. In a 1944 survey, 30.9 percent agreed with the statement that "beer is a light drink," but the 39.7 percent who agreed in 1949 had become 49.7 percent in 1954. Brewers are certainly providing the "light" and less aromatic product that is in demand, especially among women. One series of beer advertisements frankly asks, "Who says beer is a man's beverage?" and shows a female beer klatsch.

While women have been increasing their consumption of alcoholic beverages during the last twenty years, some non-alcoholic drinks that were traditionally feminine have become men's favorites. Men are drinking proportionately more soft drinks than women. There has been a substantial increase in men's interest in tea, which no longer has Helen Hokinson connotations.

Americans' enthusiasm for other bland drinks makes it less surprising that instant coffee has become so popular. Instant has moved from 7 percent of the total coffee market in 1946, to 12 percent in 1952, and 39 percent today. Once a utilitarian product favored by people living alone who made only one cup and by families whose members did not want coffee of uniform strength, instant coffee then began to attract new consumers who could not consistently brew a satisfactory cup of regular coffee. Although the instant product is simple and reliable, it has limited flavor, aroma, and texture. As a result of the ease with which its bland but standard taste could be produced, post-World War II consumers educated their taste down to fit convenience. Many young couples have never had a cup of regular coffee and would regard it as "too bitter."

The shift from regular to instant coffee is typical of the fate of many foods, whose blandness could have important effects. Food is so important and regular a part of our lives that its growing tastelessness helps to reinforce our acceptance of the neuter in other aspects of the environment. As our gustatory satisfactions become narrower, we may be content with a lesser range of other sensory satisfactions. And although there is disagreement over which comestibles are most aphrodisiac, few people would question the anaphrodisiac effects of bland foods.

It would be logical to expect our great technological proficiency to have produced foods with an enormous range of taste, texture, and aroma. Yet our marriage of technology and convenience has led to wide acceptance of many foods with a blander and less explicit taste than in previous generations. Frozen baked potatoes and french fried potatoes, for example, only approximate the natural product's taste. Although it is easy to heighten powdered mashed potatoes with butter, cheese, and sauces, the powdered product lacks the texture, taste, and aroma of freshly mashed potatoes. Children are less able to tell their mother's mood by variations in the texture of her mashed potatoes and today's working mothers have little time for such communication.

Frozen and instant potatoes are typical of over 7,000 quick-preparation convenience foods that have enabled many Americans to broaden the range of their diet. Unfortunately, the taste, aroma, and texture of such products tend to be more homogenized, bland, and less sharp than fresh foods. Convenience foods have become staples in many households where pressure cookers and infra-red broilers gather dust on shelves, although a pressure cooker can cook many vegetables in less time than is required to open, prepare, and heat frozen or instant vegetables. Fresh produce prepared with a pressure cooker retains taste and vitamins and is usually less expensive than a packaged version. The infra-red broiler cooks meat, chicken, and fish so rapidly that fifteen minutes can suffice to prepare an exotic shishkebab. Frozen meat takes several hours to defrost, is more expensive than fresh meat, and has a flatter taste.

Yet American women have not fully utilized infra-red broilers and pressure cookers, in spite of the appliances' ability to prepare food inexpensively, quickly, and with a minimal loss of essential food elements. Why? They were first available at modest prices during the decade following World War II, when many different forces were at work to bring about a leveling of taste and an appetite for blandness. American women, usually so enthusiastic about economy and new appliances, eagerly responded to the tastelessness of convenience foods. One appliance development that has further contributed to blandness is

Teflon, the no-stick coating that largely eliminates the
need for butter, oil, or other shortening—as well as the
flavor and taste they formerly provided.

More than technology has contributed to our general
acceptance of tastelessness. A homemaker who works often uses convenience foods to cope with new problems of
family life. She can express attention to her family by
serving a variety of quick-preparation foods, just as she
once might have done by thoughtful preparation of a pot
roast. Family members may enjoy considerable permissiveness in food choice by the availability of convenience
foods. Access to a wide variety of such foods enables a
wife to cope with varied eating schedules of toddlers,
school children, teen-agers, dieters, and husband. Although much of the original motivation for convenience
foods may have derived from a wife's needs, her children
and husband have learned to enjoy blander food, just as
they now prefer instant coffee.

Homogenization of prepared food can be seen in the
metamorphosis of peanut butter. The texture resulting
from mixing ground peanuts and salt was strong enough
to tear the bread on which it was spread and stick to the
upper palate. Today's smooth product has fewer peanuts
than before and vegetable oils, sucrose, honey, seasonings,
and smootheners have lessened its tendency to tear bread
and stick to the roof of the mouth. They have also replaced the nutty taste that represented a unique sensory
experience with a textureless honey-flavored butter. It
seems so wrong to call the traditional and new products
by the same name that the Food and Drug Administration has established a minimum proportion of peanuts necessary for a product to be called peanut butter.[6]

New bland-textured foods will become available in the
future as aerosol cans package more products.[7] Although
the cans have the advantage of exposing only the food
used at any one time, it has an unappetizing consistency.

A contemporary meal could consist of pâté, salmon mousse, whipped potatoes, vegetable puree, and zabaglione—each from a separate aerosol can. With so many textureless foods slithering through the mouth, the popularity of dentifrices promising to block tooth decay is small wonder.

The aerosol can and boil-in-the-bag vegetables are recent examples of softer food consistency and texture. Oatmeal is one of the many formerly strong and coarse cereals that have become more popular in smooth instant forms. Bread has lost consistency, taste, and even shape. Manufacturers know that consumers judge bread's freshness by squeezing it and have developed additives that provide a soft sponginess but blur the bread's other qualities.

American sweets and desserts may not have been gourmet favorites, but there could be no mistake about their heartiness. In our time, exiguously textured gelatin desserts with a taste that can barely be recalled an hour after eating are replacing the Apple Betty and Indian Pudding. Frozen chocolate puffs and coffee cake simply do not have flavor and aroma to compare with the fresh article.

One outpost of strong flavor that was hailed by foreign visitors used to be the ice cream parlor. Twenty-five years ago, a pineapple ice cream soda would be lined with an inch of crushed pineapple and include an ounce of milk, a heavy layer of pure whipped cream, and at least two large scoops of ice cream. Today its flavor comes from a jar of concentrated pineapple syrup, and the cream, not so much whipped as defeated, would be an ersatz aerosol product. The soda has less ice cream and milk and a much thinner texture.

The frosted of previous years, made by mixing flavor with ice cream, has now become aerated soft ice cream, a euphemism for frozen custard that consists largely of air. The malted milk has been another casualty of loss of texture and flavor and eight ounces of ice may go into a

12-ounce glass of a soft drink. One sip of a British ginger ale stings the upper palate with tang and bite that cannot be achieved by a whole glass of the American version, which tastes like club soda with sugar. Marketing research taste studies have concluded that most consumers who are blindfolded and unable to smell carbonated beverages are unable to tell one from the other, even a cola from a grape drink.

The child who once savored the strong flavors of ice cream and carbonated drinks could often predict his dinner by kitchen aromas. The homogenized smells emanating from today's foods make such pleasant discoveries more difficult as the pervasive aromatics of freshly cooked goulash and corned beef are giving way to the transparent vapors of boiling water and roasting aluminum foil. A popular children's pastime used to be the blindfolded identification of food by its aroma, but the game has become anachronistic. Redolent aromas from bread baked in homes or local bakeries are becoming memories to the millions who buy odorless packaged bread. Varied smells of fresh fruits and vegetables are giving way to the anonymous aroma of frozen or chemically treated products. Smells of many other edibles are declining in intensity and range and children are growing up with fewer cues of smell, taste, and texture.

The cues were often related to calendar changes, but today's children are less likely to experience the seasons in their stomachs. A meal used to reflect what was available at different times of the year and helped to reinforce the family's response to natural seasonal differences. The crossing of seasonal boundaries represented by our eating strawberries at Christmas has helped to blur differences stemming from the calendar. Elimination of our seasonal food traditions can only underscore other homogenizing influences, as differences disappear from the very air around us. With air-conditioning, sedatively even temperatures soothe us all year round. But the difference between a lake breeze and the coolth of air-conditioning is like the difference between fresh and frozen strawberries.

In the United States, the average temperature is eight percent higher than it was in 1890 and even the difference between summer days and nights is dwindling because of the 133,000,000 tons of aerial garbage we dump into the atmosphere each year. The average city puts out as much particulate matter as an active volcano. It includes aldehydes from automobile and truck exhausts, sulfur dioxide from fuel oil, industrial fumes, and dust. These substances mount into the atmosphere and form a shell that hangs over the earth, captures warm day air that ordinarily would have escaped with the earth's movement away from the sun, and prevents cool night air from pressing down. Day and night are barely distinguishable in terms of weather and the gas envelope over our cities tends to decrease seasonal temperature differences by making fall and winter much warmer.

The supermarkets that carry frozen strawberries at Christmas tend to be alike all over America. They are replacing the neighborhood butchers, fish stores, and groceries that catered to varied ethnic, economic, and class backgrounds. Cultural and regional differences in food are disappearing as the supermarket does even more to eliminate regional foods than the refrigerated freight cars that carry perishable products thousands of miles.

Refrigeration has made it less necessary for foods to be spiced, smoked, or pickled. Our most popular condiments are ketchup and mustard and even homes that have a shelf or two of dried herbs and spices seldom use them. Only a relatively small proportion of families, in which cooking still retains an ethnic flavor, regularly use an herb like oregano or a spice like paprika. Multiplicity and heightening of tastes become less likely as such products recede into the immigrant past.

Much of the current interest in cookbooks, cooking schools, television chefs, and newspaper and magazine food columns has developed because many third-generation homemakers had little opportunity to learn kitchen skills from their mothers. The first and second generations' desire to Americanize their cooking, an increase in the number of working mothers, and other demands of World War II led to a sharp loss in continuity of traditional culinary skills. Cooking instruction has also flourished because today's bland foods require considerable work merely to raise them to the level of taste that was taken for granted when ethnic cooking and non-convenience foods were dominant. Cooking well has become a personal achievement rather than a skill to be acquired while growing up.

The New People are travelers, and the millions of Americans who go abroad each year have excellent opportunities for sampling interesting, thoughtful, and varied cooking. Yet, very few sustain their interest in such cuisine after they return. A typical visitor to Europe may have wine with dinner for a month or two after he comes home, but such reminders of a better culinary way of life are usually soon abandoned. Our purchasing of convenience foods has increased most dramatically during the generation in which foreign travel has become so commonplace.

Although there is still some disagreement about the ultimate harmfulness of pesticides, few persons would argue with the thesis that fruits have become more bland as a result of growth acceleration by chemicals. Another reason for homogenization of fruit taste has been the replacement by suburban housing developments of many small truck farms that formerly grew the produce for cities. We are losing tart grapefruits and blood oranges and strongly flavored fruits like the sharp-tasting crabapples that were so important a part of Sherwood Anderson's world.

The ubiquitous popularity of dieting has reinforced our trend to bland foods because most foods for reducing are as tasteless as water-packed fruit. National preoccupation with losing weight has led to transformation of a single shelf of special foods into large sections that display hundreds of products. One ironic consequence of diet food blandness that could subvert many good intentions might be an increase in dieters' food consumption. Jokes about Chinese restaurants remind us that large quantities of bland food are required to allay hunger and we can expect that people will eat more as food becomes less tasty.

Many Americans have been encouraged to diet by the extensive publicity given our recent presidents' avoidance of calories. Butter is taboo at the White House and Mrs. Johnson often lunches on a hard-boiled egg and two prunes. Salad dressing is blended with mineral oil and the Johnsons nibble on unsalted and unbuttered popcorn.[8] Mr. Johnson looked at the cake that had been baked by the White House chef for his thirty-second wedding anniversary—and reached for a plate of tapioca. He fed spoonfuls to reporters, pointing out that "tapioca has less calories than any other dessert you can get . . . when it is made with skim milk and sucaryl." The President compared the 109 calories in a heaping cup of tapioca with the 250 in a serving of ice cream.[9]

Mrs. Kennedy often had a glass of skim milk for breakfast. Luncheon for the Kennedys was usually served on trays and consisted of consommé and a grilled cheese sandwich or a slice of cold beef. Dinner was also a diet-conscious meal, with the infrequent dessert consisting of an occasional lemon ice.

No one on the White House staff knew how to prepare yoghurt when President Eisenhower requested it for dessert. For Mr. Eisenhower, the chef skipped sauces and toppings and used lemon juice instead of lemon butter in serving asparagus. Mashed turnips became a presidential favorite when served with dissolved chicken bouillon cubes instead of butter. Mrs. Truman was on a salt-free diet and President Truman ate only low-calorie foods.

The dietary watchfulness of recent American presidents has undoubtedly strengthened many Americans' resolve to replace butter with margarine's tastelessness or sugar with saccharin's unpleasant aftertaste. Creamed chicken with a traditional sauce may have a stimulating bouquet and rich texture but the same dish prepared with skim milk is far less savory. One cookbook assures its readers that "your family will never know the difference" between "whipped cream" made with skim milk and the same product made with real cream. But the family can tell the difference in flavor and texture and aroma and will also be able to distinguish olive oil's texture and taste from polyunsaturated oils' blandness. Diet and convenience foods will never lead to the roistering pleasure in eating that was conveyed in the famous food-seduction scene in the movie of *Tom Jones*.

Much modern food is reminiscent of a phrase used by photographers who prepare the mouth-watering layouts that brighten many women's magazines. The cook prepares at least two identical versions of everything to be photographed. One version, called the "stand-in," is identical with the one that is ultimately photographed but remains on the table while photographers adjust their lights and cameras. When everything is ready, the "stand-in" is replaced. Many diet and convenience foods have the wilted flavor and blurred shape that the "stand-in" gets from extended exposure to hot lights.

Although the number of really first-rate restaurants in America has increased in the last twenty years, the great majority of restaurants have enthusiastically adapted to the technological changes that led to blander food. Many restaurants that buy a large amount of frozen food and thaw whatever quantities are needed to meet customer demand once bought fresh food that had to be discarded if there were not enough customers.

With food made in huge quantities for mass distribution by restaurant chains, the gradations of taste possible when food was prepared in smaller quantities are becoming historical. It simply does not seem possible to prepare food for thousands of people and keep its subtleties of texture, flavor, or aroma. Distribution by vending machines is another expanding frontier of food marketing that is helping to make a norm of sogginess and tastelessness.

At a time when food itself is losing sharp characteristics, it would be logical to expect dishes and utensils to be blander. There was a time when women lingered over the choice of sterling silver and plated silverware that had great symbolic significance and was used for decades. Feminine designs, curves, floral patterns, and names like "Water Lily" were frequent. Although domestic silverware was less ornate and heavy than imported brands, it began to change in appearance and become lighter about a decade ago. Floral patterns gave way to non-feminine silverware that had little or no pattern. One reason for the change is that silverware is now less likely to be part of a dowry than a joint purchase of husband and wife and plated silver or even sterling seem old-fashioned to the many young couples who prefer stainless steel. Since 1951, the Swedish Gense line of stainless steel flatware and its many imitators have largely replaced the lightweight alloy that was generically called "stainless." Both alloy and stainless steel have a cold texture and a hard surface that makes engraving of any pattern comparatively difficult.

For hundreds of years, better china was graced by delicate and frequently colorful patterns on the edge and sometimes center of plates, cups and saucers, and other pieces. A catalog of some older ware describes figures as "gracefully gentle as the fern in the glen," "dancing leaves," "unfolding rose." Recently, even expensive china has begun replacing femininity with blandness, and plastic dishes have moved from dime stores to elegant shops. The patterns of the dishes look stenciled and have an institutional quality. Their standardized shapes and light feel contribute to their neuter quality even when they are designed by talented craftsmen. We may ultimately even be grateful for the plastic dishes if the edible dishes that are now available in limited quantities develop wide acceptance.

The table that is set with devitalized vittles, "stainless" or steel flatware, and plastic dishes may look even more lifeless when it is graced with the plastic flower arrangements that have graduated from factories and offices to home. They look so realistic that flecks of moisture linger permanently on many a plastic petal. Freshly cut flowers arranged in a vase or bowl provided aroma, an individual touch, a reflection of the seasons and cycle of life. Replacing them regularly made it possible to communicate moods and emotions and accent a room. Plastic flowers provide a perfect accent for a wax museum but not for a home and provide additional evidence that the eye may lie but the nose knows.

Probably the clearest example of our decreasing sensitivity to aroma is the orchid's unquestioned status as *the* flower to be worn in a social situation. Although most orchids are completely odorless, they have replaced heavily sweet gardenias and delicately sweet roses, the two most popular corsage flowers as recently as a generation ago. Women's rejection of roses and gardenias in favor of orchids is, writ large, an example of our way of life.

But a Good
Cigar Is a Smoke

Not too long ago, the powerful aroma of cigars was so clearly masculine that ladies discreetly excused themselves while their men enjoyed an after-dinner cigar. The cigar's toughness was reinforced on one level by Winston Churchill and on another by its association with movie gangsters. Almost every time Edward G. Robinson menacingly swung his forefinger in a semicircle at his henchmen and said, "See here, you guys," he would chomp on a cigar.

Gangster movies' decline and the cigar industry's success in linking its product with film heroes and executives helped restore cigars to respectability. Younger men began smoking them, and many switched from cigarettes. As one result of such factors, sales have been developing a fresh glow and smokers now send over 8.35 billion cigars up in smoke each year. One reason for cigars' new popularity could be their reflection of the diminution of flavor and taste that occurred in food and drink and has characterized cigarette preferences.

The industry's most important technical development since 1900 is the recent perfection of machinery to make cigar components from chemicals that are blended with other ingredients. All three components are now made with chemicals: wrapper, or outer envelope; the binder, which holds the filler; and filler, which provides distinctive aroma and taste. General Cigar Company and American Machine and Foundry have independently developed processes for making outer wrappers from reconstituted tobacco.[10] The binder is made from powdered tobacco, which may derive from damaged leaves and leftovers instead of whole leaf. Binders mixed with a chemical adhesive agent and rolled into sheets are found in more than four-fifths of all cigars. Filler was once made by manually removing the stem from each tobacco leaf and placing its two halves on dies that were inserted into the cigar. Whole tobacco leaf has been supplanted by "short filler," consisting of small particles of tobacco that are blended and fed by machine into a device that forms the roll.

With each of its three ingredients homogenized, the cigar has become blander, milder, less aromatic, and increasingly tastes like an unfiltered cigarette. The embargo on Cuban tobacco imports that went into effect in February 1962 has not been a major disadvantage to American manufacturers because Cuban tobacco is relatively strong. With advertising now stressing that cigars are bland enough not to irritate even sensitive feminine nostrils, it is ironic to recall that many men began smoking cigars as a gesture of masculine defiance. Kipling's observation that "a woman is only a woman, but a good cigar is a smoke" may have been relevant at a time when no decent women smoked cigarettes and Amy Lowell's cigar was a reminder of her eccentricity. The comment has less meaning today, when prominent women smoke cigars without attracting any special attention and Edie Adams sells them on television commercials.

More women are also smoking pipes and tobacco shops report that women of all ages and income levels are asking for instructions. Tobaccos, aromatic and sweet and mild, are made especially for women. The increase in pipe-smoking by women has all but vanquished recollections of the hill-billy crone, corncob clenched between her teeth. Pipes come in navy blue, emerald, and rose and some have multi-colored gems and contrasting bowls and stems.[11]

Pipe-smoking by women is hardly new, since the First Ladies of Andrew Jackson and Zachary Taylor smoked pipes. But in the last five years the movement has increased tremendously as more women discover that a purse does not bulge even if it contains several pipes, tobacco, cleansers, and lighters.

Role reversal could hardly be more explicit, with women smoking pipes and cigars and the cigar becoming more epicene in appearance and aroma. Just as the Korean war helped spur the acceptance of a blander Scotch, the Cuban embargo expedited our response to a blander cigar. As we become more aware of neutering in taste, food, drinks, and smoking, we can appreciate Samuel Beckett's remark in *Malone Dies,* that nothing is more real than nothing.

5

inner and outer space

Light from her cigar may provide the only brightness on the face of a modish contemporary woman. Her makeup reflects the blandness and avoidance of extremes that characterize much food and drink. Flatness finds other important outlets in the manipulation of inner space represented by furniture and architecture's use of outer space.

One reason for our enthusiasm for classic Greek sculpture is its lack of color. If we could see the bright and varied colors in which it was originally painted, the sculpture might be regarded as offensively flamboyant. But our archeologist of the future who finds American buildings and furniture of the 1960's bereft of their color will not be missing a significant dimension, although he will probably wonder why an obviously flourishing culture preferred muted furniture and architecture.

The Beige Epoch

In spite of "living color," color television is a substantial contributor to the blunting of awareness of color in our time. The average set does not have fully satisfactory procedures for tuning and locking in true color. Nuances are often difficult to see, colors sometimes fuse into each other, and aureoles may form around objects and people. The set owner's expectations usually level off after a few months and his comparatively undemanding approach to color quality and definition is reinforced by the flatness of other colors in the environment. His children's ability to discriminate color may be muted and dulled by such technological forces.

His daughter, who in other years might have used vividly red lipstick and nail polish in fantasy and doll play, seldom finds such products on television commercials or even in her mother's boudoir. Mother and daughter pay far less attention to fingernails and lips than to the eyeliner that can give them lemur eyes.

Makeup and cosmetics stress paleness, more rhapsodically identified as the earth-goddess look of exquisite understatement. The beige or muted appearance of no-color color makes an ideal of "the suddenly, startlingly candid new beauties" whose makeup ". . . turns on the immensely touching *au courant* look of the untouched, nude complexion."[1]

Face powder and foundations are less necessary to lend non-color to the ghostly "barely there" face. Fashionable eyebrows are pale and even wispy eyebrows are less likely to require "character" from an eyebrow pencil. Lipsticks come in honey and other muted tones that de-accent the lips. Eve is urged to forget the "unnatural" and "obvious" fire-engine color with which she formerly suffered and to use a lipstick that gives her lips a pearlized, putty color no-mouth mouth.[2]

Some women have discovered that "immensely touching" putty face and lips can be theirs without the use of any lipstick or face powder, *au naturel.*[3] Carrying the present trend to its inevitable conclusion, many women will soon realize they look most *au courant* with no cosmetics whatever on their "untouched, nude" faces. And the logi-

cal next step would be agreement with Edgar Allan Poe
on the beauty of a dead woman's face and seeking the appearance of a corpse in makeup. One residual benefit of
this waxy Forest Lawn look, already to be seen on today's
chic models, should be disappearance of necrophilia as a
perversion.[4] The contemporary in-woman has a cooled-
out face that would be a perfect illustration for the Egyp-
tian *Book of the Dead* or *Thanatopsis.* Makeup's other-
worldliness is cited as a prime advantage in the advertising
of one major brand: "New silver sizzled pales with a sheen
never seen on earth before."

Color represents an outward expression of inner feelings
and responses to the world, so that its disappearance is
especially important in our society, where some 80 percent
of sensory stimuli are visual. As Kandinsky observed, a
painter who greeted a colleague with "How do you do?"
might be answered with "Deep violet," meaning that he
was not very well.[5] We know what is being communicated
when someone tells us that he sees red. President Eisenhower's aides knew he was in bad humor when he wore
a brown suit. The green-eyed monster and blue story have
become popular idioms.

Colors' meanings are fairly explicit even though sometimes contradictory. Yellow can suggest cowardice as well
as gold and the sun. Blue represents both sorrow and the
sky's openness. A color may be rough, smooth, soft, dry—
and its implications derive from its value (lightness or
darkness) and intensity (purity or brilliance), as well as
hue. Men traditionally prefer cool hues and women usually like warm hues. Deep shades tend to be masculine and
delicate tints are often feminine.

Valuable clues to color preferences can be obtained
from changes in the hair of the American women who
spend over one billion hours in our 145,000 beauty salons
each year. A latter-day Nostradamus might derive a lesson
from noting that the only other occasions when hairdress-

ers achieved such popularity were just preceding the decline of Greece and shortly before the French Revolution.

A change in hair color is one way of radically altering the body's appearance. Although tinting, rinsing, and bleaching are routine procedures for 45 million American women, their comparative lack of enthusiasm for red hair is surprising. Twelve percent have natural red hair, but since it fades faster than any other color, there is good reason to believe that the 14 percent of tinting preparations represented by red are purchased almost exclusively by women with naturally red hair.

Red has traditional connotations of sex that are extensively reflected in folklore. The red rose has been a conventional metaphor for the female genitals at least since the *Roman de la Rose* and the cherry a frequent vulgarism for virginity. It was the color of sin long before Hester Prynne began wearing the scarlet A and often characterizes the seduction game in movies. Bette Davis' red gown in *Jezebel* flaunted her sexuality and lecherous Rock Hudson's apartment in *Pillow Talk* was flaming red. The seduction theme of *Under the Yum Yum Tree* was reinforced by the red color of its sin apartment and every important character's costumes.

Somerset Maugham felt that the American belief in redheads' sexuality was a delusion. If so, it had many adherents up to fairly recently and many film actresses took pride in red hair. Clara Bow, the most important sex symbol of her time, had hair so vivid that she was called the Brooklyn Bonfire. Jeanette McDonald's lovely hair was frequently compared to a glowing sunset. Maureen O'Hara's deep bright red hair, the auburn of Martha Vickers and Eleanor Parker, Ann Sheridan's burning red coiffure, Greer Garson's flaming orange red, Rita Hayworth's waterfall of warm red hair, and Rhonda Fleming's strong red were immediately recognizable colophons. Practically no important current actress has red hair, only

a few years after the fellows were crazy about so many ladies in red. During the 1930's and 1940's when many
prominent actresses had red hair, it was also the most
popular color for American women who dyed their hair.
Actresses and other women are less easily identified by red
hair today, when so many prefer blondeness.

Yet, any color can be changed to red with a single product, but blonding requires a toner and bleach in a two-
process treatment, even if the hair is naturally blonde. For
some women, blonding is an opportunity to transcend
their ethnic backgrounds. Others see it as a symbol of the
child's light hair and towheadedness and for older wom-
en, blonding is a simple way of covering gray. There are
women who become blonde because changing hair is so
profound an experience that they want a radically
different hue. But for a substantial number of women, the
attraction of blondeness is less an opportunity to have
more fun than the communication of a withdrawal of
emotion, a lack of passion. One reason for Marilyn Monroe's enormous popularity was that she was less a tempes-
tuous temptress than a non-threatening child. The innocence conveyed by blonde hair is also suggested by the 70
percent of baby dolls whose hair is blonde.

D. H. Lawrence pointed out that the blonde women in
American novels are often cool and unobtainable, while
the dark woman represents passion.[6] Fictional blondes
also tend to be vindictive and frigid. Most men ignore
Anita Loos's emphatic statement and favor redheads over
blondes.[7] Over 20 percent of the sales of hair-coloring preparations are for blonding although only 5 percent of
American women have the color naturally. Most women
who use hair coloring reinforce their original shade, with
the exception of the many non-blondes who want to be
blonde.

The number of women who become blondes in order to
look remote is being augmented by many who use a tint

to achieve drab or neutral-looking hair. It is puzzling that so many women with lively hair choose to drab it down.[8] Such quixotic turning away from color may help to explain women's declining interest in the yellow gold wedding band. Over two-fifths of the brides who get a yellow gold band as well as one of platinum or white gold, wear the latter.

The woman who avoids color in makeup and hair and rings is likely to be ready to prefer non-color in underclothes. Formerly red, pink, white, and black "intimate wear" used to carry romantic connotations, but beige has become an important underwear color as part of the larger pattern of abstention from femininity and strong expressive color. Wearing an attractively colorful piece of lingerie next to the skin was one way in which a woman could express femininity. Beautifully colored and handmade lacy lingerie used to represent an ideal for many women but our emphasis on youth and muted colors has made it almost anachronistic in the day of the body stocking.

Every important item of women's underclothing can now be mixed, matched, and color-coordinated within the beige family. Each season has its favored tones: heather and chestnut in the fall, earth for winter, camel in the spring, sand and champagne for summer. We can see the inevitable cartoon of an old-fashioned male, Christmas shopping for lingerie and trying to buy something in black lace, but only being shown variants of beige.

Before it became a mass favorite for outer- and underwear, beige had been high fashion and characterized Chanel's knitted wools as well as the carpets in her Rue Cambon office. Ina Claire often wore pale beige dresses on stage. Chanel favored the color because she emphasized button and braid trimmings and beads that appeared to best advantage against a neutral background. Such subtleties are less relevant today when the color is now so modish that a woman executive wears beige for an important meeting in order to convey the impression of "being extremely successful, knowledgeable, and secure."[9] One response to such attitudes is represented by the bright colors and gay designs of many Mod costumes. The very extreme nature of their assertive colors suggests, however, that the reaction they embody cannot be sustained.

Withdrawal from strong color also characterizes homes. Only every sixth home is built for a known buyer, and every fifth one is resold each year, so that builders and contractors avoid color extremes in order to achieve the widest possible sale and resale appeal. The more individualized homes built before World War II frequently used white for interiors because of its brightening effect but neutral colors are more common now. In addition to beige, the other popular neutral color is a gray that is neither cool nor warm, neither blueish nor reddish.

Beige is the single most popular color on the 45 percent of major appliances that come in colors other than white. Typical is the 1966 line of Frigidaire home laundry equipment, for which beige is the keynote color and "control panels are softly color-blended with cabinets."[10] People who pay extra for a color telephone might be expected to select a strong hue but the most popular color is beige. Its very blandness probably permits easy blending with furniture and accessories and blending is more important than contrast or mixing.

The color of wall-to-wall carpeting now tends to the neuter. Expensive enough to survive several redecoratings, it is often passed on to subsequent occupants of a house or apartment. Soft and pale rugs usually have feminine connotations and strong patterns, red, and black, tend to be masculine.[11] For reasons of blending with furniture, economy, and ease of cleaning, the most popular rugs come in solid colors like beige rather than patterns or masculine or feminine colors. Color is an important part of a rug's ability to add warmth to a room, but a beige rug conveys an antiseptic feeling.

In many homes, the colored draperies that formerly punctuated and underlined a room's masculinity or femininity are being replaced by venetian blinds and similarly unemphatic covers. Window shades have moved up the social scale from tenements to luxury buildings. Plastic slipcovers have also crossed the railroad tracks into middle-class homes, where they reinforce the undifferentiated quality of chairs and sofas and may ultimately replace a previous generation's colorful fabric covers. One encouraging counter-trend in many homes is the use of accents of strong color in pillows and cushions.

It is ironic that the wrecker's ball now provides one of the rare occasions for viewing interesting home colors. The varied hues on interior walls of buildings in the process of being demolished often show fascinating stippling against the sky. Their blue and green and fuchsia and pink and brown are being replaced by beige or gray in the new buildings that are erected on the site.

Neutral colors are found in homes and apartment buildings at all price levels. In Manhattan's Kips Bay Plaza luxury apartment development, beige is found on the poured concrete exterior, shopping center, elevators, walls, tile floors, and lobby curtains. Bright red rugs that had originally been installed in the corridors were replaced by beige, which is also the most popular color for the walls and ceilings of apartments. The majority of the other fashionable apartment houses built in Manhattan since 1945 are made of beige brick or poured concrete.

A democracy of taste is accomplished by acceptance of beige at all socioeconomic levels. Seven blocks west of Kips Bay is Chelsea Houses, a state-aided low-rent apartment development. The buildings' exteriors are off-beige; all rooms except the kitchen are beige, and floors are covered with a dark beige resilient tile. Such projects are almost always repainted the same color, so that subsequent generations can look forward to a beige future.

In the days when the master bedroom had two bathrooms, it was once easy to tell a man's from a woman's. Tiles in the man's were usually gray, while the woman's color scheme tended toward delicate pinks. These colors' popularity has faded and a home's multiple bathrooms tend to be the same color, usually white or beige. Even a woman's bathroom that has an elaborate vanity is likely to be beige or white.

The tendency to avoid strong colors in home decoration has been enhanced by many American interior designers who follow the Japanese Shibui principle of soft color arrangements. Shibui uses natural color harmony and believes that strong colors and bold patterns are unsettling. Its exponents argue that most colors in nature are soft and quiet and recommend that furniture have similar qualities. The American adaptation does not reflect Shibui in Japan, where muted colors provide a background for one dominant high point, like a brightly colored scroll, a painting, or flowers. A background's ability to enhance other colors can be seen in the beautiful effects of Roualt's black bands on other hues in his paintings. But our domestication of Shibui ignored its backdrop function and helped to bring about a visual leveling in many homes.

Even supermarkets, presumably interested in getting the attention of shoppers, seldom use color to do so. Although some cases containing food may come in colors connoting specific products (blue—frozen foods; yellow—dairy; green—produce; red—meats), most supermarket walls and decorations are neutral in color, often beige. The store's rationale is that any one interestingly colored section might divert attention from other departments.

In stores as well as homes and offices, we are using neutral colors because we like them. Our situation differs from the decade after World War I, when yellow became popular because of picric acid's wide availability at low cost. A major ingredient in explosives and poison gas, it was also the basis for yellow dye. The surplus was used until 1927 in yellow paint, fabric, and clothes.

Colors in other countries are deeply imbued with nationalistic, religious, or moral taboos, e.g., yellow betokens sickness in the Sudan, white is the mourning color of Thailand, and the combination of yellow and gold has negative connotations of the Hapsburgs in Hungary.[12] Only functional and esthetic considerations need be relevant in furnishing living or working quarters in America. Yet beige is probably the most popular color in our "machines for living."

Color taboos in other cultures, e.g., purple in Laos, have inhibited the eating of some foods. Our lack of taboos has not led to a broad spectrum of color in food. Rather, its range has been declining along with the diminution in taste, texture, and aroma. A partially red apple is much less popular with shoppers than one that is all red. Green noodles have never achieved an American popularity commensurate with their taste and red is used far less frequently than brown or white for sauces.

Artists' prescience with respect to color may be seen in the beige second version of Picasso's "Ma Jolie" and Braque's extensive use of other muted browns in the years after World War I. Although the cubists used beige because they were primarily concerned with analysis of form and wanted to minimize the role of color, some also had a remarkable ability to predict later mass preferences.

Color is becoming blander at the same time that many other phases of social life reflect an avoidance of extremes. A fashionable woman might wear a little nothing dress in no color, over a no-bra bra and beige underwear. Her no-color stockings would blend with earth-colored shoes, muted makeup, and hair in drab. Sitting gracefully on the beige rug in her beige room, she might nibble on tasteless low-calorie rice wafers and sip a light Scotch or aromaless vodka. A physical environment that does not provide a significant range of experiences with form, texture, taste, shape, and color makes us less able to distinguish differences of any kind as we move toward the good non-life and non-phenomena.

The Beige Epoch is as useful a description of a mass society that minimizes extremes as the Gilded Age was for triumphant vulgarity and gaudy exteriors in the 1870's, the Brown Decades for the dun and sooty browns of architecture between 1865 and 1895, and the Mauve Decade for the political and intellectual development of the nineteenth century's last quarter. Mark Twain, Lewis Mumford, and Thomas Beer were each writing about substantially the same period of time. Yet each dealt with an outstanding facet which stood out and could be described in an identifying phrase. The Beige Epoch is an accurate description of our flattened social landscape because so many streams that feed into the river of contemporary life are giving it the monotony of a canal.

Grand Rapids and After

Bit by bit, many traditional means by which a man and a woman localized their presence in the home have disappeared and furniture has become both less masculine and less feminine. There are certain obvious aspects of furniture's gender, e.g., the masculinity of a straight line or femininity of a curve. Heavy furniture, dark colors, and coarsely grained dark woods have generally been linked with men, while women have usually favored delicate furniture, light colors, and finely grained, light woods.

Rooms with gender may soon be subjects for archeologists, as a result of the continuing displacement of rooms by areas that merge into one another. A woman formerly received friends in her inviolable sitting room or boudoir. Men used to lord it in paneled dens, libraries, and billiard and smoking rooms.[13] Such distinct domains are giving way to the recreation room, where the family can enjoy togetherness in an informal setting. Frank Lloyd Wright used to marvel at American adults' acquiescence in a situation in which children were often the only family members with their own rooms.

Consider what has happened to modern kitchens. Wood paneling left the man's room and reappeared in kitchens in birch, fruitwood, and maple cupboards. Kitchens' complexion is so important nowadays because doors or pantries are no longer likely to separate the cooking area from other rooms. A visitor can hardly avoid seeing the kitchen because it usually opens directly on the living or dining room. Once the center of social life for lower-class families, the paneled kitchen has now become the core of many middle-class homes. Its transformation has been facilitated by the warmth provided by wood veneer on refrigerators, dishwashers, stoves, and rows of appliances built into kitchen walls.

There was once no mistaking the massive masculine lines and intentions of oak. Simple, strong, and dark, it was extensively used in furniture. Oak's heavy graining stands out in strong relief because its pores absorb staining and look three-dimensional. The once-popular large oak table with iron claw legs has not been made for several decades and the Museum of Modern Art's restaurant was typical of many institutions and homes in replacing its tables of oak with some made of lightweight white plastic.

One reason for oak's decline is that almost all solid woods have lost popularity. Extremes of climate in the United States and steam heat's dehumidifying ability cause solid wood alternately to contract, expand, and ultimately split. A desire to avoid splitting is one reason for the recent popularity of veneers. Oak loses much depth and appears less masculine when veneered. The "decently dark" oak that was found in Dickens' counting houses and American banks used to awe a potential borrower and many modern banks have eliminated the paneling along with grim-lipped guards and barriers between customer and teller.

Mahogany's durability was so legendary that Victor Hugo compared it to burial in the Père Lachaise cemetery. Its masculinity was enhanced by a rich dark reddish color. Second in popularity only to maple in the 1930's, it is too massive for contemporary consumers. Ebony's somber depth and smooth blackness has also become less attractive to American furniture buyers, although it was once so popular in France that cabinet makers are still called *ébénistes*. The wood enjoys only limited use for decorative pieces—lamp bases, desk accessories, and cigarette tables, in combination with beech and similar lightly grained woods. Just as solid oak became bleached, the dark teak of the 1920's and '30's has become less popular than a lighter teak, that is usually veneered and has a severe look.

At the same time that the masculine woods have lost popularity, the two most feminine woods have become scarce in furniture showrooms. Poplar and ash have a soft and beautiful quality found in very few woods. Their grain is so delicate and feminine because it offers few harsh contrasts and is probably the reason for their lack of favor.

Not one of the woods that are traditionally masculine or feminine was mentioned in a national survey of the five woods most preferred for modern or traditional furniture.[14] The decline of woods associated with either sex is reinforced by furniture colors which tend to hover in a narrow range from light through medium brown.[15] The metamorphosis of maple is typical, from a reddish finish in the 1930's through a honey tone in the 1940's, and a more recent beige.

The finish reinforces other neuter qualities of popular woods. A small amount of linseed oil that gives the merest touch of life and minimum shine is the current favorite. One reason for teak's popularity since 1950 has been the compatibility of its natural oiliness with today's anonymous soft finish. Our busy homemaker does not have the time to maintain a wood's hand-rubbed patina.

Most consumers buy furniture for its finish rather than wood although a finish can be changed to shiny, dull, light, dark, or matte. The only attribute of a wood that cannot be changed is its grain. A wood's zebra, feather, swirl, plain, or flower grain will significantly contribute to a room's masculinity or femininity, but woods with graining that is clearly feminine (e.g., poplar) or masculine (e.g., oak) have few current adherents.

Modern American furniture's blandness is reinforced by manufacturers' tendency to use only one wood for each piece. Scandinavian manufacturers often combine more than one wood. They might use teak to provide a workable surface for a table top and oak for solidity in its legs. Multiple woods add texture and facilitate a clearer expression of gender in a piece. Complementary or contrasting woods permit an accentuation of each component's positive qualities.

Kinds of furniture that were formerly linked with either sex have become more neuter. Delicate lines and curved legs conveyed the femininity of a Governor Winthrop secretary. The mahogany kneehole desk was unmistakably masculine in size, color, materials, and appearance but is becoming even more scarce than the woman's secretary-desk, as both tend to be replaced by genderless styles. Today's popular kneehole and table desks are used interchangeably by men and women.

The man of the house is even less likely to have a

mahogany desk than he is to be looking over his fiefdom from the head of a rectangular table. Delicately shaped feminine tables (e.g., the folding pie-crust style) are more likely to be available as antiques at auctions than as contemporary styles. Avoidance of gender is also expressed in the plastic top on the occasional table that has been the country's single most popular table style for over a decade.[16]

Matched living-room sets before World War II often included a heavy man's chair and a softer-looking woman's model, Dagwood and Blondie. Pairing also characterized wing chairs during the Colonial revival of the 1940's, even though the wings' function of protecting a sitter against draft was largely symbolic. Today's living rooms are more likely to have similar chairs rather than a matched male-female set. Another design casualty has been the masculine shelf arm, for many years now the single least popular chair style.[17] The arm on a contemporary version is so small that it often looks out of proportion.

Depersonalization of the home has been further advanced by disappearance of the distinctively feminine boudoir chair, now almost a collector's item. The only large firm making boudoir chairs stopped manufacture a few years ago. There is also little interest in the chaise longue, once an ideal setting for women who wanted to present their legs in an appropriate setting while receiving guests in informal costume.[18] The chaise's slide to obscurity also reflects obsolescence of the sitting room which it used to grace.

With the near-disappearance of masculine or feminine chairs, foam rubber has become the Space Age's upholstering of choice. It is neutral and has no "give," in contrast to traditional upholstering's indentations after someone has been sitting on it. The flatness that foam rubber gives to chairs becomes increasingly evident as chair styles become more flat and influence sitting, the symbolic pos-

ture of our time. The chair mediates the sitter's relationship to the earth as it holds and supports his body.[19]

One reason for the neuter appearance of so many living
rooms is the popularity of light chairs that can be easily
moved, for ease in watching television. Our electronic
happy medium has made people unhappily aware of
lightweight chairs' inability to absorb sound and, indeed,
their provision of channels along which it zooms en route
to a neighboring apartment. We are belatedly realizing
that the heavier chairs of previous generations could act
as sound buffers as well as convey character and provide a
comfortable seat.

Comfort was a consideration with grandpa and even father, who preferred a chair to be sturdy, sprawling, and
enveloping and to provide room for a man to rest his
head. The opportunity of complimenting a host by saying
"This is a real man's chair," is diminishing as the sturdy
leather club chair joins the massive modern pieces of
twenty and thirty years ago in oblivion.

Many of today's chairs look so cold and neutral that
their predecessors were once believed to be suited primarily for a commercial establishment. Mies van der Rohe's
MR 1926 model, consisting of a cantilevered curve of continuous steel tube with leather slings laced over the frame,
and Marcel Breuer's 1925 angular "Wassily" chair of
leather and steel tubing, had become utility items for
kitchenettes and barber shop waiting rooms by the 1940's.
Breuer has recalled how revolutionary such furniture was
in the 1920's: "At that time elegance was silk and gold
and polished ebony. Today it is . . . a thermos."[20]

Metal and a "thermos" quality also distinguish the
comfort-defeating sling chair that may be the most antisexual piece of furniture ever made. When Bertrand Russell observed that political liberals tend to have comfortable old-fashioned furniture, he could not possibly have

anticipated the recent popularity of sling chairs with so many humanistic men of good will in this country.

One enthusiastic report on "a new age in metals" exults that "the shimmering beauty of steel, aluminum, and chromium-plated metals is becoming as much a part of today's office and home as mellow, waxed woods were of yesteryear's. . . ."[21] Such materials and the many other neutral substances used in furniture are likely to increase rooms' lack of gender. Glass can be found on doors and table tops, slate inlays are fashionable, and woven cane chairs grace many homes. Shiny vinyls also contribute to the Buck Rogers look of the modern home.

Another influential recent change in home decor has been the extensive use of free-standing furniture. Furniture standing free from other objects and surfaces tends to look stripped and bare. Any neuter qualities it possesses are less likely to be modified by contrast or blending with a wall or another piece.

Furniture is so indicative of basic needs because it is usually bought after considerable deliberation. People know that a piece that turns out to be a mistake will be staring them in the face for years to come. Furniture provides a unique opportunity for a woman to create a setting that expresses her taste and character, because her home is not only a symbol of femininity but an extension of her body. A man is generally happy to have his wife take over the decoration and furnishing of a home and would be unlikely to disagree with her major decisions.[22] The substantial nature of furniture purchase decisions is reflected in the over $6 billion that is spent on them annually.[23]

Modern styles account for three-fourths of the sales of all upholstered products. Medium-scale is the most popular. It is possible that much enthusiasm for modern furniture stems from the growing proportion of women with some degree of masculine identification. Modern's straight stripped lines and lack of protuberances suggest the kind of body that many American women would like to have. They avoid the appearance of upholstered curves in their figures for the same reasons that they shun overstuffed furniture.

It could be argued that consumers who purchase modern furniture are reflecting less artificial needs than the Americans who once slavishly bought all the latest antiques. People who buy modern paper or inflatable furniture are expressing their style of life more honestly and directly than the previous generations who bought homes during the Florida land boom and enthusiastically filled them with pieces purchased from Addison Mizner. He had "antiqued" them by shooting carefully sized shotgun pellets into the wood in order to simulate worm holes.

Undoubtedly, one factor contributing to the sterile look of much modern furniture is its size. The tendency to make everything smaller means that contemporary furniture is seldom large enough to be masculine and its small scale contributes to difficulties in achieving flowing feminine lines and curves. Sofas and couches, however, are actually getting longer; they averaged 76″ in length ten years ago, but 84″ and 96″ are popular lengths today. The smaller size of other pieces does not necessarily result from lack of space but is related to the larger forces that have eased acceptance of neutering in other kinds of personal and social expression.

A straight-line silhouette not only provides a protective cover for gender in furniture but also helps to conceal the function of many household items. The toaster may be one of the few appliances that do not lend themselves to much departure from a shape that is almost imposed by their function. But the once-interestingly varied shapes of many appliances have surrendered to a generalized neutral streamlining that blends with modern furniture. The same basic shapes, finishes, colors, and textures distinguish an electric toothbrush and a vacuum cleaner.

In Europe, the Phillips Company of Holland sells table radios with cabinets that are either circular or rectangular, shiny or lacquered, and are available in several strong colors and multiple woods. For the American market, the same basic radio is housed in blandly colored cabinets that have neutral shapes and a dull finish. The very successful American model was introduced after failure in this country of the original style, which had been Europe's best seller.

An advertisement for office furniture recently asked, "Does your furniture give a caller the feeling that he should be seeing someone higher up?" With offices so neutral, even an astute student of executive-suite topography would have trouble in identifying an employee's relative importance by his furniture. Materials, color scheme, layout, and floor plans may be uniform throughout the space occupied by a firm. A company's offices are likely to look far more neuter than in the days when they were decorated with more attention to sex differences and individual requirements.

Recent years have seen the growth of interior design which tries to conceal rather than communicate the work of an office.[24] One bonus of the lugubrious medical prints that used to line physicians' waiting rooms was that they helped to prepare patients for grim diagnoses. A modern waiting room may have no sign of its function except for pop paintings that fortuitously resemble bodily organs or op works that look like a case of the hives. No one can tell how many potential patients tiptoed out of dentists' waiting rooms, never to return, after studying the grim photographs of gingivitis that once dominated their walls. Chances are that when today's dentist asks the nurse to look at his etchings, she'll have to go no farther than his waiting room. Many a lawyer's office has abandoned its traditional shelves of the Corpus Juris and now looks like an art gallery. Even the ubiquitous stock ticker of brokerage houses is being replaced by prices flashing discreetly on a screen.

Replacement of interior walls by open-work spaces has enhanced the blurring of visible functions in offices. The old-fashioned wooden desk that held papers, pens, and telephones is metamorphosing into a simple slab that has the largely symbolic function of creating distance between people.

Some courageous men have taken a stand and tried to establish a masculine frontier in their offices. Now that homes increasingly reflect equality between husband and wife, many a man has been grateful for the hierarchical structure of his office, where a secretary is *not* his equal and he can sport Remington prints, hunting sketches, and fishing trophies. But such a campaign is only a delaying action, because furniture always reflects the way of life of its users.

Furniture's relationship to its culture can be seen in every historical epoch from which we have artifacts. The energetic efforts of Louis XIV in navigation, commerce, foreign policy, and enlargement of his kingdom were reflected in furniture of square-cut masculinity. Under Louis XV, it gave way to feminine frivolity and curved and capricious styles that were consonant with the personalities of Madame de Pompadour and Madame Du Barry. Their favorites included mirrors set into bureaus, graceful dressing tables, and low soft chairs with curved legs, that ultimately led to the chaise longue and sofa.

In contrast, furniture in Jacobean England was masculine, stout and staunch, often clumsy, matching the coarse manners, abrupt morals, and vigorous theology of the day.[25] Like the period, it conveyed strength rather than grace. Spanish furniture of the fifteenth and sixteenth century was also masculine, with straight lines and a massive feeling. The legs on tables and benches were heavily turned and splayed, just as the Spanish empire faced proudly outward to the world.

Early New England furniture tended to be simple, crude, and unornamentedly masculine, in keeping with the pioneer spirit. In the Federal era, and especially around 1800, there was considerable self-assertiveness and masculinity in furniture as Americans began to experience and test the ways in which they differed from European traditions. The dark and heavy furniture of the Victorian period was as appropriate for its secrets and repressions as our open and streamlined pieces are for American society today.

American furniture preferences of the last several generations have faithfully reflected the style of life of the times. Even our adaptations of older modes may convey neutering. A country manufactures history in its own image and our versions of historical styles mirror current trends in wood, color, design, and size so precisely that an Americanized Italian provincial piece is likely to be unrecognizable to Italians. Furniture expresses needs as accurately as a Rorschach ink blot, but we are using the blot's blurred shapes and in-between gray tones rather than its more assertive colors and forms.

Cities
of the Plain

There is a venerable story about a French mayor who was taking a tour of Manhattan's newer office buildings and surprised his guide by blowing kisses at each building. When the guide asked why he was doing so, the mayor explained that "Each building reminds me of a woman's curves." Observing the guide's perplexity, he smiled and added, "You see, everything reminds me of a woman's curves."

Only a person like the mayor would be able to perceive either feminine curves or any signs of masculinity in most of our large cities' new buildings. The Biblical cities of the plain were places of horror because of their perversions. Our cities may not inspire horror but are certainly not geared to joy and fulfillment. Pop architecture directly mirrors the facelessness of much American life and is the only architectural style ever to be formed at the bottom, rather than the top.[26] Many contemporary buildings represent an ultimate vulgarization and mockery of the purification accomplished by Louis Sullivan and the Bauhaus, whose clean lines brilliantly restored the psychological function of the visual and tapped new technological capabilities.

During the last years of the nineteenth and the first few decades of this century, large companies proudly associated their names with distinctive buildings—Home Insurance, Woolworth, Reliance, Chrysler, Prudential, Larkin, Schlesinger and Meyer. Each building had a personality and housed an idea as well as a company and its people, but such considerations seldom inform the group-architecture and planning of corporate headquarters today. The Colgate-Palmolive and Universal Pictures buildings on opposite sides of New York's Park Avenue could change signs without anybody knowing the difference. Large corporations often seem almost to be trying to make up for the non-identity of their buildings by energetic advertising and public relations activities that try to create a unique identifiable image.

The Colgate and Universal headquarters and their many counterparts were accurately described by a foreign architect. Looking up Park Avenue from 45th Street at the mile of featureless gray-green glass office buildings, he remarked: "They look like the members of a uniformed army, standing at attention. But it is an army without privates." The neutering he implied extends to many other office buildings and homes.

Le Corbusier's description of Manhattan skyscrapers as "hot jazz in stone and steel" was an accurate perception of the post-World War I years. Probably the last major American office building complex to seek individuality and avoid blandness was represented by the slabs of Rockefeller Center, around 1930. Some few buildings of the same period, like the New School on Twelfth Street and McGraw-Hill headquarters on 42nd Street in New York, used horizontal curves and avoided the popular clifflike neutral look that is represented by the New York Daily News building.

The graceless buildings going up all over America could be described as cool jazz in glass and metal. Like the music, they avoid strong assertions. The color, materials, and appearance of these ticky-tacky oblong boxes are typified by the neutral aluminum paneling that constitutes the exterior of 666 Fifth Avenue, a major New York office building that has been hailed for its new construction techniques. It looks assembled, rather than designed or built, and its bulky but bland appearance recalls the words of Revelation: "Let him that hath understanding count the number of the beast . . . his number is six hundred three score and six."

Many other buildings that carry "the number of the beast" are too unassertive even to have a flagpole. Sticking out of the aluminum and glass facade of a straight up-and-down building, it might provide an embarrassing reminder of masculinity. Signs of gender would be too much to expect from buildings that are not only anonymous and faceless, but lack top or bottom. The Grand Central Building is typical of many earlier structures in communicating an almost human quality of trying to get to the top, in the feeling of lift and upward thrusting provided by its shape. It becomes thinner as it moves from ornamental base to towerlike top, which set off the building's body. A few yards away is the totalitarian Pan Am monolith, typical of most newer buildings in its lack of distinguishing bottom or top. It is an enormous hollow sculpture. Use by humans is not related to its basic esthetic purpose, which is best seen at night when the people have left and the building's skeleton is brightly illuminated.[27] Watching the helicopters land on the roof of this people-eater suggests Oscar Levant's witticism about Elsa Maxwell. On taking off Miss Maxwell's mask at a costume party, he was shocked to see that he had decapitated her.

It is difficult to imagine such buildings aging gracefully, or even aging at all. One day, they will probably just fall over. The streets into which they fall have already been profoundly affected by the new structures and Park Avenue provides a useful paradigm of some effects of the glass ziggurats. The mile north of Grand Central Station was once a clearly defined street.[28] The Avenue was clearly bounded by the masonry fronts of massive buildings and its shape emerged clearly because the structures that lined it were solid, and only a solid can define a space. The buildings almost seemed to be participating in a dialogue because they were scaled to the Avenue and to each other, so that the effect was esthetically humane and satisfying.

Lever House was the first Park Avenue structure to adapt Le Corbusier's principle of a building as a free-standing object in space. The substantial buildings on either side provided an attractive contrast to the two holes that had been cut by the empty spaces surrounding Lever House and that led the eye out of the Avenue. But Lever House's green glass walls were themselves hollow and could not serve to define the street. Park Avenue's destruction as a visually definable street was assured when the Lever building was imitated by many other glass cubes, each conceived as a free-standing monument that had no relationship to any other building. One effect of the new glass office buildings, themselves excellent examples of corporate anonymity, could therefore be loss of the identity of the very streets that once helped to make our cities great. Whole Manhattan neighborhoods are following streets into limbo. Such changes are so important because of New York's enormous influence on architecture in other parts of the country.

Contemporary architecture can draw on such a huge arsenal of materials and techniques that its trend reflects a conscious choice in favor of Mies van der Rohe's famous dictum that "less is more." Functionalism is the advantage usually cited for the spayed metal and glass structures that distinguish, if that is the word, many large cities. Certainly, functional beauty can be very exciting, as in the George Washington Bridge. Originally, it was to have been cased in concrete and stone, but the beauty of the completed steel towers was so moving that the plan was never followed. The rhythm, movement, and dance-like quality of Frank Lloyd Wright's designs and Le Corbusier's strong and sensuous forms were certainly functional but could hardly be called neuter.

Although functionalism is the virtue most associated with today's architects, one boomerang effect of the appearance of the newer buildings is a blurring of their functions. With the relative unpopularity of architecture that clearly communicates a building's purpose, some people who walk into a modern bank feel that they should be asking for a Pullman reservation or an order of apple pie, rather than filling out a deposit slip. A bank, airport, theatre, apartment house, bowling alley, indoor parking lot, restaurant, office building, and church could have similar exteriors, furnishings, and color schemes. Whatever else can be said about earlier American architecture, it clearly communicated buildings' functions. When you walked into the old Roxy theatre in New York, said manager "Roxy" Rothafel, "you knew you were *somewhere.*" Today's theatres resemble many other buildings in that they might be anywhere, and hence give the impression of being nowhere.

The appearance of American hotels once left no doubt about their function and a guest could select one that suited his mood and requirements. Hotel guests are being replaced by motel travelers, even in large cities. New York City is typical in having lost thirty-six hotels and gained forty-eight motels since 1946. Motels resemble one another all over America, just as the most typical comment about a motel is that it is "all right" or "adequate." Motels appeal to the largest number of people, but hotels attracted specific groups who developed attachments to them. Who could cherish a motel?

The travel in which so many Americans are engaging is, paradoxically, often occurring under circumstances that minimize rather than broaden experience. A jet separates its passengers from any sensory experience, even from perceiving that they are moving. An expressway makes it easy to drive for days without seeing anything. Standardized motels and international hotel chains make it possible to travel thousands of miles and never leave home.[29]

Many travelers are covered by a protective blanket of musical noise, in the canned music that is a widespread dividend of the Pax Americana. This audible wallpaper is found in elevators, factories, banks, offices, restaurants, hospitals, and even airplanes. Muzak pipes its medleys to 60 million Americans each working day. Since the same music may ooze into a bus, restaurant, airline terminal, or supermarket, there is no opportunity to associate specific music with situations or locales. The music is not intended to stimulate a response, and people who react are deviants. In 666 Fifth Avenue, a man and woman happened to be sole occupants of an elevator that began playing piped music as it ascended. In response to the music, the woman began humming and swayed slightly in a simple dance step. The man was terrified by her spontaneous response, pressed the emergency button, fled at the next floor, and complained to the starter about "a madwoman in the elevator."

No art frees man's spirit as does music. But it is hard to recognize what Aristotle proclaimed as the purest of the arts in dry-cleaned sound that is meant to be heard but not listened to, and has no beginning, middle, or end. No pause separates the end of one piece from the beginning of another. Selections are not identified by title or composer, so the listener cannot orient his perceptions, especially since every piece is played the same way. As the sounds of music are replaced by noise, our ability to differentiate sounds tends to diminish, just as an earlier generation lost its ability to distinguish water gushing or a cow's mooing.

The lifelessness that is an inevitable component of canned seamless music is also communicated by the fluorescent lighting common in new buildings. Fluorescents deaden flesh tones, eliminate skin highlights, make people look flatter and neutral, and give them a ghostly pallor. Devitalization of skin inside modern buildings is especially appropriate since so many lack masculinity or femininity. Some perspectives on gender in architecture can be obtained from the Taj Mahal. Its soft pastel colors, curves, and sinuosities are almost overwhelmingly feminine, as befits a mausoleum built by an emperor in memory of his wife. The soaring masculinity of the Empire State Building is a conspicuous phallic symbol even without the bulboid efflorescence of its mooring mast.

Two structures with similar functions can communicate different feelings of gender. Sir Christopher Wren borrowed substantially from Michelangelo and other Italian architects in the design of St. Paul's Cathedral in London. Yet even though St. Paul's has a massive quality, it is softer, gentler—more feminine—than St. Peter's. Wren's use of space, and small details like his fluting of each of the dome's upper columns, contribute to the structure's feminine connotations. In contrast, St. Peter's deployment of space, simplicity, and the uninterrupted movement of its columns convey masculinity.

The beauty of the two cathedrals, each suggesting a different gender, reminds us that neither masculinity nor femininity has intrinsically superior esthetic qualities. Actually, a very rich emotional experience may be provided by a structure that combines masculine and feminine in an esthetically pleasing expression of unity. Bringing together sexual opposites, like the cave and tent shapes in Frank Lloyd Wright's Taliesin West, can be completely satisfying. Such shapes are becoming less common as architecture moves away from strong towers and rounded domes and toward organic forms that are closer to nature. Even the church's campanile and dome are giving way to more organic shapes that are less identifiable as masculine or feminine. Our avoidance of the traditional construction vocabulary of the feminine (e.g., lunette, balustre, arch, barrel vault) and the masculine (e.g., column, tent pole, lintel, chimney) is a reminder of the former importance of sexual symbolism in architecture and building (e.g., couples, male and female connections, nipples).[30]

The shape of newer buildings of all kinds is increasingly homogeneous and anonymous and is often independent of geographic locale, natural setting, and materials used. One obvious reason is the small number of new homes designed by an architect in contrast to the very large proportion planned by contractors. Abandonment of traditional vocabularies of shape may be related to changes in other aspects of our man-made environment. The rock garden, built around little flowers that creep between and over rocks, seems to be disappearing. Gardens tend to be on relatively flat land, devoid of the natural terrain that distinguished both small and large gardens of an earlier era.

A symbol of our time is the increasing use of ready-made sodded lawns. They roll onto a surface like wall-to-wall carpeting, which they resemble in being sold by the yard. The homemaker need not trouble to grow his lawn, but can order it in the spring. Gardeners can also buy a plastic grass that looks authentic but is weatherproof and can be vacuum cleaned. It even tickles bare feet, just like real grass. Such products are changing gardening's traditional role as a personal expression. Gardens of the Japanese type that use gravel and small trees rather than flowers are gaining favor. In American homes that have Japanese gardens, chrysanthemums and other plants are often concealed behind a fence, building, or in a corner, in order not to interfere with the pattern of symmetry.

Many home owners who do not have Japanese gardens use white gravel, marble chips, or paved areas on the space around the house that was traditionally occupied by turf. One reason for such materials' popularity is their ease of maintenance. A reason on another level could be the feeling of barrenness that they express and reinforce. "No more fertilizing, lime, watering, cutting, and weeding," exulted one Westport home owner whose home is surrounded by chipped stones. "And it fits with my glass-walled house." Flowers, trees, and grass are often being replaced by rocks, so literal a symbol of sterility that Red Riding Hood put one in the wolf's stomach as an expression of the male's inability to conceive. The sterile appearance of so many contemporary gardens suggests that even our fantasies may be changing, because a garden is traditionally made by man in his image of heaven.

Just how closely gardening is related to architecture

and styles of living can be observed with special clarity in Holland, which has the world's greatest concentration of population to land.[31] The neat rows of red, white, and yellow tulips are reminiscent of the colors and practiced geometric symmetry of a Mondrian painting and the horizontal and vertical planes of Dutch homes. Over 1.3 million dwellings, built since 1945, have been set in straight rows of apartment houses with square green plots. Rectangles of apartment blocks, fields, and canals lead to endless flat horizons that look as if they were laid out with a T-square.[32] Their historical antecedents can be seen in the careful organization of doors and windows and other plane surfaces in the great seventeenth-century Dutch paintings. Dutch orderliness also expressed itself in their brilliantly organized fight against the sea and the systematic planning of their resistance effort in World War II.

The rhythm of a period's style imposes itself on all of its activities and the interrelationships of architecture with styles of culture never just happen.[33] The gargoyles and fantastic carvings on buildings in the middle ages, once regarded as merely eccentric, represented monsters, demons, or fiends. Such sculptures provided methods of coping with the devil, just as the cathedrals' function as "Bibles in stone" was explicated by Ruskin and Henry Adams. Roman Imperial architecture used elegant and rhetorical materials that met the same needs as the *Aeneid's* ornate style.

Our outer and inner space has become more homogenized and drably hued, with desensitization and flattening of the range of emotion only some of the possible consequences. We need only compare ourselves to the contemporary residents of Chartres and Paris, who surely derive a far more profound sense of the human situation from their environment than contemporary Americans can from the prevalent anti-human mode of the neuter.

The occasional exceptions to the chastity and inhumanity of so many of our recently built stone deserts offer hopeful reminders that some measure of architectural boldness is still expressing itself. But the dominant architectural mode could be seen in the results of a Chicago architectural competition for a memorial auditorium to Enrico Fermi. It may have been especially appropriate, in view of Fermi's role in atom research, that the prize went to a building that was literally invisible, buried underneath a white marble plaza and undisturbed by trees, art, or architecture.[34] In an America in which less is more, nothing is most.

6

childhood,
a journey with new maps

Father calls me William,
Mother calls me Will,
Sister calls me Willie,
But the fellers call me Bill.[1]

The confusion of sex roles that pervades our environment
would be meeting more opposition if our young people
had not previously been prepared for the change. The culture which reflects our social system, which is part and
parcel of personality itself, demands that childhood reflect
our new values.

The authors of the nursery rhyme ("Natural History")
could once have easily answered questions like "What are
little boys made of?" and "What are little girls made of?"
Such positive responses cannot be given lightly today. A
number of milestones on the once familiar road of child
development have been knocked down, including traditional name preferences, dolls, children's involvement in
fairy tales, and established identities and roles of children.
Each of these changes seriously affects how a child assimi-
lates traditional ideals of masculinity and femininity. The
nursery and playroom provide ample evidence.

From Dick and Jane
to Leslie and Tane

As Jack Paar once admitted, he had answered his
daughter's puzzlement as to why she was named Randy
with a counter-question: "Why don't you ask your mother
George?"[2] A few years before his quip, Americans were
discussing two prominent women called Pat and Jackie.
Our new enthusiasm for given names that are not necessarily associated with either sex is important because personality may be shaped, reinforced, and reflected in a
name. The individuality of a given name can be seen in
the great painters whose signatures consisted only of their
first names. Vincent Van Gogh, Rembrandt Harmens-
zoon van Rijn, and Michelangelo Buonarroti underscored
their given names' uniqueness, even if others shared the
family name.

The associations of names, often half-conscious, came
from such wildly diverse sources as novels, historical
figures, movie stars, comic strip heroes, religious leaders,
friends and relatives, even places and pleasures.[3] They
identify a person's family, reinforce his status, link him
with a culture hero, provide a tie between tradition and
the individual, and help to position him in society. A person's name carries his spirit and clothes him, just as the
"soul is forme and doth the body wear," in Spenser's lovely phrase.

A given name is the only thing of value in our society
which may be taken from anywhere, without asking. Everyone must have a given name, perhaps the one aspect of
popular culture that touches us all. In several religions, to
be dead is to have no name. Although a name does not
necessarily influence self-identity, its ability to identify a
person makes it easier for his attitudes toward a name to
become closely related to feelings about himself.

As a child becomes aware of his name, between the ages of one and two, the fantasies forming around it tend to become deeply involved in the development of his idea of self. The given name is recognized as part of one's self long before the family name. Many children assume fantasy names because of concern about whether they have the "right" name. Children constantly test the effects of a name, and their ability to do so determines the extent to which they can accept it and its connotations.

Some rather striking effects of names on their owners are suggested by a finding that Harvard students with unusual names are significantly represented among students with superior personality, neurotics, and flunk-outs.[4] Another study concludes that boys with peculiar first names are more disturbed than those with ordinary names.[5] Such findings could, of course, result less from any intrinsic properties of a name than the attitudes toward a child that originally led the parents to select a particular name.

It is not unreasonable, then, to suspect that names given to children will reflect our culture's neuterization and what is becoming the game of sexual identity. One way of measuring this is to note birth announcements and to compare the names of the children with their parents'. In a large sample of birth announcements between 1948 and 1963, over one-fifth (21.3%) of the children's names were not found among the parents', and three kinds of names accounted for practically all of the difference: surnames used as given names, names linked with both sexes, and those having no established connotations.[6]

The surname as given name was originally a device to give a mother's maiden name to her son. The practice was once popular in the South, where a given name like Page, Saunders, Mallory, Logan, or Pierce was not uncommon even for a girl. Its previously established surname use tends to give such names a genderless quality.

The largest category of new names consisted of those given to both sexes. Some names have historically been given to either sex, e.g., Maria in Latin countries. England has had generals and admirals named Vivian, Jocelyn, and Joyce. But such established historical trends in other countries are quite different from our recent increase in ambisexual names.

One reason for the increase could be a more liberal interpretation of how names may be derived from religious sources. American Catholics still relate a child's baptismal name to a saint, who is a prestigious and protective model and guiding figure for the child. But today, a saint's name may appear on the baptismal certificate (e.g., Anastasia) and a related but secular name on the birth certificate (e.g., Stacey). Another approach is to add a saint's name to a secular one, so that Dana on a birth certificate might become Dana Anne at baptism. Jewish parents interpret the requirement to relate a name's initial letter to a deceased ancestor in an increasingly free manner. An ancient Hebrew name like Rachel may appear on family records but metamorphose into Robin on a birth certificate.

Another sanction for names that could be used by either sex is the growing number of prominent persons with such names: Alexis (Smith, Johnson), Babe (Didrickson, Ruth), Connie (Francis, Mack), Dale (Evans, Robertson), Dana (Wynter, Andrews), Gene (Tierney, Tunney), Jan (Sterling, Murray), Jean (Seberg, Shepherd), Jeff (Donnell, Chandler), Jo (Stafford, Davidson), Joey (Heatherton, Adams), Joyce (Brothers, Cary), Kay (Kendall, Kyser), Lee (Remick, Tracy), Leslie (Caron, Howard), Loren (MacIver, Eisely), Lynn (Fontanne, Riggs), Michael (Strange, Wilding), Noel (Adam, Coward), Pat (Carroll, Boone), Ray (Dooley, Milland), Ruby (Keeler, Goldstein), Shelley (Winters, Berman), Shirley (MacLaine, Povich), and Vivian (Blaine, Fuchs).[7]

There is a busy traffic in names from one sex to the other. Kipling's Kim was a man, but in America three famous actresses bear the name (Hunter, Novak, Stanley). Miss Novak has indicated the confusion caused by her name: "I like Kim. . . . I see a little boy or girl with a shining face looking you straight in the eye."[8] Dana and Robin, once used for boys, have become very popular for girls. A number of names (Shirley, Leslie, Michael, Sidney) that are still masculine in England are used for both sexes in this country. Many other previously masculine names are now shared with women, but fewer feminine names have been taken by men (e.g., Winifred).

Children born in the last twenty years are more likely than their parents to have similarly pronounced names, differentiated only by spelling, e.g., Barrie-Barry, Claire-Clair, Jessie-Jesse, Rae-Ray, Sydney-Sidney. The popularity of such names has further contributed to blurring of sex differences. Some formerly sex-linked names have become homophonic, with Jessica, for example, becoming Jessie.

Unfortunately, ambiguous names continue to plague draft boards—women constantly receive notices to report for military duty. Such names have also led some steamship lines—inadvertently—to pair a man and woman in the same cabin. Another side of the problem is illustrated by a young man originally named Leslie Towne Hope, who has become better known as Bob Hope. After falling hopelessly in love with a young kindergarten classmate called Leslie, he renamed himself Lester in order to assert his maleness. Names' ability to convey problems in sexual identity is suggested in two films released during the war year of 1943. Both had heroines called Charlie and a third heroine was called Chris.[9] The films were released when men were away from home and women assumed many previously male tasks. Such sexual confusion has become routine in today's movies, with Irving an attractive blonde in *Breakfast at Tiffany's,* and Charlie the heroine of *Goodbye, Charlie.*

Still a third category of children's names that differed significantly from parents' consisted of those that were freshly minted and lacked established connotations, e.g., Tane, Abar. The increase in names without antecedents among the New People may well support Ortega y Gasset's observation on the tendency of the masses to avoid history, since not using names from the past represents an excellent way of losing identification with it. After all, a name connected with nothing in particular involves loss of a ready-made identity.

The parents who made Washington the most popular post-Revolutionary boy's name were expressing admiration for the first president and a belief in contagious magic. The unfortunate child saddled with a name which has historical connotations may identify with or rebel against them. But even more importantly, beliefs about the sort of personality associated with a name may strongly influence otherwise latent traits.[10]

In the 1948–1963 sample and in earlier large-scale studies, unusual names were twice as frequent among girls as boys. Fathers have more to say about sons' than daughters' names and naturally seem to prefer more ordinary first names. Women carry and enjoy less common names.[11] Their favoring relatively unusual names is contrary to the stereotype about women being less adventurous and more conforming than men.[12] Some mothers may select masculinized or ambisexual names for daughters as an expression of identification, rivalry, or ambivalence.

All three name types found in children—surnames, ambisexual, and those without connotations—have neuter qualities. Such names may have a variety of effects on their innocent young bearers. Latent anti-masculine tendencies of a boy or anti-feminine tendencies of a girl may be reinforced. Other persons may look for sexual ambivalence in a person with such a homogenized name and the name can cause its owner to react against such tendencies.

Even the sounds of names are significant. Many neuter names have more sibilants and liquids than guttural consonants. They tend to be shorter than the parents' and many have become thinner: Mark becomes Marc and John's son is Jon.

An attempt is sometimes made to distinguish sex by pronunciation. A boy Cecil may have the first vowel short but a girl often has it long. A male Leslie can be identified by a sibilant *s* while a female might have the *s* pronounced like a *z*. For most ambisexual names, however, such distinctive pronunciation for either sex is not possible.

Other related trends reinforce the new generation's neuter names. There is a growing penchant for initials that do not stand for anything, like Harry S. Truman's middle initial. Many young people have added such initials in recent years. Among the prominent men who prefer to be identified by their initials are former presidents Kaufman Thuma Keller of Chrysler Corporation, Cyrus Rowlett Smith of American Airlines, and toymaker Alfred Carlton Gilbert. Actress K. T. Stevens is known by her initials, presumably inspired by great admiration for Katie Hepburn.

The homogenization of names can be seen in the LBJ brand. The name of each member of the First Family has similar syllabication and initials. Although the similarity among the Johnson names may inspire some names with identical syllabication and initials on the banks of the Pedernales, it has not become a national consensus and it is unlikely that many children have been named after the President and First Lady. There was not one Lyndon or Lady Bird in a large sample of children born in New York City in 1964, although a substantial number in previous years had been named after presidents or their wives.[13] The very homogenization of the First Family names could make it more difficult for parents to be emotionally involved with any one Johnson and to reflect such identification in naming a child than was possible with White House occupants who had more singular names.

Homogenization of names is also encouraged by the growing popularity of neutral diminutives and nicknames: Jerry, Bobbie, Jo, Willie, Mickey, Rusty, Bunny, Jackie, and Billie can identify either gender. Governor Nelson Rockefeller is called Rocky and his wife is known as Happy, but many a happy woman is nicknamed Rocky, e.g., Gary Cooper's widow. Happy is also a popular name for men, e.g., sportscaster Happy Felton.

Even famous athletes compound the confusion through neuter nicknames or diminutives. Consider a baseball team which included Ruby Gomez, Nellie Fox, Elly Howard, Sal Maglie, Babe Ruth, Lena Styles, Birdie Tebbets, Vickie Power, Gussie Triandos, and Gene Woodling.[14] Such neutering of sports figures' names is relatively unexpected because athletes often have complex and non-euphonious names. Typical are Zoilo Versalles of the Minnesota Twins, Felipe Alou of the Atlanta Braves, Yelberton A. Tittle of the New York Giants, Erich (pronounced Eerish, not Eric) Barnes of the Cleveland Browns, Vada Pinson of the Cincinnati Reds, and jockeys Angel, Ishmael, and Mario Valenzuela and Braulio Baeza.

The same name may even belong to two people of different sex and in different fields of endeavor: Terry Moore, a brilliant center fielder for the St. Louis Cardinals, and also a prominent actress. Such ambiguity may increase the difficulty of a boy or girl Terry in finding an appropriate resonance for his or her name.

But how are ambiguous names regarded by others? The connotations of six first names were investigated by personal interviews. Two were unequivocally masculine (William and John), two were clearly feminine (Mary and Elizabeth), and two of the recently popular ambiguous names were rotated from a roster of six (Dale, Dana, Leslie, Lynn, Robin, Tracy) that had not differentiated sex in our study of birth announcements. The majority of both younger (17–30) and older (31–50) adults who were interviewed failed to associate the ambiguous names with either one sex or the other, although neither group had any such difficulty with the traditional names. The younger persons were better able to relate a range of personality characteristics to the ambiguous names but tended to ascribe non-sex-linked qualities to them.[15]

The new American propensity for neuter names is not found in England, which does favor names that are connected with movie stars but clearly communicate the sex of their owners. A study of names given to workers and their children in London found sharp differences between generations. Older parents tended to name their children after themselves, with most (58%) husbands and many (38%) wives passing on their own names. Few (20%) of the youngest husbands and none of the wives conveyed their names to children. The inherited names tend to be simple (John, George, James, Mary, Alice, Ada), but Hollywood's influence here can be seen in the post-World War II children (Glenn, Gary, Maureen, Lana, and Linda).[16]

Although the incidence and neuter qualities of recent American names were unequivocal, the names of parents who submitted birth announcements might themselves have differed from their own parents'. When files of the same newspaper were studied and similar comparisons made for 1923–1938, some 19.4% of the names of children born during the earlier period differed from their parents' —but only 3.1% were surnames, sexually ambiguous, or lacking in connotations. Then and now, the great majority of parents seem loyal to established names, but perhaps one-fifth are responsive to other possibilities.

Yet, it is possible that people who arrange newspaper birth announcements may not be representative of the

general population. There is no complete directory of the
children born during the period studied, but spot checks
with hospital birth records and school records substantially confirmed the incidence of neuter names. Why are they
in the air at this time? Because like all names, they express attitudes toward the self, one's own sex, the opposite
sex, and toward sexuality itself.[17] To a parent, such names
may seem to be one way of being different, although, sad-
ly, they provide still more evidence of conformity. They
may also represent, along with spelling changes like
Edythe for Edith, a desire to provide a classier name and
identity for the New People who can expect to enjoy the
age of affluence.[18]

Barbie as
Baby Doll

The extraordinary popularity of *Lolita*, written by a
middle-aged Russian émigré who would hardly have
known any American girls of his heroine's age, suggests
how ready the American public was to accept the idea of
a sexually precocious young girl. The witty story of Hum-
bert's becoming the victim of his twelve-year-old mistress
was published in 1958, just one year after the introduction
of the first mannequin doll and one year before Barbie,
the most successful such doll. Four years before *Lolita*,
Susan Slept Here had been the first movie to discover the
power of the sexually emancipated teen-ager. Its aggressive girl delinquent moves in with a disillusioned script
writer, deftly eliminates his fiancée, and marries him.

The great popularity of the mannequin doll is noteworthy because it mirrors an acceleration of social and sexual
development and because doll play is traditionally so important. Dolls represent the largest single category of expenditure of the $2.68 billion that Americans spent on

toys during 1966. The more than twenty million girls of doll age in the United States average two new dolls a year and devote more play time to them than to any other toy.

Children can magically and easily transfer the qualities of living persons to their dolls. A passion for dolls is strongest between seven and ten, reaching a climax between eight and nine.[19] The old-fashioned rubber baby doll was practically indestructible. Simple, without gadgetry, it represented an ideal object for creative fantasy play that could later help a little girl to become comfortable in the role of mother. Simple dolls tend to elicit the fullest response. Elaborate mechanical dolls that sucked, drank from bottles, wet diapers, cried, kissed, waved, and burped have also been popular but tend to stifle rather than stimulate creative impulses. A gimmicky baby doll may be so robotlike and have such specific physical detail that imaginative play is difficult.

Many girls learned to sew by working on doll clothes. By taking care of her doll, a girl could project into the future and see herself as mother. At the same time, the child could identify with the doll, since both were being taken care of by a mother. The baby dolls looked young enough for such identification and projection. Long before Freud, Victor Hugo wrote: "The doll is one of the most imperious necessities, and at the same time one of the most charming instincts of female childhood."

The ability that dolls once had to evoke such rhapsodic responses and help a girl ultimately to prepare for active nurturing motherhood became historical with the extraordinary popularity of mannequin dolls. They have far outsold their predecessors and radically changed the satisfactions provided by dolls. Every fourth girl between four and twelve owned a Ginny mannequin doll by the mid-1950's, when another popular favorite was Betsy McCall, whose extensive wardrobe included mink stoles and muffs.

The prototype teen or full-figured doll was introduced in 1957, and Barbie appeared in 1959, followed in two years by Ken, her male consort. Three Barbies have been sold for every Ken. An average of over six million mannequin dolls have been sold each year for a decade. A minimum standard wardrobe for Barbie costs an elegant $588. Auxiliary equipment includes a car, ranch house, and fashion wigs that can be dyed. The mannequin dolls have very adult and sophisticated clothes, and one of their contributions to acceleration of young girls' social development has been a sparking of interest in grooming and fashion. Little girls have been buying a weekly average of 125,000 dresses for fashion dolls, including costumes for cocktails, dancing, and traveling. A girl can purchase a *boutique* shop, with her doll as the proprietress. To complete the adult charade, Ken's chums include Ricky and Allen, Barbie has relatives, and her "best friend" is a doll called Midge. The girl with a Barbie can get a Midge and practice the game of competing with Ken as the target. Ten or fifteen years later, our Barbie may find that it's not all that simple. Her expectations may prove inadequate because love cannot, like Barbie's wardrobe, be purchased at the corner store.

What is the effect of these mannequin dolls on their millions of owners between four and twelve? Such girls may be less able to achieve the emotional preparation for being a wife and mother that they received from baby dolls. Barbie is a sexy teen-ager. A girl who projects and sees her doll as a mother figure is seeing her mother as a teen-ager, which is certainly confusing. If the youngster identifies herself as the mother, then she is taking care of a child who is already an adolescent.[20]

The role of the new woman in the larger world is suggested in fashion doll owners' play, which typically involves social activities for the doll and her escort. The girl selects a situation and dresses her doll accordingly. If she owns a male doll, he is also dressed—just as if she could control the way the man in the mating game would dress. She also gains experience in mixing with the opposite sex and competing for a male. On the make, in control of the situation, she is preparing herself to be the aggressive woman who flourishes in novels, plays, and movies. On television, her most obvious expression is *The Dating Game,* which is so successful that it can be seen weekdays and Saturday. Its format involves a girl who puts questions to a panel of three young men, evaluates their answers, and then selects one who will accompany her on a date. By the time the Barbie owner reaches the age at which she can actually participate in dating, she is likely to have a definite idea of just how her escort will play his part. For this mechanical bride, little will be left to chance or to disturbing human impulses.

Alas, many a young man, already two years slower in achieving puberty, may well be overwhelmed by his date's aggressiveness. For the Barbie-weaned girl, a relationship with the opposite sex may not be marvelous and exciting; it could rather be a routinized aspect of our culture's material assembly line, lacking mystery or momentum because of its predictable outcome. The Barbie girl may learn to expect to be valued because of her ever-increasing wardrobe and ability to manipulate her father and, later, husband into buying clothes and more clothes. During the latency years, she is being introduced to precocious sexuality, voyeurism, fantasies of seduction, and conspicuous consumption.[21]

As the sexy automatized doll displaces the baby doll, some effects may be seen in recent studies of figure drawings by girls from twelve to sixteen. Although such a tendency was not reported before the mannequin doll's popularity, girls now frequently draw male figures with feminine characteristics.[22] The girls are aware of basic sexual differences but insist on tagging the male with feminine qualities—a symbolic castration. Their confusion about boys' appearance may be related to some characteristics of the dolls. Barbie has a very substantial bosom, but Ken has no visible genital signs of masculinity. Many girls who have put Ken's head on Barbie do not appreciate the significance of Barbie's bosom or hair. They will find Ken-Barbie in the flesh when, in later years, they look for "men" and discover how many have feminine characteristics.

So much time separated the nine-year-old with an old-fashioned baby doll from her role as mother that she could enjoy fantasies about motherhood and not be concerned about doing something about them. But the distance in years that separates a Barbie fan from a socially active ten- or eleven-year-old girl is frighteningly slight, and she can easily translate doll-play fantasies into real social life. The girl's confusion of fantasy with reality was only increased when stores began selling "Barbie-coordinated fashions" that could be worn by the dolls' owners.

Barbie's wardrobes, homes, stores, playrooms, automobiles, and other elaborate equipment are an elaborate and rigid script for fantasies. Mannequin dolls' great popularity comes directly from their provision of vicarious experiences which are far beyond the emotional ability of their owners. One unanticipated consequence is that more and more teen-age girls who have gone through a Barbie phase later buy stuffed baby dolls in an apparent attempt to make up for earlier deprivation of symbolic motherhood via a baby doll. There is already some evidence that the teddy bear frequently ends up as the third person in the honeymoon bed.

We can only speculate on the ultimate effects of play with a doll that is relentlessly geared toward courtship rather than motherhood. Children can confirm their sense of identity by play with dolls, which is a "royal road" to understanding the infantile ego's efforts to come to terms with the real world and the other components of self.[23] The small world of toys that the child can manage is a harbor to which she can return for the purpose of redefining her ego, but mannequin dolls can accelerate psychosexual development and transform doll play into a turbulent and disruptive voyage.

Barbie and her counterparts are so recent that there really has not been enough time to assess their ultimate results. But there is already good reason to fear that some effects on many young girls were not anticipated by their purchasers, any more than Rabbi Löw could predict how much trouble would result from his golem, which followed instructions until the charm was removed from its mouth. The rabbi originally used the golem with good intent, just as parents want to please their daughters. Premature learning of later social roles, however, could cast a shadow into the later life of many a child who is currently enjoying her Barbie.

A parable with some ominous implications for the future may be divined in the history of the wheel's development in Mexican culture. Wheels were never used to lighten labor or to facilitate transportation in pre-Conquest Mexico, although archeologists have found children's wheeled pull toys from the same period. The Barbie craze may be predicting later trends in adult life, just as wheeled pre-Conquest toys were precursors of later developments.[24] The Mexicans regarded their children's play with wheeled toys as a game without implications for adult life and American parents view the fantasy play that Barbie provides as a curiosity without practical consequences. Although nothing in play is final and play itself usually occurs within the charmed circle of reversibility, Barbie may be providing experiences that are ultimately irreversible.

Sleeping Beauty
Wakes Up

The centenary of the Grimm brothers' death provided
an opportunity to recall fairy tales' former role in giving
innumerable young people abiding impressions of love
and romance. Once upon a time, the tales used to be the
most important literature of most children. Barbie is coming to the attention of little girls at an age when they were
once heavily involved with such tales. The frequency with
which children appeared in fairy tales made it easy for
young people to identify with the few but fabulous
characters.[25]

Part of fairy tales' granite power over young people derives from adherence to basic principles of good storytell-
ing. There is considerable repetition. The characters are
types with few but outstanding characteristics: very good
or very evil, ugly or beautiful, huge or tiny, enormously
wealthy or terribly poor. Animals, often anthropomorphic
and superior to humans, frequently appear at crucial moments to help virtue triumph.

In this world, people pass from poverty to riches and
the pauper knows how to be a king. Fairy tales' expression
of these transformation myths provides the child with one
method for transcending reality and overcoming obstacles.
Childhood is the only time when we really believe in mir-
acles and the tales' miraculous action often breaks down
into independent single events that casually violate the
thermodynamics of everyday life. Although changes in
imagery occur with dreamlike rapidity, the story makes
few demands on a reader's power to combine ideas simultaneously because it is seldom necessary to think of more
than a few objects or persons at a time.

The impact of fairy tales on imagination and fantasy
was reinforced by their often being read aloud by a mem-

ber of the family, as Lewis Carroll observed in his introduction to *Through the Looking Glass*:

> Child of the pure, unclouded brow
> And dreaming eyes of wonder!
> Though time be fleet and I and thou
> Are half a life asunder,
> Thy loving smile will surely hail
> The love-gift of a fairy tale.

Young people may find more truth about their own
lives as well as about anger and love, excitement and danger, power and chance in fairy tales than anything else
they might read. For many youngsters, fairy tales also provide comfort and hope in a world which seems increasingly barren. They can help a child to feel that his questions
about origins and goals are not senseless.[26]

The nursery-school or kindergarten-age child whose
fantasies flourished on Grimm could respond, a few years
later, to the less powerful adults in Andersen's fairy tales.
By ten or eleven, the imagery of Andrew Lang's tales and
the poignant moralism in Oscar Wilde provided additional satisfactions. Children of this age could enjoy looking
for incidental clues that led to resolution of the story.[27] A
child was able to follow the scent of romance in fairy tales
from the age of three to adolescence.

The kiss that awakens Sleeping Beauty represents love
coming to a girl after the right man has first kissed her. It
is not necessary to consider her lips as displaced genitals
in order to respond to the theme of the miracle of virginal
affection. The thornhedge surrounding her can be understood by a child to be maidenly restraint, independently
of the story's deeper meanings. Psychoanalytic interpretations of the frogs and serpents who figure in fairy tales has
called attention to some of the deep psychological truths
that contribute to their appeal.[28]

Within the last generation the traditional fairy tales

have declined in popularity, perhaps never again to approach their former importance for young readers.[29] Most new editions of fairy tales in the last twenty years have been of Grimm or Andersen. Former favorites like the colored fairy books of Lang are often out of print and it is sometimes difficult to find Wilde's tales even at well-stocked libraries. Most of L. Frank Baum's pre-*Wizard of Oz* tales are unavailable.

Why did the cake of fairy tales crumble? One reason has been the almost pejorative meaning of the name for many young people. "Fairy" now has such negative loading that it may cause even girls to giggle. In our contemporary withdrawal from stories of marvels, we have forgotten that fairies had gender. Identification of the stories as "marvelous" or "wonder" tales might help to overcome the semantic barrier to their acceptance.

As the social learning represented by parents and grandparents reading aloud has increasingly become the province of the school and other institutions, fairy tales have become less important in imprinting ideas about heroes and villains, beautiful women and romantic men. Traditional sex roles have moved to comic books and to "classics," which are often ignored because of their designation as such.

Another reason for fairy tales' loss of popularity is the popularity of language arts and individualized reading of contemporary books in school. Two generations of young people have been weaned on "here and now" and "easy to read" books and watered down and "realistic" fiction that presents a world without peaks or valleys.[30] Science and "how-to" books, controlled vocabulary reading, curriculum-related material, and biography have also been crowding fantasy material to the wall. The parents and librarians who believe that reading should be "useful" and who buy most children's books have made it easier for a child to pick up a new book about a space ship than the story of a magic carpet. Fantasy will not be enhanced by a coloring book that has numbers marking the areas to be covered by each color.

A larger reason for the decline of interest in fairy tales is that their strange events are now part of our daily lives. Children are so accustomed to television's routinely presenting remarkable things that they are less excited by magic and extraordinary actions in fairy tales. The unconscious of young people was probably often tapped by the fantasy tales that provided material for dreams, daydreams, and fantasies. With the strange and bizarre so available via mass media, young people may have less need to draw on such facets of their unconscious. When you have learned the details of a fire bomb that can eat you up, the dragon who blows fire and can swallow you is far less frightening. An astronaut who walks in space is more real than the fairy who flew through it.

One possible result of such developments is that today's young people may be developing less of the kind of collective unconscious that Jung identified than previous generations. Many of the archetypes that constitute the collective unconscious are less likely to be activated in the minds of young people who absorb vast quantities of information about matters that were once subjects for fantasy. Even though much of the goal of psychoanalytic treatment involves replacing the unconscious with the conscious, we can be concerned about the effects of young people ignoring part of their unconscious or replacing so much of it by the "real" world that something akin to atrophy may occur.

One function of fairy tales was to prepare young people to expect the worst and to be ready for the dire. Indeed, a complaint of some parents against fairy tales is their inclusion of such material. With our society not expecting destruction by traditional calamities like the plague, the tales' aid in helping to provide resilience against extremes is less relevant.

Many publishers respond to parents' fears about reinforcing childish terrors by stressing sanitized text, cute art work, and "interesting" covers. But the publishers do not dupe the children, who go out and buy comic books which feed their interest in extremes of emotion. One factor in the decline of fairy tales undoubtedly is the availability of bowdlerized Puritan versions that remove much material of interest.[31] Leonard Baskin has observed how important it is to "let devils and witches and evil old men cavort," so that the pages of children's books can truly be "mysterious windows opening onto a world beyond the bed, the desk, the bureau."[32] These windows, once invitingly opened to a world of fantasy, seem to be closing and sealing off many opportunities for reinforcing positive attitudes toward romance.

Replacement of fairy tales by more prosaic reading material is removing the child from an atmosphere in which imagination can assert itself, and alienating him from a traditional feature of childhood itself. Our knowledgeable young Admirable Crichtons run the risk of being less able to respond to an autumn leaf. The hierarchs in Eugene Zamiatin's *We,* probably the most brilliant satire ever written about Communism, believed the best insurance against disobedience to be removal of the brain area responsible for imagination. Downgrading fairy tales could represent a step in the same direction.

Our equivalent of Cinderella is Lana Turner being discovered while sipping a soda in a drugstore, Kim Novak spotted while bicycling, or Colette's first noticing Audrey Hepburn in a hotel lobby. The little girl raised on fairy tales and legends who dreamed of a pure and brave knight who would carry her away on a white horse, now sees him regularly on television, where the only transformation myth in which he engages is making clothes white. The bumbling husband and witty wife of the situation comedy are replacing the powerful wise king and his beautiful queen. In such a world there is no place for the fantasy, imagination, and romance of fairy tales.

Playing and Wearing Roles

At a government conference on recruiting women scientists, a major toy manufacturer stressed that "we need to develop new lines of toys which have no 'sex,' which would appeal equally to girls as well as boys. Giant magnifiers, our lens comparer, incubators, stethoscopes, flexible mirrors, etc., are precisely such items. . . . Let us start recruiting women scientists . . . during the years from two to seven."[33] Science-oriented, neuter toys are receiving more attention as playthings specifically designed for each sex decline in popularity.

Play preferences of boys and girls now overlap at a relatively early age, in addition to traditional shared sports like hiking and roller-skating. Girls are learning to play with model cars, Erector sets, baseball equipment, and guns, and are "pretend" space travelers or western heroes. High-riser bicycles, with handlebars resembling the horns of a longhorn steer, are rapidly eliminating the need for boys and girls to own different bicycles. Pangloss's buttockless people would have been delighted with the very high thin seat that tops the high risers' small frames and wheels. The crossbar connecting the seat of a boy's model with the steering apparatus is low enough not to injure a girl while she is mounting or dismounting. As a result, many girls are now using their brothers' high-riser bicycles, and sales of girls' models have declined.

Just as the profile of boy and girl cycling on their high

risers is indistinguishable at a distance, the profile of
school studies for both sexes shows much overlap. A number of schools offer boys sewing in the fifth and sixth
grades. Many eighth-grade boys learn cooking, while girls
study tool and die work, plumbing repairs, metalcrafts,
and lathe work. Both sexes are taught to type in high
school.

Once upon a time, young people used to have masculine or feminine fountain pens. Boys' pens were long and
stubby while girls' tended to be thin and short, but the
use of standardized ball-point pens has largely erased these
differences. Sex differences in handwriting were easily
communicated by nib pens, but are now relatively
difficult to identify because ball points make strokes of
uniform width.

Young people of each sex are more likely than ever before to have read books formerly associated with the other
sex. Girls who never owned a *Nancy Drew* story may have
read *Treasure Island* or *Huckleberry Finn.* Many boys who are
oblivious to the appeal of the *Hardy Boys* enjoy *Heidi* or
Peter Pan. Some very successful recent books have a girl
hero but seem of equal interest to both sexes, like *Island of
the Blue Dolphins* and *The Moon Spinners.* Except for boys'
interest in sports, both sexes are now almost equally interested in all categories of books, although there were distinct reading preferences even twenty-five years ago.

Television programs watched by children also seem to
be devoid of qualities that appeal to one sex or the other.
The most extensive study of television and children found
little support for the view that girls are more squeamish
than boys in connection with violence. Other studies concluded that middle-class adolescent girls took greater responsibility than boys for aggressive action toward a frus-
trating authority.[34] The girls will probably be even more
forceful in the era of the mannequin doll.

In the past, parents tended to punish boys more often

than girls with beatings and other physical measures. Recently the frequency with which such punishment is administered to boys and girls has become less distinguishable. Many a mother who never was physically disciplined as a girl has spanked her daughter, perhaps reluctantly at first, as she has learned to make few distinctions between measures applied to sons and daughters. Twenty-five years ago, when little girls were perhaps still believed to be made of "sugar and spice and all things nice," Talcott Parsons could accurately observe that "there is really no feminine equivalent of the expression 'bad boy.' "[35] But today we do not hesitate to speak of and punish a "naughty" or even "bad" girl. Contemporary parents are more willing than the previous generation to recognize that their daughters can behave unpleasantly and even destructively.

The formerly considerable gap that once separated the allowances given to girls from those received by boys has been dwindling steadily as girls have been getting more money from parents. Eleven-year-old girls in one study received 76¢ a week while boys of the same age averaged 97¢ a week.[36] Girls of thirteen tend to get and spend more money than boys and many fourteen-year-old girls expect allowances to be large enough to cover their wardrobe expenses. Barbie owners are especially likely to press for money for clothes.

Many other lines of evidence support the view that a wide range of forces is helping to cast boys and girls in the same mold. Even before a name is selected, the blurring of sex differences may begin. Parents once bought pink for a girl and blue for a boy. The pink-clad girl was "darling" and "beautiful" and the boy in blue was "handsome" or "strong." Although pink is still restricted to girls, blue is now worn by infants of either sex. But an even more important change is the popularity of maize, aqua, pale green, gray, and other neutral colors for both boys and girls. The near-disappearance of clothing differences should prepare the toddler for later blurring of visible signs of masculinity and femininity.

The signs are even disappearing from diapers. A diaper folded in front conveyed masculinity and one folded in the back connoted femininity, because of differences in the direction of the child's urination. In the last fifteen years, this difference has almost vanished, as a result of the disposable diaper and the "ready fold" with a rectangular panel along its center, both front and rear.

Diapers are only the beginning and children soon learn to wear other desexualized clothing. Identical coats and jackets are favored by both boys and girls.[37] Colors like sage seem to have been created because children of either sex wear similar clothing. As designer John Stephen summed it up: ". . . the hottest story in young fashion: boy/girl, his/hers, either/or clothes and haircuts."[38]

Even in the first years of school, girls wear trousers so often that some school systems have required them to wear dresses. Young boys' footwear is almost indistinguishable from their sisters'. Boys' sneakers were formerly ankle-high, but today are often cut as low as girls'. Many a boy strolls down the street in sneakers and bobby sox interchangeable with his sister's. Little boys and their sisters wear shoes of similar colors. Brown boys' shoes have gone the way of the black or white that formerly accounted for most little girls' footwear. Ten years ago, the Mary Jane that once was available only in black patent leather or white kid blossomed forth in a variety of colors and fabrics on young feet.

Boys are letting their hair grow longer. Now that girls are cutting their hair shorter, they are relatively unlikely to have the pigtails that boys of an earlier generation used to enjoy pulling. The ambisexual Oliver haircut, which represented one mark of a well-dressed young person, led logically to the Beatle non-haircut. The many other similarities in the appearance of boys and girls provide a bridge to adult clothing and help to explain why leading designers of women's clothes, like Courrèges and Gernreich, have been so successful in creating children's wear. Parents in our psychoanalytically sophisticated times are so tolerant of neutering that they permit crisscrossing of sex roles in children's appearance that would have been considered pathological just one generation ago.

The word "sissy," which derives from "sister," was once a terrible fate for a young man. With so many boys resembling and adapting clothes from their sisters, perhaps "sissy" should be retired. The phrases used to describe boys' wear sound as if they had been taken directly from women's fashion magazines ("the ultimate in wash 'n' wear," "the elegance of simplicity").

By 1963, young girls began saying good-bye to ruffles and bows and adopted the little-boy look. Now that a typical girl's costume consists of a shirt with a bib front and suspenders, worn with a boy's cap, there would seem to be considerable understatement in a report that identified twelve as the age at which a girl begins to raid her brother's wardrobe.[39] Girls' clothing is sold in quantities commensurate with the proportion of girls in the population. Boys' costumes are, however, sold in much greater quantity than the proportion of boys, suggesting that girls are far more likely than boys to dress in the others' costumes.

Over a generation ago, when writing anonymously, three times as many girls as boys wished to be of the opposite sex.[40] The many traditional boys' attributes that have been taken over by girls make it likely that fewer girls would express such a wish today, and in a more recent investigation, only 40 percent more girls than boys wanted to be of the opposite sex.[41] If current trends toward role reversal continue, and literary critics continue to raise questions about Huck Finn's masculinity, more boys than girls will soon be expressing a desire to change gender.

7

costume and custom: the vanishing difference

One way to stop wars, Shaw suggests, would be for soldiers on the battlefield to remove their uniforms and face each other in the nude. Their aggressiveness would presumably be dropped along with their trousers. Whether or not this proposal would work, it reminds us that clothes make the man and that major consequences can result from the loss of gender of clothing and appearance since World War II.

Clothing reflects its time even more strikingly than do furniture and buildings. When we look back at historical periods that experienced dramatic changes in clothing, we can see that the shifts were inevitably and directly related to other modifications in the quality of life, and were all of a piece with modifications in architecture and furniture. We strongly associate the carved ornamentation on bulbous Elizabethan table legs with men's trunk hose; women's caps in the late seventeenth century and the William and Mary chair's back; overelaboration of women's costume with plumed beds of the Louis XVI period; silhouettes of lamps and lady's costumes circa 1895; art nouveau fireplaces and women's costumes of 1900;

straight lines of flapper dresses and buildings of the 1920's.[1]

Our furniture and architecture are abandoning character and gender so rapidly that it would be logical to expect similar confusion and bastardization in costume and appearance. The same complex forces that have influenced the style and meaning of so many cultural artifacts of the New People have led to each sex's borrowing from the other's clothing, wide use of perfumes and jewelry by men, and inevitably, each sex's adaptation of the other's shoes. Such forms of self-expression may represent a more eloquent language for many a person than the ten or eleven minutes of conversation that he may average each day.

Dear Sir or Madam, As the Case May Be

A wedding described as a "quiet, elegant affair" took place at New York's Plaza Hotel on February 18, 1966. The bride wore pants, because pants are "very much me."[2] The bridegroom was said to be "very enthusiastic" about his wife's costume. For her wedding trip to Europe, the bride wore navy blue slacks and a blue and white muted houndstooth jacket. Our acceptance of a pants bridal ensemble suggests one important direction of the $18 billion a year women's fashion industry.

Much more than time separates us from May 1933, when Marlene Dietrich was refused admittance to a Broadway musical (*Take a Chance*) because she was wearing men's clothes. Today a woman could be well dressed in a costume totally derived from men. The adaptation of men's styles by women's fashions is important because the clothing tastes of most people are guided by tastes and values shared with friends, so that a successful style reflects a wide spectrum of acceptance. The public is prepared for a new fashion by small and subtle changes. If a style is introduced too abruptly, it may fail because it has become a fad rather than a fashion.

Synthetic fabrics have played some part in defeminization of women's clothing. No one could mistake the lovely femininity of the ostrich boas, delicate laces, soft embroidered velvets, dripping sables, and sensuously clinging and luxuriously revealing silks designed by Orry Kelly and Travis Banton for the "movie movies" of the 1930's. Detailing and fabrics were elaborate, with chiffon appliqué on chiffon and a great deal of lace and handwork. Today's artificial fabrics have limited ability to flatter the wearer. A satin-finished nylon crepe simply does not have the life, softness, "give," and flesh-hugging femininity of satin crepe. And the new paper dresses, whatever their other merits, can hardly do very much for a woman's femininity.

Simultaneously with wide use of lifeless materials in every item of women's clothing, its styling has become significantly masculinized. For over ten years, the blouses which women have been tucking into their trousers or skirts have used masculine paisleys, foulards, and regimental stripes. Like men's shirts, they have shirttails, and button-down collars. The cotton knit T-shirt has also become a favorite of women, who now buy 20 percent of the yearly production.

Casual suburban living has contributed to the popularity of women's shirts since the 1950's. The twenty shirts in a typical girl's wardrobe resemble men's shirts more than women's blouses in tailoring, separate neckband, and lack of darts.[3] Several brands have broken with tradition by placing buttons on the right side. One brand (h.i.s. for her) has a label that reads "don't envy h.i.s. . . . wear them." Some shirts that use a zipper are made in one style for both sexes and manufacturers often employ the same nomenclature for sizes in both men's and women's shirts. Much of the shirtwaist dress's popularity derives from its origin as a lengthened man's shirt.

Oldsters who remember the sweater girl can recall when "Danger—Curves" was a double entendre. The woman's sweater is no longer designed to show off a woman's figure, as it was when Lana Turner bounced into stardom in a 1937 film called *They Won't Forget*. Depending on the woman, of course, a tight sweater is now more often vulgar than charming. Many women favor bulky and shapeless men's sweaters, mackinaw styles, and heavy cable knits. Even sweaters of Italian knit and other body-hugging fabrics are designed to be loose-fitting.

Women's adaptation of men's sweaters began in the early 1940's, when Clark Gable's famous white turtle-neck became a significant woman's fashion. Soon after, the Sloppy Joe's crew neck and baggy lines became a uniform for women and the man's Shetland pullover sweater found distaff favor in the mid-1950's. Long and low-buttoning cardigans, formerly synonymous with Perry Como, Rex Harrison, and Dean Martin, are now available with embroidery and designed to be worn with dresses and evening gowns. Traditional feminine rounded neck and blouse-style sweaters are less popular.

When a woman first tries on a new coat, she usually puts her hands in its pockets to take symbolic possession and to see how she will be able to live with it. Time was when a woman's coat's silhouette was as identifiable as a knight's coat of mail. But such times became almost more remote than the coat of mail as women increasingly tended to wear the male's coat. The classic man's Chesterfield has been a woman's fashion since 1945, perhaps spurred by Merle Oberon's portrayal of George Sand in *A Song to Remember*. A few years earlier, the classic man's tan poplin raincoat had been adopted by women, along with the man's belted trench coat, modified into the full-backed duster look. When men began wearing raincoats of black synthetic fabric in the mid-1950's, so did women. The man's fingertip coat was dubbed a car coat when worn by women, but the polo coat did not change its name after becoming a woman's style several years ago.

Knee-length socks, originally worn by men with their Bermuda shorts, began to become women's favorites in 1955. Seven years later, Balenciaga's heavy man-styled, textured stockings became a craze. The stockings' striations and tree-bark nubbiness give even the most attractive legs a slightly bloated quality. Although manufacturers originally expected that older women would buy textured stockings for warmth and cover for protruding veins, younger customers have been the stockings' most enthusiastic fans.

Uglification of legs was more fully achieved in 1965, with the introduction for evening wear of spats-like gaiters over the ankle and instep. Other models that cover the leg from knee to instep were made of wool and jersey and worn with casual daytime clothes. Although Leopold Bloom was a fetishist, his "Watch! Silk flash rich stockings" reminds us that the sight of women's transparent silk stockings has titillated men for decades. Contemporary American men looking at women's no-nonsense stockings or gaiters may shiver, but not with delight.

Men once smiled at the flower-bedecked women's hats that inspired two generations of cartoonists. They are probably smiling more warily these days, when so many styles derive from men: Daniel Boone hats, military campaign headgear, jockey and boys' caps, stocking caps, swagger brim casuals, Sherlock caps with earlaps, snap-brim hats, Scotch berets, aviator helmets, sewer cleaners' helmets, and crash helmets with and without goggles. Since the Johnsons moved into the White House, the wide-rolled Stetson brim has become an outstanding woman's fashion.

The most visible adaptation of men's clothing by women is their replacement of the protective enmeshment of corsetry with the freedom of trousers. The proliferation of trouser formats for women has led to short shorts, stretch pants, regulation shorts, Jamaica shorts, Bermuda shorts, pedal pushers, deck pants, cabin trousers, Capri pants, toreador trousers, ankle-length pants, tapered trousers, bell bottoms, harem trousers, ranch pants, pantaloons, and jumpsuit pants. The Ivy League back-buckled belt has moved over to women's slacks, and jodhpurs are popular with teen-age and college girls who have never ridden a horse.

Blue jeans are so chic that designer Mary Quant measures every new outfit against them and diamond-studded jeans have been shown for evening wear.[4] The zipper's location on the front of men's blue jeans had a lasting effect on its relocation away from the left of women's trousers. After moving to the rear, it is often in front, frequently without a fabric covering, so that its tab hangs very conspicuously. Courrèges's trousers have a large exposed tab that swings luxuriously from side to side.

After all the jokes about who wears the pants in an American family, there is suddenly nothing to smile at.[5] Perhaps only the pants manufacturers are laughing, now that women's clothing stores may sell more trousers than skirts. Over 45 million pairs of trousers are now bought by women each year, a four-fold increase over a ten-year period. For every situation where a dress could be worn, designers have developed an appropriate pair of trousers.

The trouser motif continues at night, as women increasingly wear pajamas rather than nightgowns. Rudi Gernreich's little-boy pajamas for women were very popular, although they may have driven some husbands to consult analysts. Trousers are favorites for at-home or leisure clothes. The Chinese houseboy costume, with tight calf-length pants, became a mass-produced item, along with ankle-length and wide-legged pants.

No important style has ever been adopted because of its practicality, and trousers are no exception. They have been becoming tighter, more tapered, and less comfortable than the looser styles of previous years. The traditional belief that pants' practicality increased their popularity with Rosie the Riveter in World War II is wrong, because they are less comfortable and more binding than skirts. During and after the war, working women constituted a small minority of trouser wearers. One of the practical reasons for wearing trousers is the barrier they present to extemporaneous sex and dalliance in taxis and automobiles.

Even if goals of sexual differentiation or esthetics are not advanced by women in trousers, one positive result of the trend may be greater semantic accuracy. Imprecise words like "rippling," "ballooning," "quivering," and "bulging" have previously been used to describe this modern condition. The need for a single noun that succinctly describes the situation has been met by combining "jiggle" and "juggle" in "juglipidity." A large woman walking along in stretch pants can be described as having "acute juglipidity," however inadequate may be the words we use to describe our reactions to her appearance.[6]

Six months after Courrèges predicted the wearing of pants to most social functions, the majority of Paris and American couture houses were showing pants costumes. Today, pants are even more masculinized than Courrèges' hard geometry, with American designers featuring trousers designed to be worn with double-breasted blazers, side vents, and brass buttons. For many women, basic black no longer refers to a dress, but to the color of a pants suit costume and its accompanying leather jacket. Seasoned fashion commentator Eugenia Sheppard, in 1964, noted despairingly that every third woman strolling along New York's Fifth Avenue on a Saturday wore pants.[7] Today the proportion of women doing so would be greater.

Culottes, which were worn by American frontier women, made a brief reappearance at the New Frontier in designs by Balmain and Norell for evening and dressy daytime wear. They were not immediately successful, perhaps because they represented an embarrassingly literal expression of women's split role. Culottes have recently become popular as more women have come to terms with the ambiguity of their roles, which may contribute to the extraordinary success of Norell's mood of quasi-masculinity and as-if femininity. The relative straightness of his skirts is softened by their tucks or gathering at the waist; his masculine belts and vests are often counterbalanced by the femininity of large bows. Norell's designs for Lee Remick in *The Wheeler Dealers* typically included a very mannish tailored cape and an evening dress with a man's revers.

Women are able to wear culottes, minipants, and pants dresses because of modifications in their underclothes. Many women wear one-piece tights and others who resented thigh-length underpants as girls are delighted, as adults, to wear the same garment, variously called pantislip and petti-pants. In rebellion against the businesslike quality of matching girdle and brassiere, a number of women have begun wearing the chemise as an undergarment. Very similar to the 1920's "teddy-bear," it helps give women a flatter rather than contoured look and a willowy rather than pillowy silhouette. Other lingerie to go with short dresses is simple and resembles men's athletic clothing.

Another contributor to role and sex ambiguity is the speed with which the hemline of women's formal dresses has been shifting. The formal floor-length dress used to epitomize femininity. World War II Regulation L-85 on economizing of fabric raised the formal dress to ballet length, midway between calf and ankle, but this attempt to bring some order to escalation of hemlines quickly became as obsolete as price control. There is no longer any established silhouette, line, or length for the social situation in which a woman is expected to be most attractively feminine.

Sportswear and "Le Sportive" Look

The sportswear revolution that represents America's unique contribution to fashion has helped to annihilate categories of clothing that go with specific situations. Before World War II, sports clothes were worn for special occasions, by a limited number of women who had the leisure and opportunity to participate in sports activities. Now they are worn by practically everyone for everything. A woman can wear trousers through a day and merely change her cotton overblouse for one of silk in order to be well dressed for a formal evening event.

Sportswear involves a continuing adaptation of men's clothes by women. The post-World War II sportswear boom owed much to Chanel, who derived inspiration for a scarf from ditchdiggers, modeled a blouse after a mechanic's jacket, modified sailors' jackets and men's pullovers, and borrowed knitted wool jersey from men's polo sweaters.

Some of Chanel's qualities could be seen in Claire McCardell, America's most influential sportswear designer, who used everyday materials like cotton and thin wool and learned much from men's work clothes and cowboy attire. Typical of the McCardell approach was her famous soft felt modified sombrero. Bonnie Cashin continued the trend with suede, leather, and tweed clothes and Emilio Pucci provided a new look with stretch pants and overblouses.

John Weitz, who has adapted car coats, knickers, coveralls, and shirts from men's styles, has observed that "in a country where a woman has been a candidate for the presidential nomination, sportswear can no longer reflect the marshmallow quality of the life of women in earlier generations. That is why I include pockets even in evening clothes that I design. Pockets come from men's clothes, but today's woman wants and needs them—and my job is to provide them. Blouses that fit under jackets are necessary for a woman who leads a busy life. She picks her husband up at the station, and when they go out at night and he gets looped, she drives him home."[8]

Although Mrs. Lyndon B. Johnson does not have to collect a looped husband on the 6:33 at Greenwich, she is representative of other celebrities who are identified with sportswear. Less well known for her Adele Simpson evening dresses than for western outdoor clothes, Mrs. Johnson and her daughters have been photographed in cowboy shirts, work pants, blue jeans, boots, overblouses, ten-gallon hats, neckerchiefs, wide belts, and sneakers.

Leather vests and jump suits, farmer-boy smocks, fishermen's oilskins, leather-trimmed and rivet-studded knits, gauntlets, riding crops and shillelaghs are part of "le sportive" look that matrons across the country have been adopting. What might be called *"The Story of O"* look includes hardware jewelry from carpenters' tool kits, heavy chain belts, and industrial zippers. One rationale for this combative quality argues that it makes the wearer feel more feminine by contrast. With such logic, perhaps a revolver will be the next accessory.

Following the Straight and Narrow

Changes in women's clothing must be considered in the light of its historical function of attracting the opposite sex. Much of today's stark clothing, when it calls attention away from rather than to the body's traditional erogenous centers, is unlikely to perform the function very effectively. Before World War II, the preferred look in women's costume was an implicit roundness conveyed by clothing that just skimmed the body. The wartime hiatus was followed by the New Look in 1947, when Dior's slashed bod-ices focused attention on the waist and bosom.

After the interlude of the darted and beltless sheath dress, American women had an opportunity to respond to the chemise, the most energetically publicized fashion since World War I. The chemise's lack of a waist was very flattering to most American women, who are short-waisted. In spite of the style's sinuous line, the chemise was a resounding failure. Regressed sexuality implicit in Dior's stress on the bosom had been acceptable, but American women were seemingly threatened by the chemise's call-ing attention to hips. With an almost audible sigh of re-lief, women turned to fashions that transferred attention away from bosom and hips and onto the body's appen-dages. Geometric styles like the A-line and shift remained dominant for a decade. They are short and often sleeve-less, so that the focus of attention has become the arms and legs, which are sexually undifferentiated.

Geometric fashions blot out details of the torso, which seldom has an upper and lower half. A dress that hangs from the shoulders has little draping, fluidity, and move-ment because its line remains constant regardless of body movement. St. Laurent's shifts resembled modern office buildings in their lack of top or bottom, and could almost be worn upside down. Since 1957, fashion has replaced roundness with angularity and straight lines. Unfortunate-ly, the female body is not geometrically constructed, and clothes that look as if they were designed with a T-square cannot really accommodate bosoms and hips. A woman confronting a rack full of dresses with hard lines and fab-ric asked a salesgirl at Lord and Taylor, "Don't you have any dresses that move?" "They all do," came the reply. "I mean with me, not against me," demurred the shopper.

Contemporary designers can congratulate themselves on having squared the circle, a feat which has baffled mathe-

maticians for hundreds of years. We may ultimately have
to look into old magazines in order to recall the range of
female silhouettes. Large hips are unlikely to return to popularity because they express the womanliness that society
is contradicting in many ways.

Few men are bold enough to emulate Sir William Roper, who appears to have selected his wife on the basis of
her feminine hips. He had been courting Thomas More's
two daughters but could not decide between them. Roper
had a conversation with More in which he praised the latter's recommendation, in *Utopia,* that young people should
be able to see each other in the nude before deciding to
marry. More promptly took Roper to a bedroom where
the daughters were asleep in the same bed. As Aubrey put
it, "they lay on their backs, their smocks up as high as
their armpits."[9] More yanked the blanket off the bed and
both daughters modestly and promptly turned over onto
their stomachs. Roper slapped one on the rump and said,
"I have seen both sides; thou art mine." His marriage to
More's oldest daughter was so happy that he became her
father's official biographer.

In the last few years, the bosom has become flatter as
the result of overall fashion trends and brassieres made
with padding of spun dacron rather than foam rubber.
Although sales of such padded brassieres are moving forward, their contours are not. The padding is not intended
to provide a bigger bosom, but a smoother and more symmetrical silhouette. It compensates for cyclical or other
differences in size and calls attention away from the bosom.

Styles in hair are likely to be subdued in length as well
as color. Women are wearing their hair shorter than at
any time in the last generation. The bouffant, froufrou
curls and round, full balloon have been replaced by shorter cropped hair-dos that convey a blunt and hard chic.
The girl who had a wig wardrobe for her Barbie may cover her Vidal Sassoon geometric skullcap with a wig. If

she wears her hair longer, she may iron it into lifelessness. Further progress toward the mechanical bride can be seen in the enthusiasm for angular or square curls. Sharp geometric shapes became popular in hats at about the same time as hard-edge geometric earrings, so that the chic face can be completely framed in 90° angles.

Another element in dehumanization of appearance and fashion is the importance of models. Some, like Suzy Parker and Anita Colby, have become more celebrated than the designers for whom they work. Today's high fashion models are hardly paradigms of warm and inviting femininity. They resemble catatonic schizophrenics, with a frozen face and a non-human posture, pelvis thrust forward at an angle of 15 degrees from the vertical. Their barrenness is especially evident when they walk, because a model successful in still photography generally looks stiff when she moves.

One of the very few women who is not an actress or model or synthetic creation but became a fashion goddess is Mrs. Jacqueline Kennedy, who developed The Look and who adapted some of her most influential costumes from men's clothing. Her preferred clothing included a loose overblouse, semi-fitted jacket, semi-fitted coat, and dress with an easy waistline. She favored formless dresses and especially a loose A-line. Mrs. Kennedy's coat, with long thin sleeves, a pleat in back, and a buttoned-down front was a modification of a man's coat. The Rajah coat that she brought back from India for dinner and theatre costumes was worn by Indian men and her pillbox hat was essentially an unbrimmed fedora.

American women shoppers are knowledgeable and independent enough to wear non-feminine clothes because they like them rather than because merchants or artificial fashion celebrities recommend them. Ten years before their ruthless rejection of the chemise, they had vetoed Claire McCardell's tight-fitting trousers. Another product that did not find favor with women in the 1950's was the bias-cut, non-uplift brassiere, which more recently has won acceptance as the no-bra bra. In the fall of 1963, the Dior-Bohan plunging neckline was praised for being nicely naughty, but could win no more acceptance than the knickers that were widely publicized in the same year.

Women have amply demonstrated that they accept or reject clothing on the basis of their needs. How those needs have changed can be inferred by recalling the discussion between Marie Dressler and Jean Harlow as they walk toward the climactic dinner party in the film version of *Dinner at Eight* (1933). Miss Harlow expresses concern about machines putting people out of work. Miss Dressler, looking at the Harlow curves very conspicuously implied fore and aft in a delightfully feminine gown, remarks: "My dear, that is something *you* won't have to worry about." But a modishly dressed actress in a contemporary film is likely to look dehumanized, vaguely menacing, and resemble one of the machines that troubled Miss Harlow.

Fine Birds
and Fine Feathers

Surely the most with-it wife in our diplomatic corps abroad is Mrs. Frederick Reinhardt, wife of the American ambassador to Rome. Discussing a blue and black flowing caftan with peek-a-boo openings down the chest, she dutifully admitted at a Florence fashion show, "I just bought that dress for myself. Now I'm going to give it to my husband and buy something else for myself."[10]

At a time when an ambassador might wear a caftan, it is not surprising that the constitutionality of the New York State statute prohibiting a man from wearing a woman's clothes has been challenged, for the first time in one hundred nineteen years. In 1964, the American Civil

Liberties Union appeared *amicus curiae* to defend a New York City man who had been arrested in high heels and a fur cape, wearing a woman's wig, lipstick, and powder.[11]

Questions could be raised about the statute because men's clothing has been abandoning its former Puritan severity. Apparel may oft proclaim the man, but many bells are jangling out of tune in the current proclamation. The bright colors that once identified country cousins or Mediterranean immigrants are now worn by well-dressed men who have increasingly been heeding the advice in the Epistle of Saint James: "And ye have respect to him that weareth the gay clothing, and say unto him, 'Sit thou here in a good place.'" More men wear "gay" clothing as a large part of the $9.4 billion spent annually for men's wear goes for styles that differ radically from previous decades' somber hues and may represent a throwback to lower species in which the male is more colorful than the female. Observe the suits worn in old movies on television. A typical 1940 suit jacket had broad padded shoulders, tucked-in waist, loose-fitting sleeves, a square bottom, and wide lapels.[12] Today's straight-line jackets have little or no waist or shoulder padding and give literal meaning to Carlisle's remark that man was made by the small clothes of society. Lapels are just half their former four-and-a-half inch width. Jackets follow the torso and may be cut on the bias and have side vents.

Trousers that were once pleated, high-rise, cuffed, and full now tend to be pleatless, low-rise, cuffless, tapered, and slim. If the trousers are held up by a belt, it is likely to be thinner than in earlier generations. The once-staid brown or black leather belt has been yielding to belts of colorful fabric with a variety of patterns and decorations. The old-fashioned simple intialed belt buckle has been partially supplanted by works of jewelry.

Under their slim trousers, many men's bulges are restrained by rubber and nylon girdles and spandex shorts, the demand for which is outstretching the supply. Millions of men wear shorts of nylon tricot, the most popular fabric for women's undergarments. An advertisement for men's nylon tricot underwear stressed that "mothers and wives will like the no-iron fabric." They probably do, because they can treat it just like their own underwear and maybe even wear it in an emergency. Men's underwear regularly comes in feminine shades that are given euphemistic names, so that pink undershorts may be called "rust." As a New York lawyer said, "Why do they still call these pink pants made of nylon with a flower decoration 'boxer shorts'? Maybe only a boxer would have the courage to wear them."

Today's well-dressed man might strut in a rakish sports jacket with bright corduroy epaulets. His raincoat could have a leather and suede collar and cover a suit of fabric formerly worn exclusively by women, like silks, iridescents, or even kangaroo-skin. Gaily colored vests grace many a manly chest. In one recent season, 80 percent of the new men's clothes came in colors like gold, coffee, banana, clay, wheat, sand, pewter, and sterling. What a contrast to the clothes worn by Dodsworth and Babbitt!

At a Zenith dinner party of the 1960's, a guest might feel hurt if nobody said a word about his new purple cummerbund or shawl-collared, brocaded or velvet, pink or magenta dinner jacket. His costume might include satin-piped edging, silk-faced trouser waistbands, jacquard, and glorious but unseen pastel underwear. Men's evening clothes are becoming so sporty that even conservative stores supplement the traditional business, sportswear, summer, and formal lines with a fifth major department, for evening casual dress items like black trousers with tartan side stripes and solid red or yellow jackets.

Men's interest in color has contributed to the blossoming of a dickie section in some men's shops, and others feature separates and coordinates. Before too long, men may routinely accessorize their costumes, and such touches may be needed to differentiate shirts worn by men and women. Three female models, each wearing a different man's shirt, were shown in an advertisement which ungallantly noted that "these shirts wash and wear even better than Heather, Margo, and Lillie, and never lose their shape, either!"[13]

The models could feel at home in most men's shirts of the last decade. Business shirts are made of batiste and voile, have frilled, bibbed, and pleated fronts. They are tapered and come in blue, yellow, gray, pink, eggshell, russet, gold, and even polka dots. Contrasting collars and cuffs have become extremely popular. The new freedom in men's shirts was facilitated by the "Mr. B" model after World War II. It had a long wide collar and came in mauve, yellow, mint, and baby blue. Although the colors have remained, assertive collars have given way to more effete narrow styles. Today's tabbed collars provide a less rugged tone, just like the Tab Hunters on the screen.

What ties are worn with the new shirts? The sincere masculine tie that identified well-dressed executives in *The Hucksters* has given way to slender and more feminine neckwear that often comes from Trigere, Cassini, and other women's designers. Assertive regimental stripes are declining in favor. The width of the tie has decreased in the last decade from 4½" (the "belly-warmer") to 2". A Slim Jim is only 1⅜" and resembles the edging on a Chanel suit in providing a continuation of the shirt rather than the contrasting visual focus of a wide tie. The countermovement back to wide ties has not been very successful.

Another opportunity for self-expression is provided by the hat. Brim widths narrowed from three to two inches in the last decade. In order to retain proportion, crowns were made smaller. The soft felt that is today's favorite comes in willow, dove, and other light colors. Boater straws and even derbies draw on a rainbow range of colors, and so do the ribbons that wave at the world from men's hats. The sort of man who would never dream of climbing any mountain could be seen gaily decked in a Tyrolean covered with feathers and a medallion certifying at least four successful ascents of the Matterhorn.

Colorful geegaws on men's hats go well with the gaiety of their sweaters. A vivid riot of colors and fabrics greets anyone walking past a men's sweater counter. Sweater fabrics often have elaborate patterns and the traditional V-neck has been yielding to the feminine boat neck and mandarin collar. Short-sleeve styles have also been adapted from women.

There are a variety of "looks" for desk-bound males. The "surf look" attracts many men who have never seen a surfboard. The real or fantasy surfer can walk to the beach in a madras parka and sand-colored levis over his laced-front swim trunks. Or his cabana swim-and-lounge set could match his wife's. Now that men's swim trunks have begun appearing with the zipper on the left, and even in the rear, many a man struggling into swim trunks undoubtedly asks his wife to "zip me up, dear."

Although women seek exclusivity in clothing, most men want to be reassured that "everybody is wearing this." Their conservatism makes it astonishing that men have accepted so many new colors, shapes, and fabrics. A few years after World War II, the leading clothing trade association concluded that men represented only a limited market for clothing made of gay colors and materials, a condition identified as a frantic flight from Beau Brummel fanciness.[14] Today, the race is being run in the opposite direction and Rotary Club chapters are happy to book men's fashion shows.

Why have men's clothes changed so radically? Among the many reasons are a new interest in style, men's growing enthusiasm for sports clothes, our youth cult, changes in the self-concept of men and in women's perception of men, transvestism in mass media, exhibitionism, the model provided by some celebrities, and changes in the economy. Not to be underestimated is the enthusiasm with which millions of American men, after World War II, turned away from the standardization of costume imposed by their uniforms.

Our new stress on style has made it gauche for a man to display too much shirt cuff. Wearing socks that fail to cover his calves may hurt the chances of a job applicant. Style took a representative community like Indiana, Pennsylvania, by storm. Saul Waxler, owner of a store there, has summarized the experience of many retailers: "In selling clothing we've found that style is it. Our customers will not sacrifice style for anything."[15] Young men are so preoccupied with style that the same rather wry joke is told at a number of different colleges. A coed and a male classmate went out on a date. The coed ignored a mirror that they happened to pass—but the man stopped and checked his appearance in it.

Another reason for the increase in men's finery is contraction of the work week, which has led to more leisure and to costumes for specific leisure activities. Men's enthusiasm for gay sports clothes is reflected in the colorful outfits worn by the touring professionals who set styles for pleasure golfers.[16] A leading pro golf money winner and major fashion pace setter is Doug Sanders, who often wears an all-shocking pink outfit at tournaments. Sanders matches and color-coordinates his sweaters, slacks, gloves, and patent leather golf shoes. He is developing a white golf bag with detachable pockets, so that each day the golfer can have a pocket of a color that matches his costume. Such outfits are a far cry from Bobby Jones's simple knickers and Ben Hogan's grays and browns, and have developed simultaneously with the revolution in women's sportswear.

Youth is an arrogant dictator in the styling of new

clothing. Energetic and vital young men are the style leaders. How many men are willing to admit that they are too old to wear young-looking clothes? Contemporary clothing stresses youthful slimness and reinforces our animus against obesity.

Just as there is little occasion for a man to play at being James Bond, there is less need for him to function psychologically in a masculine manner. With less opportunity to be stalwart in one direction, there is more of a requirement to be assertive in quite a different way. A man who doesn't feel manly is not likely to want to look or speak the part. Wearing clothes with feminine overtones may provide secondary and tertiary reinforcement of the feminine identification of some men. The Ivy gilding of even midwestern lilies has led to a convenient gelding of old-fashioned masculine self-perception.

Some purchases of men's clothing reflect women's changing concept of men. Women *buy* over half the men's shirts sold and 85 percent of the ties. Approximately one-fourth of American men used to buy their clothes in the company of a woman, but almost two-thirds do so today. A woman who does not think her man is very masculine would naturally select appropriate clothing when shopping with—or for him.

Transvestism on the part of men figures increasingly in plays and movies. Ray Bolger, Jose Ferrer, and Jack Benny have played in a version of *Charley's Aunt* in the not-too-distant past. One reason for Mr. Benny's enduring popularity is the signature of his vaguely feminine walk and clothes. Cary Grant wore drag in *I Was a Male War Bride*. In *Psycho,* Anthony Perkins played both a young man and his mother. Jack Lemmon and Tony Curtis in women's clothes were largely responsible for the great success of *Some Like It Hot.*

Another aspect of men's interest in clothing exhibitionism could be seen in their response to wash-and-wear shirts of dacron and similar synthetic fabrics. Both opaque and transparent models provide similar washability, light weight, porousness, and low cost, but transparent shirts outsell the opaque by twelve to one. Motivation research studies have identified the great attraction of the transparent shirt to be the wearers' knowledge that others could see their undershirts under the transparent fabric, just as many women enjoy wearing transparent blouses through which the straps of their underclothes can be seen.

Celebrities have been reinforcing and helping to inspire men's enthusiasm for colorful clothing. Cary Grant builds film wardrobes around his leading lady's color scheme. The floral sport shirt so frequently worn by our former president is still called the Truman shirt. Other famous men wear florid checked shirts that once had the practical function of helping to avoid bagging fellow hunters but have evolved into the gay plumage worn by men hunting for compliments or hoping to pass unchallenged through the Amazonian lines.

New patterns of distribution and increases in income and the number of men's apparel stores have made it easier for men to buy clothing.[17] Technological advances have provided new materials. Men's fashion columns, fashion magazines like *GQ*, and newspaper supplements flourish to an extent that would have been unthinkable in the days of the boiler-plate two pants suit.

As men's clothes become more visible, their designers are emerging from anonymity. Well-dressed men might have known that Henry Poole and Kilgour and French were the two best tailors on Savile Row, but the tailors themselves always shunned publicity. Long after Worth established the couturier as a social arbiter, men's tailors remained far beneath their clients in social acceptance and standing. Designers of men's clothing have become culture heroes as it was discovered that they bathed regularly, spoke English, and could be quite amusing. Now that prominent creators of women's clothes have begun designing men's clothes, men are beginning to derive panache from wearing items from Hardy Amies, Pierre Cardin, Emilio Pucci, or John Weitz.

Are men wearing the newer clothing by choice? Emphatically yes, because they will resist what they do not want. Traditional masculine clothing is available but has little appeal, even though more comfortable than the skimpy cut and binding armholes, tight pants, high collars, and narrow cuffs of Ivy League styles. Men have not hesitated to reject a number of new products. From 1948 to 1951 and again in 1961, the shirt industry unsuccessfully tried to interest men in heliotrope. Burgundy failed to generate male enthusiasm for its use in outerwear and sweaters in the early 1960's. Bottle green was heavily advertised during 1964, but never got out of the cutting room.

Many styles have followed these colors into oblivion. In 1959 and 1960, sweater manufacturers could not succeed in popularizing the shawl collar. A sweater with a half belt in back bombed out in 1961. The pork-pie hat never caught on, even after strenuous promotion. The continental suit, introduced in 1957 and originally designed for shorter European men, never really became popular. But the large number of feminine styles that men have embraced add up to a trend toward a combination of adornment and neutering that is unique.

A new domestic problem has been created in homes where the wife has observed guests sidling over to her husband in order to get the name of his shirtmaker, shoemaker, or tailor, but no one seems interested in her suppliers—unless it's a very "in" party with some marihuana smoking. The most ironic, but completely logical, turn of the screw came in January 1966, at an annual presentation of men's sportswear by the J. M. Fields chain of stores in New York. The complete spring and summer line of men's merchandise was modeled—by four women. No wonder that William Doniger, president of one of the country's largest manufacturers of men's and boys' fashions glumly stared at the whole line of clothes at his company's fashion show and growled, "If my kid looked like this, I'd kill him."[18]

The Sweet Smell of Success?

In the Scented Sixties, men's purchases of fragrance-containing preparations come to three times as much as women spend on perfumes, toilet waters, and colognes. The men's market is growing so rapidly that estimates of its volume become dated as quickly as they appear, but it is well over $500 million annually. One sign of growth is the new identification of the products as men's "cosmetics," rather than by the utilitarian and functional bathroom associations of men's "toiletries." The cosmetic and toilet goods field's most rapidly growing segment is the manufacture of perfumed products for men, which has increased 400 percent since 1950.[19] Sales of utilitarian toiletries with little or no fragrance have not grown proportionately during the same period.

There have been steady increases in the proportion of men who have switched to perfumed preparations rather than fight the trend. The extent of use of after-shave lotions by American men jumped from 68 percent in 1948 to 93 percent by 1965, and they represent the largest single use of fragrance, in gallons. Such lotions were once astringents that burned the skin, reinforcing any masochistic component in shaving rituals, but today's skin bracers heal more wounds than those left by the razor, do not burn, and are so aromatic that men often slosh them onto chests and shoulders.

The well-lacquered male has come into his own. Acceptability of a grooming product once rested on its being a necessity that was bought quietly and used almost surreptitiously. But the new man revels in the glory of sweet smells. The bolder "modern" scents are now so popular that traditional bay rum and verbena-scented eau de cologne have become almost historical. As one perfumer put it, "Why shouldn't a man smell as good as he looks?"[20] It has been suggested that many men use perfume and cologne so that their lives may seem harder in contrast, just as it has been argued that femininity emerges more sharply from women's wearing masculine clothes. Such unusual theses seem to be anxious rationalizations of our society's muddling of sex differences.

The fragrant years began in 1939, when scented toiletries and packaged toiletry sets for men first became available, and wartime prosperity provided money for civilians to buy such articles. They represented attractive gifts when other items were scarce. Military personnel learned to use the products from observing their barracks- and shipmates, and many came into contact with foreign cultures in which upper-class men regularly used "scent." With a limited number of outlets for their money, servicemen began to purchase scented grooming aids. Wearing the uniform probably helped to allay any fears that the products' users might be unmanly or were indulging themselves.[21]

The most recent postwar impetus for fragrance products was the great success of Canoe in 1959. College men traveling abroad began to bring back the sweet and citrus-scented French cologne, used it for themselves—and gave it to their girl friends. Its sales tripled in one year. The appetite of college students and teen-agers for strongly scented products in turn influenced their fathers, uncles, and older brothers. Scent is a method of adornment by which a man of any age can unbutton his emotional self and attract attention, in frank recognition of women's growing freedom to pick and choose.

The older man who buys fragrance products has displayed so much enthusiasm for them that one Revlon official has tried to explain some reasons for its impetus: "When a man reaches forty or fifty these days, he simply doesn't want to be old. He wants to swing a little . . . is also open to something for his face. He's open to something for his hair. He's open to something for his body. That's what's happening."[22]

The fragrances to which both men and women are "open" are essentially similar, except that men sometimes stress the fragrances' masculine connotations in discussion. Men usually say they like a fleeting and mild fragrance, but typically select one which is lasting and strong. A manufacturer has happily pointed out that "if there is a fellow in the room with our scent on, you know it." Mark II describes itself as a "zesty essence for the male animal."

Very strong fragrances may have special appeal to men who are suffering from feelings of depersonalization. Just as anointing and incense helped to extend the body's boundaries and reach toward God, a man using a strong fragrance transcends his body's boundaries and creates a unified atmosphere that projects him toward people. Other men who are confused about their body-image may use "zesty essences" as one way of reassuring themselves, in our deodorized age, that their body is recognizable and has exudations. Today's correct male no longer projects the smell of "the sweat of his brow"—or, God forbid, his armpits. Seducer and seduced dance in a Perfumed Garden—and no one can tell the dancer from the dance.

Some men buy cream sachet, a concentrated solid perfume that penetrates deeply into the skin. Others use bath

oils with a concentration of odor three to four times as
strong as regular perfume. An executive of a scent company noted that "men . . . want . . . something more lasting, more unique. Men want to be identified with their
scent, just as women do."[23] The average man who starts
the day with a fragrance product wants it to last at least
until noon. Many men have bottles in their offices and
touch up before lunch.

One unexpected problem posed by the multiplicity of
fragrance products is the bewildering array of personalities now available to a man.[24] He must choose between
being either the sort of fellow who can "make things happen" with York Town, a cad whose use of Gant "gives a
man an unfair advantage," or really shed his inhibitions
with Centaur ("half man . . . half beast. . . ."). He can
splash on a Jaguar personality ("only for the man who
gets a bang out of living"), become a more self-congratu-
latory Dante type ("for men who know how to handle
women"), or the subject of gossip with British Sterling
("You may both go down in history"). He can identify
with the dubious male of the north through Teak ("what
Scandinavian men have"), or with the simmering Mediterranean man via Signoricci ("suave, persuasive"). It's a
lucky man indeed who can sample ocean travel with Old
Spice Lime ("the romantic aroma of the trade winds") or,
with St. John's Aged Lime, exude "a robustness never before captured." The strain of conducting the self-analysis
needed to make a wise choice may be so nerve-racking
that many men will be unable to employ their new exudations to best advantage. And women are left to puzzle
whether it was "Him or his Piping Rock?"

Scented togetherness for couples is a new trend, with a
woman's product like Ambush hardly distinguishable
from the same maker's Canoe. Many fragrances frankly
identify themselves as suitable for both sexes. The Royall
Lyme label indicates that it is "a delightful essence . . .

to be used by gentlewomen as a cologne, and by gentlemen as an after-shave lotion." 4711 identifies itself as a "refreshment cologne . . . both men and women can use it after a bath or shower, or as a brisk all-day freshener." Kanaka is "the 24-hour cologne" for "Him and Her!" Where there are differences, men's scents tend to be complex and women's to be simpler.

Pine is named by the majority of men as their favorite fragrance, probably because of its established connotations of outdoor maleness. But when asked to choose their favorite from several odors, one of which is pine, it is almost always at the bottom of their preferences. One reason that most men rely on pine is their rather inexact fragrance vocabulary. A fragrance is described as smelling like something else, e.g., wet lilacs, or the adjectives are borrowed from the sense of taste, e.g., sweet. With such paucity of language, men have felt more confident about a fragrance that is as unambiguous as pine. As men increasingly accept products frankly designed to give them a sweet smell, manufacturers will find it less necessary to stress the "whistling clean fragrance from a man's world of wind and northern pine."

There previously was enough onus attached to fragrance preparations for many men to need the justification provided by their "tough beard" and the executive, masculine, and military names that some products boast: Aztec, Big Shot, Branded, Caesar, Career Man, Denim, Executive, Figaro, Grit, Moustache, Musketeer, Pardner, Secret Service, Stampede, Sweat, Top Brass, Waterloo. Gravel is as tough as anyone could desire—it has pieces of gravel embedded in its bottle.

Users were further reassured by masculine bottles with strong-looking caps and pictures of horses and Indians. The figure of a court jester constitutes the bottle for one brand, so that its user can feel an element of the amusing and childlike in the product. If it is all in fun, how can he be compromising his masculinity? But this sort of masculinized packaging has become less necessary as men more openly accept the cosmetic implications of the products. After-shave lotions, once made exclusively in cool green and blue, now come in amber and pink. Gone is the diffidence that characterized marketing of perfumed colognes in the days when men made subterfuge purchases and the products were discreetly displayed in women's cosmetics departments for a few weeks before Father's Day. Today, more than 450 brands of men's cosmetics are sold openly in drugstores, men's shops, and haberdasheries.

American industry cares for the new man from head to manicured toenail. Hair spray for men was an instantaneous success when introduced in the early 1960's. Face creams, mudpacks, vanishing cream, night cream, and perfumed lip balm are in many men's medicine cabinets. An artificial sun-tanning cosmetic (Man-Tan) was successfully sold to men before it was even marketed to women. Home manicure sets are increasingly popular gifts for men, and many a man who once could not distinguish a buffer from an orange stick is doing his nails at home. Men who formerly sheepishly inquired about cuticle scissors "for my wife" now ask directly for advice on accessories.

The new popularity of perfumed bath soap, fragrant talc, perfumed bath oils, and similar products among men may be partially responsible for changes in bathing habits. Although data from earlier periods are not available, the proportion of men preferring baths and of women favoring showers appears to have increased in recent years.[25] The stereotype of a husband briskly showering, while his wife lounges in her tub in water softened by bath oils is almost obsolete. Some women are taking showers rather than baths because they have limited time to get ready for work in the morning and second bathrooms often have showers instead of baths. Men's increasing use of bubble and similar bath products probably contributes to their loss of interest in showers. No doubt there are even households in which the wife apologizes to dinner guests because her husband is still getting ready upstairs.

What of the future? The national merchandise manager of Sears Roebuck has estimated that men's cosmetics, which now account for 20 percent of total cosmetic sales, can soon reach 50 percent.[26] New products are continually being introduced, including some that have adopted traditionally feminine formats. A fragrance sachet to be kept in a man's shirt drawer and a man's spray cologne in its own atomizer have already been successful.

A woman's magazine rhapsodizes over the new male: "With a toss of his long, extremely tossable hair, he makes Old Mr. Muscles—that crew-cut idol of the day before yesterday—look suddenly as square and wiped-out as the Hupmobile. . . . He . . . chooses his shampoos with the gravity of a connoisseur, and scents himself with enormous care . . . wears his vanity as an ornament. . . . He will order unguents for his complexion, masks for his circulation." The magazine concludes: "You must reckon with him. He is here—and now."[27]

Poor Mr. Muscles! He has probably been abandoning his barbells along with his crew-cut. No more tell-tale bulging biceps or broad shoulders. The new man knows how terribly important it is that he use the right beauty products. We can understand how confused he might become to learn that as he buys more fragrances, women have been buying fewer. Most American women are seemingly oblivious to the Song of Solomon, since only one-half of one percent use a fragrance daily. For the past two decades, the heavily seductive floral scents (Joy, Bellodgia, Muguet) have been giving way to light modern blends (Arpege, Sortilège, Chanel Number 5).

A related recent tendency is for women to favor perfumes with masculine-sounding (e.g., Woodhue) rather than feminine names (e.g., Surrender). Another possible direction for women's perfumes is suggested by a new scent that smells like salt and was developed by Pucci for sophisticated modern women. Even Aldous Huxley would have thrown down his pen before a situation in which men smell sweet but women's fragrance is salty.

At just about the time that men were beginning to use more perfumed hair products, they were also spending more time and money on other hair-grooming products. The Census Bureau reported that 1953 was the first year in which men spent more money in barber shops than women did in beauty parlors. The old-fashioned barber shop, along with Mr. Muscles, has undergone a face lifting. White tile floors, spittoons, and bare white walls are being replaced by color coordinated vinyl flooring, pastelized wallpaper, and modern paintings. The new look includes partitioned booths, soft indirect lighting, and lampshades of Tiffany glass.

In sensible Lincoln, Nebraska, the Cornhusker Hotel has changed the name of its barber shop to the "House of Shears." Barbers in many other cities refer to their work with appropriate deference. The Manhattan telephone book lists Men's Hairstyling Studios, Haut Coiffure Masculine Francaise, Continental Hair Stylists, Physiognomical Personality Haircutters, Hair Salons, and Tonsorial Specialists. The shops' waiting rooms are more likely to display current issues of men's fashion magazines than ancient copies of the *Police Gazette*.

The barber himself is less likely to be a technician who is hailed by his first name than a professional who requires a respectful "Mister" or "Sir." The new breed of hair stylists is less likely to provide gossip, discuss baseball, give advice on marital problems, or take bets on policy and races than the neighborhood barber. The hair stylist wears dark trousers, stylish jacket, and Ben Casey jerkin rather than the old-fashioned white uniform.

In many a shop, after the apprentice has worked over and prepared the head, the artist in hair design sets about cutting and setting. Many a Continental Cut, Natural Shoulder, Ivy Swirl, or Cavalier, carefully expressive of its owner's personality, takes final shape as he has his nails done. The client may be cautioned on how to comb his hair before he makes an appointment for another treatment. Men's barber-shop expenditures have been soaring at the same time as their interest in toupees, and wigmakers report a sharp increase in men customers.

A man's right to wear his hair in any style and length has been hailed as an essential feature of a free and democratic society.[28] The Nazi crew-cut and the prisoner's shaved head represent suppressions of individualism. One ominous clue to the reactionary temper of the military junta that seized power in Greece in April 1967 was its proscription, four days after taking over, of long hair for boys. With man's ability to select his own hair-do now hailed as a free society's crowning glory, we can expect that our civil-libertarian age will see a proliferation of new and daring hair formats for men.

Many headquarters for tonsorial artistry are rising to the challenge and straightening, curling, and shaping their clients' hair. A man's hair net is discreetly called a "trainer" and a permanent wave is "hair processing." One hair stylist identified the new trend as ". . . a rebellion against the electric clipper, toward shaping with a razor, and it's marvelous."[29] Their customers seem to agree. As one advertising executive said, "I felt pretty silly sitting in a barber chair with two things like milk bottle caps over my ears and a hair net, but now I don't feel self-conscious at all. I used to ask for a booth, but now I don't mind sitting in the open." The future will doubtless have many his-and-hers hair-dressing establishments like Hair Design Associates on St. Mark's Place in New York, where the same coiffeurs trim the hair of both men and women.

Up to fairly recently, many men customers were embarrassed about receiving hair-coloring treatments, once associated with actors and gigolos. Of America's 37 million men with gray hair, from two to three million were using a hair-coloring product before Clairol registered the slogan, "Does he . . . or doesn't he?" and in June 1966 introduced Great Day. National advertising for it and similar preparations has helped to make men much less uneasy about their open use of a gray-covering product. It is likely that every sixth man will be modifying the color of his hair in the very immediate future.

With even hair coloring now so accepted, many businessmen readjust their schedules in order to keep an appointment with a favorite hair stylist. Stanley Kramer and Jules Stein are among the prominent men who go to the Golden Door near San Diego.[30] Such spas offer a wide range of services, including facials, massage, and cold-cream treatments, and one spa advertises that "here a hairy man can become a charm boy."

Even the eyebrows of "a hairy man" are now evaluated in terms of esthetic criteria. Fortune telling manuals, dream charts, and popular tradition lauded bushy eyebrows as a sign of good character, in the days when a heavy reef of eyebrow was almost the single most reassuring facial feature that a man could have. But now, his eyebrows are shaped to eliminate excess hair and accent the eye. Yet at the very time that men's eyebrows are becoming thinner and more delicate, Audrey Hepburn and Elizabeth Taylor helped to popularize heavily defined eyebrows for women.

It would seem that the male most successful in obtaining a raise, wife, date, or an important business interview, should be charmingly coiffed, sweet-smelling, and young-looking. Martha Hyer has warned that "on the Sunset Strip these nights you can't tell which are the girls and which are the boys. It's not only confusing; it can be dangerous."[31] Just how "dangerous" emerges in an incident reported by a young male writer to his psychoanalyst. "I was at an art gallery," he mused, "and I was attracted to this beautifully dressed and nicely smelling creature in slacks and with wavy blond hair. But I honestly couldn't tell its sex, or whether it was a man who needed a haircut or a woman who had just got one. So, what do you think, Doctor, am I a pervert or not?"

Popular humor is already reflecting the change. There is a story about the Harvard man who was telling a Princeton friend about his successful recipe for seducing girls. "Invite her to dinner at your place. A thick steak, lettuce with Roquefort dressing, Italian bread, a baked potato, soft music in the background, and candles. You chat quietly, and when dinner is over, discreetly blow out the candles." His friend thanked him profusely. The two met a few weeks later and the Harvard man hailed the son of Nassau. "How did you make out?" "Not too well," he muttered. "I followed your advice exactly, and things seemed to be going according to plan. But by the time I finished with my hair and applied skin lotion, she was already sound asleep."

The Rings on His Fingers

The most successful single product of our new era in men's cosmetics is a $4.50 scented cologne called Jade East. Introduced in 1963, its key television commercial showed a Chinese girl bathing in a fountain. "She senses your presence before you speak a word," says a male voice. "It's something about you that excites her."

An average woman's hearing is more acute than a man's, and his jewelry's jangling may have enabled her to sense him long before Jade East's scent wafted over. Men are not yet wearing bells on their fingers and rings on their toes, but they may be doing so before too long. It is not surprising that Jade East comes from Swank, Inc., the largest maker of men's jewelry, because similar needs are met by a man's wearing jewelry and scent. The cologne's success is probably related to the enthusiasm which many men have displayed for jade rings during the last decade, as technical problems of mounting it have been overcome. Men's recent interest in precious stones and other jewelry has provided far more sales for jewelers than traditional items for women like matinee or opera-length pearls, charm bracelets, and pearl and diamond clasps.

Never before, for example, has there been such a proliferation of cuff links. The most successful new shirt style in years is the convertible cuff, which permits a man to wear links without actually having traditional foldover cuffs. Three different people connected with a testimonial dinner independently came to the only jeweler in a small community and each wanted to order a pair of cuff links to present to the guest of honor. After the dinner, the guest of honor himself came to the shop. The proprietor was afraid that he would return some of the cuff links. Not so; the man wanted a fourth pair that had been suggested by combining several designs on the other pairs. Few men are as enthusiastic about cuff links as former Presidential aide Robert E. Kintner, who owns 200 pairs, but fifteen or twenty pairs are fairly common.

Many men select the device they use to keep their ties in place in the same way that a woman chooses her earrings. The simple tie clasp has given way to tacks, bars, buttons, and pins. Among the stones used in tie tacks are garnets, rubies, sapphires, white pearls, blue pearls, black pearls, and even diamonds. The tie tack's popularity was originally enhanced by many women, who bought them as gifts that involved precious stones and yet were not intimate. Today, most men buy their own tacks.

Men are also buying more rings set with precious stones. Many a man has adorned his little finger with a garnet ring and men have begun to wear rings on other non-traditional fingers. A major impetus has been the recent availability of artificial star sapphires, emeralds, and rubies, for around $100. Men unable to afford the natural product are happy to sport a man-made stone, or diamond.

We have come a long way from Tipperary. Up to World War I, it was considered effeminate for men to wear wrist watches. Officers began using them only because combat conditions made it impossible to carry pocket watches. Since then, men's wrist watches have become routine and are now items of jewelry. Their evolution into things of beauty can be seen in the watch band, once a utilitarian brown or black leather strap. Today watch bands come in many colors and a variety of semi-precious and even precious metals, and it is often difficult to tell a man's from a woman's except by its width.

During the last twenty years many masculine wrists have been clanking with a gold or silver identification bracelet that has its wearer's name engraved on the outside. Like the tie tack, it originally developed as a gift from a woman to her husband or beau, but 80 percent of the sales are now made to men. Consumer studies suggest its appeal to be the provision of a socially acceptable opportunity for a man to wear a bracelet. Many a contemporary scented and gaudily bedizened man may well need the bracelet as a reminder of his identity.

The head of the family may no longer wear a crown, but some of its glittering baubles now shine forth from his costume. At the same time, men's jewelry is becoming more popular with women. Many a salesman who showed a man's wrist watch to a woman has volunteered, "I think he'll like that one," only to have her reply, "It's for me." Women are taking to men's watches because their own tend to be too dressy for sportswear. Men's dials are larger and easier to read, especially those with white faces and Roman numerals.

Men's cigarette cases are popular with many women for similar reasons: designs are simpler and the cases larger. Men's money clips often nestle at the bottom of women's handbags. Perhaps the most popular style has the shape of a large paper clip and is made of gold that is twisted like a rope. Sets of gold buttons originally intended for men's blazers are bought by women for their own costumes, along with men's cuff links. Some women carry men's key chains and others wear men's rings with semi-precious stones set flush in plain settings, or signet rings with a coat of arms or crest design. Still others wear a man's pocket watch on a gold or silver chain around the neck.

Women's growing preference for men's jewelry and men's new interest in lapidary adornment may lead to domestic problems that did not previously exist. We can imagine the husband bringing a new ring home and eagerly showing it to his wife. "Thank you, darling," she could say, "it's beautiful." "But," he might stammer, "it's for me."

The Shoe
on the Other Foot

In the confusion over the gender of clothes, the question of who wears which shoe becomes a pressing one. Shoes are terribly basic: people die with their boots on, are down at the heel, step into someone else's shoes, put their foot into it, pussyfoot around, and are tenderfeet.[32]

One reason for great interest in Greta Garbo's shoes was audience difficulty in reconciling her luminous beauty with the unattractive shoes she often wore, because the single most revealing item of a woman's costume is the shoe that holds her outfit together. The shoe is the point at which attention stops, the period at the end of the sentence, just as gloves are parentheses that set off the words in between. It is the platform on which the costume stands. A woman will show the shoes in her closet shoe rack with a pride that she has for no other article of clothing. Women realize that they cannot do much about the reality of their legs, but can modify their legs' appearance via shoes.

Women tend to be diligent shoppers for shoes, although fashion magazines provide little shoe coverage and window display mannequins are seldom shown wearing shoes. Neither are high fashion models, whose size-nine shoes are too clumsy to photograph attractively. Newspaper accounts of women's costumes seldom describe shoes, even those worn at weddings. In spite of such media neglect, women at practically all age and socioeconomic levels tend to be better informed about footwear than any other item of clothing.

Even women in prison are sensitive to shoes. Upon leaving New York's Women's House of Detention, each inmate is given a complete change of costume which is generally one season old and comes from women in the community. The inmates are usually pleased to get a going-away outfit, but many reject the shoes, saying, "I would rather go barefoot than wear shoes that are so out-of-date." [33] Interviews suggest that a prime reason for the vigor with which they reject the shoes is a sensitivity to what shoes reveal about a wearer.

Shoes permit a woman to remain a lady and still suggest an aspect of her personality that would be vulgar if conveyed by the cut of a sweater. It is possible that they reveal sexual attitudes because encasement of the foot in a closely fitting shoe may symbolically suggest the positioning of sexual organs during coitus. Not only is the shoe the most popular item of clothing with fetishists but deities of sensuality like Bacchus, Hecate, and Lilith have

animal's feet. Foot modesty is found among the Siberian
Koryak and an Eskimo woman who removed her boots
would be communicating a sexual invitation.[34] When
Joan Baez took off her shoes during a concert at Philhar-
monic Hall on April 19, 1963, the audience applauded
more enthusiastically than to any of her songs.

The women in Arthur Miller's *After the Fall* are often at
the feet of the hero, but he is unable to respond sponta-
neously to them, a failure that he expresses via inability to
remove his shoes. Miller uses a similar metaphor in *Death
of a Salesman,* when Biff throws his sneakers into the fur-
nace after finding his father in a hotel room with a
strange woman.

The intimate significance of shoes lends particular importance to the fact that women's footwear has adapted so
many features from men. A number of spectator pump
variations stem from men's golf shoes. The stacked heel
that once identified better men's footwear has been trans-
planted to women's shoes, as a result of style's backward
droop, with dresses and jackets worn up to the chin and
off the back of the neck. Modern women have so little occasion to take mincing little steps that the three-inch heel
is now a museum piece. Roger Vivier's two-inch heel
started its descent a decade ago, and today's chic shoe has
a heel that is ½″ to ⅞″, just about as high as a man's.
Such shoes were once considered unesthetic when they
were called "flats" and worn around the house. Now they
are the height, or non-height, of fashion.

The most radical change in women's shoes has been
their recent abandonment of light and slender shapes for
clodhoppers' clunkiness and stubbiness. But blunt toes
and squatness seem almost fey in comparison to the boots
that cover many otherwise attractive legs. Some men won-
dered why women were walking around in white galoshes
when it wasn't raining, before headline writers learned to
spell Courrèges. Boots rise above the knees and cover the

thighs. They come in fur, satin, and leather, and are worn regardless of weather, their ugliness, or even the wearer's discomfort. Fashion columns discuss how to get boots to wrinkle attractively.[35] There are even bridal boots. Some of the fantasy once associated with hair-dos and dresses has shifted to boots, and their popularity suggests that it may have the undercurrents of sadism found in the song "Boots."

The harsh horizontal lines of boots often graze the knees and underline their lack of curves. A woman with today's fashionable slender legs has thin and bony knees, and gyms have been doing a thriving business in teaching exercises that trim the "ugliest spot in a woman's anatomy." There is a new "dread fashion disease . . . dowdy, porky, dumpy, doughy fat knees."[36] The miniskirt gives no quarter.

Fashionable women who are lucky enough to have knobby knees sometimes accentuate the knobs by sporting a walking stick. Some of the sticks have a whiplike quality, and a whip is a logical accessory for a woman striding along in high boots. Edwardian women used to carry long walking sticks to clear a path through a crowd so that their elaborate hats would not be disturbed. Today's woman might carry a whip in order to clear men out of her path, although her boots help to frighten them away.

As the work week becomes shorter and automation spreads, men need fewer heavy work shoes. Men buy shoes frequently, currently averaging 2.7 pairs each year.[37] Shoe repair shops have reported a tremendous decline in the resoling business as men increasingly prefer to buy a new pair rather than salvage old ones.

As women's shoes became heavier, men's turned lighter. Men sport tapered, long, and narrow pointed shoes and low-cut and laceless models. Slender slip-ins and lightweight square toes are replacing heavy moccasins. Shoes with a decreasing number of eyelets are in vogue. The popular two-eyelet model resembles what was once called the "nurse's shoe." Some men's shoes have elasticized panels and others have the medium Cuban heels that women gave up a generation ago.

A few months after colored patent leather became popular with women in 1961, men had begun wearing it.[38] Men's shoes are now available in ochre, taupe, red, mauve, purple, sage, canyon, java, chianti, blue haze, gray mist, shadow, buffalo, birch bark, olive, desert sand, golden fog, turquoise, and fishsilver green. Slippers have emerged from black, brown, and plum into a wide range of colors. Hues once regarded as flamboyant are also seen on well-dressed ankles, as socks have become splashier.

The unique ability of the costume to convey sex roles emerges with devastating clarity as women's shoes increasingly resemble the orthopedic footwear of the past. Although they look heavy enough to act as ballast for astronauts landing on the moon, light colorful styles dominate the men's market. Both men's and women's shoes are also becoming more neuter as a number of styles are made of the synthetic Corfam. It springs back to its original shape and smoothness after not having been worn for a while. The deep lines left in leather by wear are partially responsible for many people's reluctance to discard worn shoes, because they feel that the lines reflect the wearer's personality. Men's and women's footwear made of Corfam will have the depersonalized smoothness of a foam rubber surface, making the shoes of both sexes even more look-alike.

Vive
la Différence

Ever since Eden, the most provocative thing about each sex has been that it looked and smelled so different from the other. Women liked men whose tweeds made them look stronger and bigger and whose tobacco and leather exudations were ineffably male. Men responded to women whose softly clinging dresses discreetly hinted at curves beneath and whose perfume was promises.

In *Lady in the Dark,* the hero notices that the heroine's tailored costume is very similar to his. "We must go to the same tailor," he says. Each sex has increasingly been adapting the fashions and secondary external characteristics of the other in the quarter-century since Moss Hart's play. If clothing becomes much more intersexual, we may need "His" and "Hers" on clothing in order to be able to tell the players apart without a score card.

Designers have always drawn inspiration from the opposite sex, but the current borrowing of one sex's costume by the other is taking place on an unparalleled scale. Clothing represents the furniture of the mind, and today's trans-sexual changes in these things are likely to have profound effects. Clothing changes affect the styling of automobiles and other products. Television has intensified the speed with which styles move and large chains like Sears Roebuck and J. C. Penney reach thousands of communities with new fashions almost overnight.

The profound interrelationships between clothing and behavior are built into our language. A costume embodies custom, and there is a continuing relationship between habits we have and the habit we wear. One aspect of the relationship is suggested by a finding that emotionally disturbed women are more likely to experience their body as masculine than normal women.[39]

One interpretation of clothing neutering is in terms of morality. Silhouettes tend to be sharply defined, broad-shouldered, and small-waisted when morality is rigid, as in the days of the Spartans, Saxons, Cromwell, and Victoria.[40] In times that are less moral but more uncertain and complex, like those of Louis XIV, the Edwardian period, the 1920's, and the post-World War II years, a more blurred silhouette seems preferred by both men and women. We project our uncertainty about the ambiguous future onto clothing silhouettes. The times decree our security, security influences morality, morality affects shapes, and shapes lead to fashions.

Another reason for clothing changes is its reflection of each sex's relation to the other. Women of the mid-nineteenth century showed helplessness by rigid corseting, sweeping skirts, and high heels. Contemporary men may wear gaily colored clothing, perfumes, and jewelry as one reflection of their increasing tendency to become the objects, rather than the initiators, of courtship. Today's preferred shape for both men and women is loose fitting and formless and expresses and reinforces our blurring of maleness and femaleness. Clothing further deepens the internal conflict and confusion of each sex in fulfilling its role.

War and its aftermath provide another reason for radical changes in clothing. During a war, women at home mute their femininity as one response to the absence of men. Postwar clothing is usually regressive, with women looking like little girls and men borrowing from women's costume. In the years following the French Revolution, as well as the two World Wars, women shortened their hair and discarded restraining undergarments. They moved the waistline up after the French Revolution and down after the two World Wars. In both the 1920's and 1950's, men blossomed forth in colors. It is almost as if war's grim dictation of the roles of men as defenders of the home and women as mothers could be erased by radical postwar changes in clothing.

In war and peace, clothing always reflects role and style of life. Joan of Arc wore men's clothes when she took over an army and Amazons distinguished themselves from other women by knee-length skirts as well as cutting off one

breast. The color and banding on Roman togas desig-
nated status and sex and only royalty could once wear er-
mine and purple. The Mandarin in China was recognizable by his ankle-length gown and Queen Christina of
Sweden wore men's clothes to indicate that she was a rul-
er and not a queen.

But the French Revolution is the classic instance of how
clothing reflects social change. Pre-Revolutionary law prescribed that only duchesses and princesses could wear silk.
Gold braid, lace, jabots, and brocade for men were eliminated by the Revolution. A bland middle-class costume
replaced the aristocracy's frequently changing and elaborate trappings. Balzac deplored how difficult it was for
men of his time to look elegant in clothes that reflected
the abolition of class distinction. Today's clothes represent, if not the abolition of sex distinction, the closest we
have ever come to it.

Writers before and after Balzac have been aware of the
importance of costume in masculinity or femininity. Sten-
dhal, Balzac, Flaubert, De Maupassant, and Proust responded to the meanings of clothing. When Jane Eyre
looks through the stair railing, the description of the costumes of women at the dinner party is so insightful that it
became unnecessary to say more about them. Katherine
Mansfield actually designed her characters' clothes and
described them in detail, like Bertha's white crepe dress in
Bliss.[41] John Dos Passos showed great sensitivity to costume in *Manhattan Transfer* and *U.S.A.,* but fractionation
of character in more recent fiction has led to a decline in
novelists' interest in clothing. Young people who read older novelists today often skip over descriptions of clothing
because they seem antiquarian to readers weaned on contemporary unisexual costume.

Some implications of women's interest in wearing men's
clothes were anticipated by Shakespeare in many plays.
Portia appears disguised as a man in *The Merchant of*

Venice, and clever Rosalind and cunning Jessica want to look like men and have rehearsed the role in their imagination. The modern dramatist is necessarily alert to clothing because he gives as much attention to each character's costume as he does to the appearance of a room. In pieces as diverse as *Peer Gynt, Arms and the Man, The Prince and the Pauper, My Fair Lady, High Spirits, The Sound of Music,* and *The Music Man,* a costume change connotes a shift in personality.

Movie roles have long been communicated by clothing. Yesterday, Humphrey Bogart wore a dark and well-cut overcoat as a gangster, but a trench coat as a private eye. Today, the wife in *Juliet of the Spirits* wears trousers throughout most of the film, but switches to a dress when she realizes that her husband has been seeing another woman.

One occasion for clothing change is a modification in its wearer's self-concept. We have had the experience of seeing a friend in a dress or hat or sweater or coat and saying "That *is* you." William James once observed that clothing is as much a component of the self as the body and is part of the "material me."[42] It also communicates impressions of maintenance of the body by the very manner in which it conceals such maintenance. The clothing worn by a person helps to create a mood which can be validated in what other people see in him. How different Theodore Roosevelt would seem without his pince-nez, Franklin D. Roosevelt without his cigarette holder and black boat cloak, or John F. Kennedy *in* a hat and vest.

Interest in wearing clothes of the opposite sex is growing rapidly, and a number of magazines (e.g., *Transvestia* and *Turnabout)* are devoted to the subject. In questions submitted by the general public to a leading popular magazine concerned with sex, three times as many men as women asked about cross-dressing.[43] This ratio probably reflects the ease with which women can already wear men's clothes, although social pressure still exists against men in women's clothing. Less than half the men interviewed in one study had dressed in others' clothing as children, but 85 percent of the girls had done so.[44]

More liberal attitudes may make transvestism more visible today. But it could actually be increasing, because normal costumes already contain so much that is borrowed from the opposite sex. The existence of a substantial group that wants to wear even more clothes of the opposite sex, at a time when each sex looks like a transvestite parody, suggests that genderless clothing is meeting important contemporary needs.

The needs that have brought about this interchange appear not to have taken deep root in other countries. While London is the pace-setter for neutral *youth* fashions, and some Scandinavian teen-agers clutch look-alikeness to their indistinguishable bosoms, unisexual clothing has not become popular with adults in most of Europe and the rest of the world. Perhaps the only major exceptions are English women's adaptations of the man's jersey V-neck sweater and pants suit.

Some items of costume have gone back and forth between the sexes in America. Men complained about the clumsiness of women's handbags, but women could point to the long-handled and tipped men's umbrella, which was difficult to carry, easy to trip over, and had to be discarded if the wind blew it inside out. The woman's umbrella had a practical carrying cord, a convenient handle, short shaft, and lack of a tip made it easy to carry. A collapsible version could be carried in a purse and withstand the wind.

The traditional female umbrella, with so many advantages, has given way to newer umbrellas which are modeled after men's. They are long, tipped, canelike, sheathed, and have the high trip-over quotient of men's umbrellas. Parallel with women adapting men's umbrellas has been a reciprocal shift: men's umbrellas now resemble the newer women's models, which are adaptations of the former men's style.

Men used to laugh at jokes about the hundreds of objects carried in women's handbags. By the mid-1950's, similar quips were leveled at the range of goodies carried by men in attaché cases, which had become part of the businessman's uniform. By 1957, the case had itself begun to develop into a woman's fashion accessory. More recently, the roundness of women's change purses began to give way to the hard edges of men's foldover billfolds and women's handbags have become smaller in order to go with short skirts.

Men's gloves were once fairly heavy and had a variety of striations and ribbings, but in the last decade have become light and sleek and lost much of their nubbing. Women's gloves have tended toward heaviness and striation. Some copy men's motorcycle gauntlets and others derive from men's racing gloves and conspicuously expose the knuckles and back of the hand. They may be fine for karate, or a quick uppercut to the jaw, but are unlikely to encourage a man to hold hands.

Many women wear a man's watch chain as an accessory; men who carry a pocket watch often decorate it with chains, charms, and fobs that resemble women's costume jewelry. College men have reclaimed the loafer, but its gay colors and lightness bear witness to its several years of popularity on Sorority Row. Women's boots of the early 1960's were adapted from cowboy footgear. A year or two later, men began buying Wellington Boots, which rise four to six inches above the ankle and are copies of the women's boots—which came from cowboys.

The vivid designs and colors of women's sweaters led to men's ski clothes, which in turn provided inspiration for women's ski costumes. Soon after Vienna's Willy Bogner used stretch fabrics in women's ski pants in the 1950's,

American manufacturers began making stretch ski pants for women. Electric blue became their most popular color, and in two years had also become the leading color for men's pants.

Crisscrossing will probably occur more frequently as look-alikeness becomes more accepted. It is already so routine that exactly the same product may be sold to men and women. The sweater-styled Swiss velour shirt with a knitted neck is one style that has been enthusiastically received by both sexes. Some couples save money by buying storm coats and similar outerwear in a size larger than the wife's usual one, but smaller than her husband generally takes, so that they can wear it alternately.

Just as the middle classes have adopted the rock-and-roll music that was once an exclusively lower-class favorite, they have also taken over many items of clothing and appearance from previously outsider groups. Clothing not only blurs age and sex distinctions but now also crosses the class lines that were exemplified in formerly pariah characteristics, like colored stockings, light lipsticks, boots, leather jackets, and long hair for boys.

One aspect of clothing that has not changed is the sequence in which men and women put on their garments. Most American women get into their brassiere before their panties or girdle, but the typical man dons his shorts and then his undershirt. The representative women slips into blouse or shirt before getting into skirt or slacks, whereas her husband is likely to step into his trousers before putting on a shirt. Women may cover the upper body first for several reasons: the breasts' relationship to feeding of infants, women's feeling that breasts are more individualized than pudenda, vulnerability of the bosom, and the American preoccupation with bosom and milk. Men may cover their genital area first because they are more puritanical than women or because of concern about castration.

Some items of clothing are being adopted by both sexes simultaneously, like bikinis and fur hats. The French waistband, which is a continuation of the skirt rather than a piece added to it, became fashionable at the same time that women were abandoning belts, and a self-belt can be found on three-fourths of men's trousers. Neardisappearance of the waist and belt has made the body line smoother and the genital area less conspicuous. College students of both sexes began wearing similar jeans, coats, sweaters, and footwear at about the same time.

There has not been much of a counter-movement of each sex wearing sexually indigenous clothing. One masculine trend is greater visibility of men's legs and genitals, as more trousers are designed to show a handsome thigh and well-turned calf. In the last few years, non-homosexual men at East Hampton and other resort areas have been wearing snugly fitting jeans over women's thin nylon panties. Men's tailors increasingly ask customers, "Do you dress left or right?" a euphemism for genitals "favoring" either side. Today's average customer is much more likely to have an opinion than was his father.

Some few changes in American women do represent a more feminine feeling. The belt gave way to the loose sash, which moved down to the hip and is being transformed into a hard belt that has little suppleness or softness. Some signs suggest that bosoms may reappear and the growing use of beads and pleats involves an accentuation of the feminine. Women can choose among many more shades of nail polish than the light, medium, or dark of the 1930's. The gloppy earrings now worn by women would be more feminine if they were less hard and brittle, but at least help to distinguish women from men.

Many other aspects of outward appearance no longer differentiate the sexes. During the last two decades, in which clothing has permitted fuller expression of individuality and also become more "free" and "fun," it has also contributed to our renunciation of both masculine and feminine. A vivid picture of the New People's unisexuality can be seen on many a Main Street. A teen-age boy and girl might be wearing the same pea jacket, sweater, jeans, and boots. Otherwise, we might watch a woman striding vigorously along, in hip or knee-length boots over textured stockings. She would wear a black leather coat, helmet, racing gloves, and a Harris Tweed pants suit. Her button-cute male companion could sport a pastel sack suit, soft and smooth suede gloves, a bright feather in a mauve hat. His delicate tie would be set off by the ruffled front of a Tom Jones pink shirt. Semi-precious stones would grace his cuff links, tie tack, rings, and watch. He would exude fragrance that was sweet and thick, like Ashes of Roses. His pointed toe, low-cut shoes or low quarter boots would rest on high stacked heels. Both man and woman would be fashionably dressed, but their more than seven types of ambiguity would make it difficult even to speculate on who would be whispering sweet nothings to whom.

8

men, women,
and other minority groups

Former Prime Minister Sir Robert Menzies of Australia
was once engaged in a bitter debate in Parliament with an
opponent who wanted to suggest that Menzies was the
creature of pressure groups. He identified Menzies as
". . . the merest instrument of a power in the background."
But the Prime Minister appeared to misconstrue his meaning and snapped, "I'll thank the honorable gentleman to
keep my wife out of this discussion."

Today's American wife is hardly likely to be a power in
the background. Her work role has moved to the fore-
ground; she adapted to the sharp decline in the ideology of
romantic love. And both she and her husband have grown
up in a society lacking many of the benchmarks that once
identified each developmental epoch. Loss of such markers is crucial because our identity is discovered in interaction with others over a long period of time. In an age in
which only counterfeit coins of sexual identity are available, we may be handling wooden nickels, without sus-
pecting that we are, in fact, being cheated.

Dagwood
and Blondie

Women are better able to compete for jobs with men as the United States has become the first nation in which less than half the workers are involved in the production of tangible goods.[1] Women hold 46 percent of all jobs in service industries, in contrast to 19 percent of those concerned with manufacturing goods. The application of automation will provide new role conflicts for many men, as our society becomes increasingly service-oriented. With more work consisting of the kind of person-to-person relations that represent a woman's traditional province, the recent pattern of women competing with men for men's jobs may be replaced by men vying with women for women's jobs.[2]

Over 2,300,000 wives earn more than their husbands, and the discrepancy in income could contribute to domestic problems. An extreme example of the problems posed by work role is provided by what some people saw as a possible conflict between Mrs. Charlotte Spiegel's work as head of the New York County Democratic party's executive committee and her husband's post as a judge of the Civil Court. The New York City Bar Association suggested that the conflict might be resolved by her withdrawal from active politics or his resignation from the bench. In other quarters, it was urged that a divorce provided the best solution. The voters appear to have felt that each spouse should feel free to pursue his and her own career and not only promoted Judge Spiegel to the State Supreme Court in 1966 but gave him more votes than any of the other twelve candidates.

Title VII of the Federal Civil Rights Act of 1964, which bars job discrimination because of sex, has already given rise to the "bunny problem," or what might happen to the man applying for a job in a Playboy Club. Since bunnies serve drinks, there would seem to be no reason why a man could not do the work. For similar reasons, a man's sex should not preclude him from being hired as a clerk in a women's corset shop. An employer who insisted on a secretary of either sex might be as guilty of denying fair employment rights as a railroad that would not hire women locomotive engineers.

De-sexing the job market may require a substantial rewriting of the English language.[3] Housemaid, meter-maid, milkman, iceman, foreman are discriminatory terms. So is handyman, although he seems to have disappeared in real life. A maid could be a man, and Girl Friday and saleslady now represent offenses. Newspaper classified advertisements for Help Wanted–Female and Help Wanted–Male are obviously discriminatory and will have to go. These changes represent more than adjustments—they are examples of the role revolution through which we are living. Another facet of the revolution is the decreasing age at which mothers are returning to work. Half the members of a sample of 1957 women college graduates surveyed by the Bureau of Labor Statistics were working ten years after graduation.

Neuterization of work roles reinforces a situation that already exists in many middle-class homes, where external conditions make it difficult for a woman to sustain the traditional feminine role.[4] She is unlikely to cook with materials that are inherited from grandmother and mother and carry feminine lineage and connotations. The maple kitchen table that was once handed down from mother to daughter has been replaced by an expandable formica or metal table. Many utensils and accessories are made of plastic, with which women cannot have the established relationship possible with earlier materials.

Other aspects of social life have made it easier for women to exercise leadership in courtship. Girls are likely to have had extensive experience in taking the social initiative as a result of previous practice with Barbie. Many a teen-age girl will not hesitate to pick up the telephone and tell her boy friend that "there's a party over at Mary's house next Thursday. I'd like to go. How about it?" She will also often suggest what clothes her escort should wear to Mary's.

A few years later, Mary will feel free to visit a "dating bar," where the single woman looking for a man can go without embarrassment. In the last few years, such bars have opened in many large cities. Two-thirds of the more than 2,000 singles who tried to get into Boston's Mad Russian bar on its January 1967 opening night were girls.

Even the jokes told by teen-age girls often deal with their leadership in later life. A current favorite among teen-agers deals with a woman who had been widowed four times. A friend asked her, "How did you come to marry first a banker, then a theatrical producer, a bishop, and last, an undertaker?" "Well," replied the widow, "one for the money, two for the show, three to make ready, and four to go." Such stories suggest how women today bridge the gap between childhood games and adulthood.

Middle-class teen-age girls also learn subsequent role behavior by financial as well as social leadership. Among the 30 percent of teen-agers who go steady or date frequently, a substantial proportion follows the girl's lead in money matters.[5] Joint bank accounts are common, and some girls put their boy friends on budgets, decide on their purchases, and badger them into demanding larger allowances. Boys' career, school, clothes, haircut, automobile, and music preferences are substantially influenced by the teen-age matriarchs. The girl may easily make such decisions because she could consistently identify with her mother, in contrast to her brother who shifts from identification with the mother to a masculine role.[6] The boy's role is often defined as what he should not do, and such negative goals can create anxiety because reasons for the prohibition are often vague.

Girls often get more affection and are more amenable than boys at similar age levels.[7] Such sex differences have probably arisen because the development of initiative in boys requires a relationship between affection and authority that differs from the approach usually taken with girls. Folk wisdom suggests that "it takes a man to raise a boy," but recent stress on love-oriented procedures for raising children could be making boys less enterprising and aggressive.

Other elements in modern socialization contribute to girls' superior equipment for later life. A girl's goal of being a date and later a wife is more easily implemented than a boy's push toward a career. Girls have more chances than boys to develop an awareness of the continuity of life and to relate to a wide range of people. Baby-sitting provides an opportunity for contact with children, and girls are more likely than boys to visit relatives and neighbors and open up the world of older persons. Girls also participate with peers more freely than boys. They shop, give parties, belong to voluntary groups, visit one another, share interests with siblings, and otherwise engage in more varied social activity. Girls have a better opportunity than boys to establish a repertory of emotions and behavior for the demands of later life.

With the head start provided in youth, it is not surprising that women seem to have a wider range of behavior than men, even on the level of unconscious processes. The dream is one art form that is available to all. Every character in a dream represents an aspect of the personality of the dreamer, just as his ability to recall the dream is a direct reflection of relationships to other people.[8] Men tend to dream more about men than about women. Women, however, dream about both sexes in almost equal proportion, suggesting that their role repertory is expanding in sleep as well as daytime activity.[9]

For many middle-class men, social living emphasizes impulse restraint and conformity to external demands, although traditional masculinity emphasizes self-expressive and individualistic characteristics.[10] Modern living makes physical strength, bravery, or aggressiveness less necessary for men, the redefinition of whose sex role has not kept pace with reevaluation of women's. But men who compromise an assertive role in favor of restraint may experience severe problems of identity. One early sign of the tribulations of fashioning a convincing and contemporary sexual identity may be reflected in the disproportionately high rate of psychiatric referrals among boys from seven to twelve (2.6 boys for each girl).

Contemporary jokes like the two boys' exchange of "My daddy can beat your daddy," and "Big deal, so can my mother," remind us that we really haven't found substitutes for the traditional stereotypes of masculinity. Today's middle-class boys are less likely than those of previous generations to see their fathers functioning in a masculine way. Dad may cut the roast with an electric knife and relax after dinner in a chair that massages him while he sits passively. He could use an electric eraser to correct errors in his shopping list, brush his teeth with an electric toothbrush, and cap his evening with isometric exercises. Relatively few fathers are likely to be blacksmiths or hunters or otherwise use strength and agility in their work. Moreover, few sons ever see their fathers engaged in any work activity.

Sex-linked behavior like working, cooking, and house cleaning reflect larger patterns of role behavior.[11] Only one boy in four in a midwest community helped his father with male chores.[12] Boys in all parts of the country seem to have a diminished opportunity of learning traditional man's work around the house, and father's decline is suggested in one finding that he was a less significant figure to junior and senior high school students than the school bus driver or janitor.[13] One factor in the father's change in status, as the division of labor by sex inside the home has dwindled, is his involvement in nursery or kitchen tasks that were once the exclusive province of the wife and of domestic help. Most husbands help to wash dishes and almost half assist in cooking, so that many a husband could almost be said to be a part-time wife. Even motherhood is becoming a joint experience, with many fathers taking Red Cross courses that enable them to empathize with their wives during pregnancy and birth. Children who observe these newer solutions to household roles will be the parents of tomorrow.

Boys also have less opportunity to identify with adult male behavior because smaller families and geographic mobility have largely eliminated the grandfathers and other alternative father figures formerly provided by large families when the several generations lived near each other. Roots of later hero worship were established in childhood, through boys' identification with heroic figures of history, sports, and adventure novels. In an age of anti-heroes, the abridgment of childhood and decline of childhood fantasy make it less likely that boys will receive inspiration from male heroes.

A young man who starts his working career with fantasies of retirement rather than becoming boss, and with latent feelings of passivity, may find few obstacles to their assertion. Now that governmental programs make provisions for the old, the sick, and the unemployed and the state performs more functions of a symbolic mother, it is likely that many men will be under less pressure to exert themselves. We can applaud the desirability and even necessity of such welfare programs and still note that they reinforce our drift toward neutering.

Another reason for neutering in our time may be that many of today's young adults were born during World War II. Sons of servicemen had no male figure with whom to identify and girls were deprived of a significant aspect of their psychosexual development.[14] As a widespread result of having been born between 1940 and 1946, many young people may have been predisposed to difficulties in sexual identification. Separation of the father from his family could have contributed to the wife's anxiety, and negative alterations in her mood further exacerbated effects of the father's absence on young children. Comparisons of boys from homes where the father was absent with boys from father-present households concluded that the former tended to behave like girls in fantasy and overt behavior, especially in their lack of aggression.[15] With over 12,300,000 persons in uniform at one time during the peak of the war, the father's absence may have been this country's most widespread example of an unhealthy situation affecting normal personality development.

Adults born between 1940 and 1946 may therefore be specially vulnerable to difficulties in sexual identification that predispose toward acceptance of, and find outlets in, the aspects of our culture that reflect sexual depolarization. The outlets could provide a non-pathological channel for what might otherwise have become homosexuality, pseudomasculinity or pseudofemininity resulting from reaction formation, and obsessive chronic self-doubting behavior. The prevalence of depolarization among persons born during World War II may lead to a chain reaction by creating an atmosphere which facilitates other age groups' acceptance of neutering.

Several aspects of sexual role reversal recently found expression in a popular commercial for Noxzema shaving cream. To the brassy background of David Rose's "The Stripper," a fierce-looking Valkyrie clenches and unclenches her teeth and throatily murmurs "Take it off—

take it all off!" to a meek-looking man. He smilingly and obligingly cuts away at his beard with a razor. Each stroke is synchronized with the music's driving bump and grind beat. Viewers can enjoy the man's obeisant removal of the manhood symbolized by his beard while the woman grinds her teeth and usurps the male role in urging the shaver to "take it off."

One potentially desirable effect of sexual depolarization is the possibility of its summoning forth new resources of personality and character as people are forced to reexamine the bases of their feelings of identity. Some may achieve an authentic individuality as persons more easily, as traditional roles become almost anachronistic. The future may witness new kinds of sensibility and role expression—if we survive this tumultuous period of accelerated social change.

Marriage for Moderns

The aftermath of World War II helped to bring about an atmosphere hospitable to depolarization in social life as well as clothing. Just as existentialism flourished in France under wartime occupation, our epoch's neutering may be related to our no war–no peace way of life. We used to remind ourselves of the existence of peace by celebrating Armistice Day, but the cold war has blurred the distinction between peace and war. One expression of this cloudiness is the replacement of Armistice by Veterans' Day. Our living in a gray area between war and peace could be facilitating acceptance of the in-between in daily life.

Depolarization could have profound effects on the characteristics sought in a mate as well as levels of marital satisfaction. Love is not really blind.[16] Husbands and wives

select one another on the basis of similar social backgrounds and complementing personality characteristics.[17]
The typical dynamic of sex attraction involves a man and
woman whose characteristics are interlaced but complementary. If each sex has fewer clear-cut characteristics,
its ability to find reciprocal and complementary qualities
in another person will diminish, because complementary
implies differences. Neutering might also have effects on
the incidence of marital problems because the lesser polarization of a married couple might result in a decreased
level of satisfaction. With fewer peaks, there would also be
fewer valleys. Such a situation has developed in Australia,
where marriage is a union with less than total involvement and intensity and marital discord is far less common
than in America.[18]

As a result of their not having fully adjusted to the radical shifts in American sex roles, young Americans often
have contradictory expectations of a mate. A young woman says that "I am looking for a husband who will be an
equal to whom I can look up." A young man describes his
ideal mate as "an equal who will listen to me." In spite of
the incongruity suggested by such expectations, the contemporary eradication of polar extremes is more likely to
lead to equality than to looking up or listening.

Changes in marriage in America are more important
than they might be in a country like France, where there
is a tradition of mistresses and lovers. The elder Dumas
once remarked that the institution of marriage was so
heavy that it required two people to lighten it, and sometimes three. But in America, the participants in a marriage are likely to adapt to the situation rather than seek a
long-term extramarital relationship.

Some dimensions of the new American marriage were
suggested by a special assistant to President Johnson, who
denounced the "glamor girl in a negligee" as an unaccept-
able feminine symbol.[19] The new woman has a "serious

acceptance of her responsibility as a contributing person to her society." It may be more important for her to be mature, intelligent, adjusted, or poised rather than feminine.

La Rochefoucauld's aphorism that people would never fall in love but for hearing love discussed is relevant here. It reminds us that one reason for vanishing romantic attitudes among contemporary Americans is that they hear much more about adjustment than about romance. Our downgrading of romance and femininity helps to explain why America is probably the only country where the husband's love for the wife often has the same quality and direction as the wife's love for the husband.[20] By the time they are old enough to think of marriage, the emotional posture of each sex has often become blurred with that of the other. It is probably as difficult today for a man to be aggressive and forward as for a woman to be romantic and compliant. Love that is masterful and dominant or humble and grateful is less possible in the United States than elsewhere, even though we still half-believe in the stereotypes that specify such expressions of love on the part of men and women, respectively. Many American wives are too self-sufficient for husbands who would like to be romantic or gallant, and husbands often do not know how to express such qualities. Spouses tend to function as partners whose relationship is parallel rather than complementary.

The decline of complementarity that begins in childhood is likely to be well established by the time of courtship, and can be seen in small but revealing social customs. A young man escorting a young woman across the street is unlikely to hold her arm in the old-fashioned way. If he bothers to link an arm with hers, he will probably do so in the same manner in which he holds the arm of a male friend.[21] One reason for the absence of such small cues of gallantry is that they imply the ability to say, "I'm stronger than you are, so I do not hesitate to be polite to you." "Gentleman Jim" Corbett was walking with a friend one day when a man bumped into him. When Jim apologized, the friend asked, "Why did you apologize to him? He walked into you." The man who had defeated John L. Sullivan explained, "I can afford to apologize—I've got the punch to back it up."

Some men behave as if they anticipated the same disastrous consequences from politeness as befell the French at the Battle of Fontenoy in 1745. The commander of the English troops is said to have urged the French commander to fire first. The latter refused, because the British invaders were his guests. The British fired one huge series of volleys by companies, inflicting tremendous casualties on the foremost French regiments, which broke and fled.

American men often flee from exhibiting politeness in what many regard as the battleground of their relationships with women. The decline of politeness is one reminder of the new relationships between the sexes that may gradually be replacing satisfactions of mutual dependence for many young people. Two generations ago, a man might kiss a woman's hand. One generation ago, he would shake it. Today, in extreme cases, he might expect a slap if she proffered her hand.

Language and speech patterns identified with each sex began to disappear at just about the same time as politeness. Although James Joyce was master of the seamless web of prose, his readers could usually distinguish the observations made by men from those made by women in *Ulysses* and even in *Finnegans Wake,* though Joyce did not use usual methods of identifying the sources of conversation. English and American contemporaries of Joyce generally wrote dialogue that was clearly associated with either men or women in content and grammar. Hemingway and Henry Green produced pages of sharp-edged dialogue without one "he said" or "she said," because they wrote at a time when separate masculine and feminine vocabularies still existed. The last two generations have seen a steady attrition of sex-linked language; words like "delicious" and "tough" are no longer linked with either sex (feminine and masculine, respectively) and have joined the great pool of neuter words. Most novelists who accurately mirror contemporary life use relatively non-sex-linked language. Women's relatively casual use of four-letter words that were once regarded as too strong for their delicate sensibilities has eliminated another important linguistic sex difference.

The Godiva
Principle

It is paradoxical that what appears to be a sexual economy of abundance could actually be suffering from a recession. Why should there be less sex at a time when it seems so available? A major part of its attraction in the past has undoubtedly stemmed from curiosity about sexual intercourse as a forbidden activity that cast its own unique shadow. Part of its pull has been the defiance of taboos and obstacles in the way of sexual expression and the yearning that comes from wanting but not having sex.[22]

Every society, present or past, has some sexual taboo. We may identify as the Godiva Principle the proposition that people tend to be attracted to sex in direct proportion to the extent that it is prohibited or surrounded with mystery. Peeping Tom violated Lady Godiva's proclamation that all persons should keep indoors, shut their windows, and not look at her. Instead, he looked at Godiva riding naked through the streets of Coventry. It was inevitable that he would look because of the prohibition, and be punished by the symbolic castration of being struck blind.

Sexual desire has been pleasantly complicated by difficulties in winning the loved person from the age of the Troubadours to the day of the flapper. The truism that the value of something increases with difficulties in the way of acquiring it is especially applicable to sex and love. The woman who is difficult to attain establishes a prohibition similar to the restrictions imposed on her suitor by his own parents. A man who overcomes this taboo feels stronger as the result of achieving fantasy gratifications of omnipotence similar to those experienced in childhood.

The seeming accessibility and demystification of sex may eliminate some gratifications for people whose fantasy satisfactions are seldom approached by actuality. Some young people who have had premarital sexual intercourse engage in less sex after receiving the social endorsement of marriage. There are even those who have had a very satisfactory premarital sex life but become impotent or frigid after marriage.

Ovid's descriptions of his illicit love with Corinna have continued to delight the western world. In the latter days of the Roman Empire, when sexual freedom and licentiousness were common, the repressive ideas of Christianity were required to revive interest in sex. Dante never once spoke with Beatrice, and probably would have been less in love if he had. He represents the most famous case of love that thrives on mystery and non-contact. A married Romeo and Juliet would hardly have excited the world's imagination.

One contemporary appeal of the forbidden could be exemplified in cigarette smokers' response to the possibility that smoking is dangerous to health. During the decade in which reports suggested the possibility of a positive relationship between smoking and lung cancer, cigarette sales continued to rise. In 1964, a decade after the original cancer-smoking reports were published, consumption of cigarettes in the United States had risen to 509 billion, a substantial gain over the preceding year. During 1965, when there was extensive Congressional and public discussion of smoking's dangers, Americans bought 532 billion cigarettes, an increase of 3.4 percent over 1964. Sales for 1966 were higher than the preceding year and per capita consumption continues to rise. Indeed, within a few short months after the report on smoking and health of the Surgeon General's Advisory Committee, most of the persons who had previously stopped smoking had returned to cigarettes.[23] It is possible that identification of the potential hazard could have contributed to making it *more* attractive to some smokers. Teen-agers are spending an unprecedented $10 million a week on cigarettes and it is likely that a substantial proportion begin smoking each year in response to its negative connotations.[24]

The power of anticipation and excitement stemming from the romantic quest can be seen in the extraordinarily successful films made by Fred Astaire and Ginger Rogers, which had filled theatres all over America—until their eighth film *(Carefree)* appeared in 1938. Because the couple had never once kissed in previous films, audiences could enjoy their fantasies of what might happen if and perhaps even after they kissed. It was decided to show their first screen kiss at the end of the color-blind dance sequence in *Carefree*.[25] The kiss was splendid, but probably helped to seal their doom as a team. Their next film, *The Story of Vernon and Irene Castle* (1939), did not do well at the box office and was their last RKO film together. It is likely that many fans began to lose interest once the tension had been eliminated by their kiss.

Excitement generated by non-consummation could have attracted many television viewers to the *Dr. Kildare* television series. The handsome young doctor went on from week to week without ever getting a girl, in spite of near hits with some misses. Dates with Nurse Lawton were often canceled because of a medical emergency. Perhaps the ideal Kildare romance was with a girl who died of leukemia, just as the perfect medieval romance ended with the death of one of the partners. David McCallum of *The Man from U.N.C.L.E.*, the single most popular teen-age idol since 1964, attracts his fans less because of his blond bangs, turtleneck sweater, and neuter cool, than as a result of his avoidance of physical contact with girls. He disappears before they can reward his bravery with a kiss.

The quest can be seen on another level in the public's relative interest in political candidates' campaigns as compared with their consequent performance. The very same Americans who follow candidates up to election day with great intensity tend to pay little attention to the winner's performance in office, because the contest's tension and excitement constitute the attraction. There was considerable apathy about the hotly contested 1964 Republican primary fights, once computers began eliminating tension by predicting the results. Now that computers are increasingly used to match dating partners, the search for the idealized mate may become a relic of the past. While a return to the sexual repressiveness of earlier generations is unthinkable, we ought to be aware of some of the hazards of our loss of interest in the quest.

Rites of Passage,
Hail and Farewell

One reason that many young people are selecting their own ethic and becoming defiantly retreatist or activist is the loss of many of the outward boundaries between young and old. There is a story about a lighthouse keeper who slept soundly through the firing of a cannon every midnight. When the cannon failed to go off for the first time in twenty years, promptly at midnight the lighthouse keeper jumped out of bed and called, "What's that?" He had responded to the absence of something that ought to have happened at a specific time, but didn't.

Less dramatically than with the lighthouse worker, young people since World War II have increasingly been deprived of significant experiences that represented modern equivalents of rites of passage. Benchmarks represented by the rites have been eroded by larger social forces of our urban industrial society. An increase in geographic and social mobility and in compensatory social welfare services, a decrease in social and economic rights of inheritance, and modifications in the structure of kinship have helped to eliminate rituals.

The rite's ceremonial used to help its celebrant to achieve an emotional state that bridged the gap between old and new.[26] He could anticipate the rite as he approached it and look back later, knowing that it would be available for those who followed. The rite gave meaning to the conclusion of one phase of the life cycle and the commencement of another and helped cushion the conflict that is an almost inevitable part of human development. It provided a sense of community and showed the participant how he resembled others. The rite was also a public affirmation of its subject's sexual and personal identity and his move from one age and status group to another.

Birth, puberty, marriage, and death were some key changes that gave rise to rites of passage. Birth is now a routine activity that occurs in hospital anonymity. The bride participates in fewer showers and bridal suppers and the groom is less likely to figure in a bachelor's dinner. Brides are less likely to be virgins, and elaborate wedding ceremonies have become unpopular among many younger people, who prefer to be practical and save their money toward furniture. Death used to represent a major American rite of passage, but the recent outcry for quiet, func-

tional dying has led to minimal funeral ceremonies and
the denial of open mourning.

Our most significant and influential rites were probably
the series of benchmarks that led toward and away from
puberty. They were fairly effective, although lacking the
pain, terror, and drama of the rites that often marked ini-
tiation into puberty in non-literate societies. The American
puberty observances included changes in costume and appearance at various ages, graduation ceremonies, fraterni-
ty hazing procedures, and an established sequence of socialization with the opposite sex. As these modern rites have
all become subdued, young people have had a lesser opportunity to develop a sense of self and a sexual identity.
The birthday party is a poor substitute for rituals of an
earlier day.

One specific sign of a person's place on the life cycle
was his costume and appearance. Every little girl's dream
was to progress from short wool skirts, flat-heeled and
round-toed shoes, and middy blouse, toward her mother's
longer skirts and high-heeled and pointed-toe shoes. She
could look forward to advancing from socks through knee
socks, cotton and wool ribbed stockings, to cotton lisle and
finally, silk stockings.

Girls' dresses used to get longer as they became older,
but the dress of a modern first-grader breaks above the
knees, just about where her mother's hem falls. A mother's
shoes, overblouses, and sweaters and separates are essentially the same as her child's. Both generations are likely
to look bare-legged in summer and wear identical tights
and textured stockings at other seasons. Women's clothing
reflects the contemporary ideal of wishing to look like a
young girl—female, but somehow sexless, with long thin
legs that do not have to be hidden with skirts.[27] The desire to look like a nymphet has helped to make skirts
shorter than ever before. Many Mainbocher clothes are

inspired by little girls and Givenchy's most famous customer, Audrey Hepburn, is essentially an older boy-girl—thin, coltish, flat, big-eyed, with straight hair.

The youthful, non-fitted look got fresh attention in 1957 when Givenchy's A-line obliterated the waist. In the same year, the first teen mannequin dolls caught the public fancy, and *Lolita* came in 1958. Ever since, the loose straight-line nymphet silhouette has characterized everything from Lilly Pulitzer's beach shift to Ferdinando Sarmi's evening gowns.

The ultimate vulgarization of *Lolita* can be seen in current fashion's drum-majorette look. Today's chic mini-skirt, bare knees, and white boots represent a traditional uniform for the leggy teen-age drum majorette who symbolizes midwestern small town parades. Because Americans have had a semi-mocking attitude toward drum majorettes, lusting after them has represented an acceptable fantasy. Counter-Oedipal guilt resulting from an older man's involvement with a pretty majorette is a theme of Elia Kazan's *A Face in the Crowd,* released one year before *Lolita.* The guilt may be less likely in the future if more men follow the example of Xavier Cugat, Nelson Rockefeller, Frank Sinatra, and George Jessel in marrying a much younger woman.

The chic mother who wears today's popular smock dress could look exactly like her one-year-old daughter. For both mother and child, it has long full sleeves and moderate fullness falling down from the bust. The tiny flowers that once characterized a child's dress are now found on her mother's. More than time separates a child from Velasquez' prinked out little Infanta and Renoir's button-booted girls whose clothing clearly differentiated them from adults. And their mothers' appearance and way of life were far removed from today's matron who visits a pre-teen shop and says, "My daughter would love

that coat. . . . Let me try it on. I'm about the same size."
She is not fooling the salesgirl, who suspects that she is
buying the coat for herself.

Such subterfuges are less necessary now that teen-agers
(Jean Shrimpton and Twiggy) have become the most popular models and as our sandbox set becomes the acknowl-
edged style leader for grown-up women who wear Mary
Jane shoes and white stockings. Dresses with puffed
sleeves, streamers, and ruffles adorn many an aging matron who spent her youth laughing at Baby Snooks and
now looks like her. Just a few years ago, in *What Ever
Happened to Baby Jane?,* Bette Davis was appropriately
grotesque as a grown woman who continued to wear the
clothes that she had sported as a child star. Today, such a
woman would be chic.

One ultimate comment on clothing's adultification of
children and infantilization of adults is the recent popularity of bridal gowns that are copies of their wearers'
christening costume. A current bathing-suit style is modeled after a diaper and held together by teething rings or
safety pins.

The brassiere used to be a token of impending woman-
hood, but today a bosomless seven- or eight-year-old may
be encouraged to wear a training, or starter, pre-bra bra.
The same girl might already be wearing curlers to bed.
Before they were thirteen, 70 percent of the subscribers to
the official Girl Scout magazine used lipstick, 73 percent
wore nail polish, and 77 percent had a permanent.[28]
Readers of the magazine are probably more conservative
than many of their contemporaries, who are already too
sophisticated for lipstick but wear considerable eye makeup. Even a youthful sensibility can respond to the symbolism of an iris surrounded by firm long lashes and shad-
owed eyelids.

Boys used to wear short pants before making the jump

to knickers and reached the moment of truth when eligible for long pants. Today, there is practically no intermediate step between diapers and long pants. Boys once graduated from hip to mid-calf length coats, but now father and son wear the same mid-thigh coat. Youths formerly wore caps until they were ready for adult hats, but even seven- and eight-year-olds now sport fedoras. Many boys even smell as sweet as their fathers. New York fifth-grader Anthony Moreno revealed that "I use Score, the hair jelly, and Command, in spray form."[29] Interviewed at a Madison Avenue barber shop while Anthony was having his hair styled, his mother added that the boy also uses cologne. Pebbles, his favorite scent, is a junior edition of Gravel.

Clothing's ability to separate boys from men began to vanish in the 1940's. The costume of a contemporary lad hardly differs from his father's, especially since President Kennedy. Although a conservative dresser, Mr. Kennedy's youth and stress on physical fitness helped men want to look young. The teen market now sets the pace for the whole men's clothing industry.

Boys and girls have largely been deprived of their former awareness that clothing and appearance bound different stages in life. The people in their environment look alike, almost regardless of age. Boys' and girls' ability to develop fantasies about and rehearse the next steps in their development is being undercut by the near-elimination of the stages of life symbolized by appearance.

The day of total elimination is being hastened by the recent popularity of clothing that can be worn by young and old of either sex. A father who had carefully treasured his World War II sailor's watch cap and Navy pea coat may now find his wife, son, and daughter arguing over who might wear them. A ribbed undershirt can be worn by father and son and becomes a poor-boy sweater on mother and daughter. A double-breasted coat or blazer with brass buttons and military tailoring can do similar quadruple duty in a family.

As the male-female and adult-child delineation of clothing gets to be more a matter of size and proportion than cost or style, some obvious advantages will result. Hand-me-downs may become chic. The whole family can shop together for the same item of clothing because every member may ultimately wear it. Closet space will becomes less urgent. And the Sears Roebuck catalog will become shorter and lighter, if less interesting.

As children have been losing the identity and visibility once provided by clothing, they have also become less visible as subjects of fiction, in spite of Holden Caulfield's great popularity.[30] Influential novels like *Lord of the Flies* present children as monsters who seem to have been born with the innocence of a 35-year-old. Such children represent extreme statements of a continuing decline in the differences between age groups. Mass media and biographies in popular magazines stress that many a young person comes into the world practically ready to function as an adult. Some adults who have achieved prominence, perhaps with the wisdom of hindsight, seem to have been adults while they were very young. Hildegarde's ability to hum a whole aria at the age of eighteen months and Paderewski's identification of the child Liberace's musical talent are typical of widely publicized prematurity.

Administrative policies of some school systems help to diminish the student's awareness of epochs in his life. The thin ceremonies surrounding completion of the first six grades contribute to a blurring of benchmarks. Completion of the sixth grade seldom occurs simultaneously with the child's biological maturity, so that the school benchmark has become less important. Before the junior high school became so ubiquitous, the double milestone of graduation from elementary school and onset of puberty helped reinforce a young person's feeling that the community was helping him move from one important stage of life to the next. With so many young people going to college, even graduation from high school has been downgraded. The new name for the "closing exercises" that mark the completion of sixth grade and junior high school suggests their triviality, in contrast to the more elaborate graduation exercises that celebrated the end of eight years of schooling. On the college campus, the rituals surrounding acceptance of new members by fraternities have diminished since 1945, because the GI students were impatient with what they regarded as juvenile hazing tactics and the antics of Hell Week.

In addition to changes in appearance, clothing, and educational benchmarks, western civilization had established a track of psychosexual development that arose from the interplay between the child's pattern of accepting things and the culture's way of giving them. The psychology of Freud can be viewed as a study of what happens when an infantile wish comes up against prohibitions represented by parents who speak for the social system. Now that the imprintings left by society and parents on children are no longer constant, the track of psychosexual progress has lost many of its boundaries.

The markers that once set off the years between seven and twelve have been leveled by bombardment with stimuli that call attention to the opposite sex. During this period, there was traditionally a decline in instinctual interests and biological drives, as fantasy is replaced by fact-finding and acquisition of skills.[31] Although data from other cultures suggest that the latency period is not universal, it has been part of western civilization for long enough to have possible residual biological effects. Encouragement of contact with the opposite sex during latency may have awkward consequences because many such children are not fully ready for such contact.

Some implications of lowering the age at which sexual expression is approved by a society are suggested by Arnold Toynbee's belief that the western world's creativity was related to its ability to postpone the sexual interests of young people while they concentrate on acquiring knowledge. Although it is difficult, in our emancipated day, to accept Unwin's thesis that the intellectual vitality of nonliterate cultures is proportional to the restrictions they impose on premarital sex activity, it has not been disproven.[32]

In the past, sexual interests began to find socially approved outlets around adolescence, with maturation of the glands of internal secretion that are related to the reproductive system. An adolescent became aware of the opposite sex just about the time his body could respond. The sexual interest that was dormant during latency used to assert itself by the dating years, when there was a healthy overlapping of readiness, opportunity, and interest.

Many non-literate societies went to great lengths to create opportunities for privacy and avoid undue excitation during the years from childhood to adolescence. One goal of such procedures was to minimize the possibility that children would be overwhelmed by too much sexual stimulation. Our own social acceleration may be compared to a fuse box without enough fuses for its electrical load. There are children of nine who have a separate telephone and even telephone numbers. Some junior high school students exchange rings and play husband and wife, and there are parents who are unhappy if their children of thirteen do not go steady. Many a youngster of eleven or twelve prefers to have parties in the absence of his parents, who often obligingly leave rather than harm the child's status by remaining.

Parents' anxiety about advancing their children to the next age level is reinforced by widespread use of terms like preschooler, prepube, preadolescent, subadolescent, pre-teen. Dean Martin's nine-year-old daughter wears "pre-subteen bell-bottom trousers."[33] Concern about the allegro tempo of children's social development has become so widespread that the newspaper with the country's largest circulation has asked, "Is Childhood Old-Fashioned?"[34] The question was answered affirmatively by the president of the Westport P.T.A.: "When this trend toward early dating and socializing began, perhaps the parents didn't see the implications. They thought it was harmless and cute. We now see that if the children have all these experiences at ten or eleven, there is little left for them when they are teen-agers except to engage in activities which all our society disapproves of." Girls are growing older sooner, all the time. As one parent said, "My daughter is eleven going on seventeen." The relaxation of parental controls can be confusing to children, who often need assurance that their own inner controls will be reinforced by caveats from parents who represent society.

During World War II, society sped up the movement of adolescents into young adulthood. The trend has continued into the present, with a continual lowering of the age at which teen-agers enter young adulthood. Mobility and privacy are available to the three-fourths of high school juniors and seniors who have drivers' licenses, most of whom have access to a car.

Mass media help to flood young people with adult experiences and contribute pressure to develop relationships with the opposite sex before it is Too Late. Is there any reason to be concerned that marriage is increasingly regarded as part of adolescence rather than its termination? Women who divorce marry an average of two years before those whose marriages continue. The divorce rate of women married between fifteen and nineteen is three to four times greater than that of any other age group. Youthful

marriages are often being terminated because the participants cannot cope with one another. For some, marriage
is a banquet at which the dessert was served first.

Many a youthful marriage has ended unpleasantly because its principal attraction to a couple was a special
status as one of the few remaining rites of passage, a ritual
that clearly identifies its participants as adults. Young
people who have been deprived of other rites by parents
and community can make their own decision to participate in marriage, but divorce may result after the novelty
of the new status begins to wear off. Premature pressure to
make other decisions may trouble some of the young people who do not marry early. A substantial number may
experience subclinical symptoms and seek relief in antiso-
cial behavior, which brings its own attendant problems.[35]
The young people may "mature out" of such deviant behavior only when they feel less threatened by society's
demands.

Our society has not yet established guidelines for its
members' accelerated sexual and social development and
many never become aware of the experiences with which
they are uniquely equipped to cope at each stage of life.
Perhaps even more tragic than the young adults who by-
passed a significant transition are the middle-aged men
and women who, like septuagenarian Jack Benny, are forever 39. Clothing, cosmetics, hair dye, and sun lamps help
to camouflage their shame at growing old and their belief
that the only desirable stage of life is youth. Slogans help
to extend the conspiracy to make youth last a lifetime.
The plot is reinforced by television commercials, which
concentrate on Young Actives, under twenty-five, who appear to go underground until they become Lovable
Grandparents at sixty.

We can profit from Thomas Mann's parable of *Death in
Venice*. Gustave von Aschenbach heeds the advice of a barber who assures him that he has a "right" to his natural

hair color ("permit me to restore what belongs to you") and makes his eyes look larger, lips fuller, eyebrows arch, and facial lines disappear ("we are all as old as we feel").[36] By thus abandoning the humanism, e.g., acceptance of the cycles of life, that has made him a famous writer, Aschenbach is building a sarcophagus in this city of palaces, so illusory that they are built not on sand but on water. Among the many things that Mann is telling us in this greatest of all long stories is that an inability to accept one's age is itself a profound illness.

As a result of such emphases in American culture, parents, teachers, and other authority figures have largely lost their ability to identify age-graded levels of emotional readiness and to convey appropriate preparation and instruction with naturalness and gentleness. Plato's remark that each of us is at once older, younger, and his actual age was never as true as it is today. The decline of age-graded experience reflects the fragmentation of our mass society, in which the component parts have only a tenuous connection with each other.

9

the seventh veil

Salome's taking off of each veil revealed another aspect of herself, and a look at each dimension of our social milieu can clarify a different facet of the style of life of the New People. Just as removal of Salome's seventh veil revealed the total of all that had been exposed by each previous covering, an examination of sexual behavior is one way of understanding the many changes in sexual identity and social role that have occurred since World War II. How a person behaves in a sexual relationship is a result of how he views himself, his partner, and their mutual roles. Bedrooms accurately reflect what is happening in other rooms in the house of society.

Love
in Runes

We are moving toward the permissiveness, non-mystery, equalitarianism between men and women, and early sex interest that already exist in Denmark, and a comparison of the two countries provides some clues to future levels of sexual behavior in America. The reputation of Scandinavian countries for permissiveness is closely linked to legislative measures like the legalizing of homosexuality and abortion.[1] Such laws date from the 1940's, but reflect attitudes that have evolved there over the last half-century. Young Danes give considerable sanction to premarital coitus and the desire to meet peer standards is an important motive for sexual activity.[2]

Denmark has the third highest population density in Europe, insuring considerable opportunity for contact between men and women. Although the relatively large size and small population of Sweden and Norway provide fewer opportunities for sexual contact, sexual patterns in the Scandinavian countries appear to be fairly similar.[3] A scale of attitudes toward sexual permissiveness and a questionnaire dealing with sexual behavior were administered to samples of male and female students at a university in (a) the intermountain region of the United States that has a predominantly Mormon student body; (b) the midwest; and (c) Denmark.[4] The Danish students had the highest scores on permissiveness and the most accepting attitudes toward premarital coitus and premarital pregnancy. The Danes were more liberal than the midwesterners, who in turn were significantly more open-minded than students from the intermountain area.

When the students were asked about the length of acquaintanceship that would be appropriate for sexual intimacy, the Danes favored the shortest and the intermountain group recommended the longest time spans for various degrees of intimacy, with the midwestern sample again occupying the intermediate position. Male students in all three cultures tended to have more permissive attitudes than females, although the difference was smallest in Denmark.

Information was available, for each student, on attitudes as well as actual premarital coital activity, and the relationship could be expressed as a ratio of those endorsing premarital sex to the number experiencing it. A ratio greater than 1 suggests that more students approved than experienced premarital coitus, less than 1 that fewer students approve than have premarital relations. The ratios for the three groups are:

SAMPLE	MALES	FEMALES
Danish	1.47	1.35
Midwestern	.92	.82
Intermountain	.59	.33

More Danes expressed approval of premarital coitus than experienced it. But the reverse was true for the midwesterners and was even more so for the intermountain students. A similar pattern for both sexes represents additional evidence that the ratios reflect real cultural differences. It would seem that the less permissive a culture, the greater is the likelihood that persons who disapprove of premarital coitus will nevertheless have engaged in it. The more permissive a culture, the greater is its proportion of persons who approve of premarital coitus but have not experienced it. Median age at the time of the first intercourse tended to be lower and premarital petting was more frequent in the less permissive cultures. In spite of more emancipated attitudes, Danish students start petting and initial coital relationships at a later age than Americans.

Another comparison comes from a report on the sexual behavior of Danish women which was published in the same year as the Kinsey volume on women.[5] Although the attitudes of Danish women toward sex were far more permissive than their American counterparts, the former had substantially fewer coitions per month than the comparable American sample. There appears every reason to believe that Americans have more coital activity than Danes, although the latter's attitudes are much more permissive.

Why should people with a liberal outlook have less sex

than those with conservative viewpoints? One reason could be that American attitudes toward sex included ambivalence and tension that made it opaque, forbidden, and secretly prized. Sex as forbidden fruit could be attractive, by operation of the Godiva Principle. Contrariwise, the relative absence of ambivalence and tension in Denmark may have led to taking sex for granted, with a resultant diminution in actual sexual behavior.

It is also necessary to consider factors like the availability of sexual partners, economic and housing conditions, the occasions and circumstances in which sexual intercourse is possible or appropriate, national levels of activity-passivity, and similar aspects of social life. In spite of such caveats, countries with a rigid culture and repressive religion (e.g., Presbyterianism in Scotland) generally have a high level of sexual activity. Scandinavians represent the most conspicuous western example of an emancipated culture, and there seems little doubt about their comparative sexual inactivity.

It should also be possible to demonstrate a decline in the frequency of sexual intercourse in Denmark, parallel with the development of permissive attitudes. Although modern survey techniques did not exist a half-century ago, trends in the incidence of coition in Denmark can be approximated by a study of the venereal disease rate, which should be especially sensitive to non-marital sex. Such data may be regarded with confidence in Denmark, where one laboratory conducts all serological testing and venereal disease is reportable under law. Except for participation in the worldwide increase during war, Denmark has had a steady drop in gonorrhea and syphilis over the last half-century, a decline that can be extrapolated to suggest less sexual activity as the country's attitudes toward sex became more emancipated.[6]

Although we do not have any substantial post-Kinsey data on the incidence of sexual activity in this country, we can speculate that as Americans develop more liberal attitudes, they will not necessarily behave more permissively. Paradoxically, discussing sex and having information about it do not necessarily influence actual sexual behavior. College students in California, Minnesota, and Indiana were questioned about their beliefs and behavior before and after a semester devoted to discussion of sex.[7] By the semester's end, attitudes were more tolerant and understanding but there was no change in the students' sexual behavior. Less than one-tenth of a New York State sample of high school and college students with permissive attitudes toward premarital intercourse had actually engaged in it.[8] Columbia University's guidance director noted that most of the students were not achieving much sexual expression, although 83 percent of them believed in premarital sexual intercourse.[9]

In America as in Denmark, permissive attitudes do not mean permissive behavior. The campus orgies that are regularly denounced in mass media are simply not occurring to any significant extent. Several independent studies have reported that a minority (20–25%) of college girls are non-virgins and a far smaller proportion (2–3%) are promiscuous.[10] All available evidence suggests that these proportions have been fairly constant since the 1920's and that there has been an acceptance and consolidation of attitudes toward sex in the last 40 years. Worrying about the alleged promiscuity of youth may titillate some older people but the liberation of sexual attitudes and conversational freedom do not necessarily imply behavioral changes. Inhibition and cautiousness still characterize the behavior of most college students.

Even teen-agers may be engaging in less sexual intercourse than is commonly believed. Frequently cited as "proof" of the growing incidence of teen-age sexual activity is the increase in teen-age illegitimacy. It would seem, however, that disproportionate publicity has been given younger unwed mothers. Between 1938 and 1957, females under the age of 20 had a *smaller* percentage of increase in illegitimacy than any other age group. Between 1957 and 1963, the greatest percentage increases in illegitimacy were for women over 20, while the teen-age rate *decreased.*[11]

Illegitimacy is not running rampant among teen-agers, although their attitudes are becoming more liberal. Additional evidence of an inverse relationship between sexual attitudes and behavior is provided by a comparison of interview data with the findings of Kinsey and his associates. Roper and other polls conducted at the same time as the Kinsey interviews suggest that persons of low socioeconomic status are more likely to express disapproval of extramarital intercourse than the middle or upper classes.[12] Yet male Kinsey interviewees with a grade-school level of education engaged in 10.6 times as much extramarital intercourse as college men, with the high school group occupying an intermediate position.

In sex it seems relatively easy to "go away a little closer" and adapt to an incompatibility between attitudes and behavior: those who do, say they don't; those who don't, say they do. Those who coo, don't bill and those who bill, coo less.

The Troubadour's
Farewell

The comparison with Denmark underscores the vast importance of cultural factors in modifying biological forces. War, depression, or social change may catalyze, modify, or mask some determinants of sexual behavior. Attitudes of contemporary middle-class Americans who enjoy "black novels" are quite different from those of the ruling-class Provençals who were exposed to troubadour lyric poetry and romantic gallantry.

People who live under the threat of imminent death or disaster may engage in more sex than under ordinary circumstances, like the men and women in the *Decameron* distracting themselves by revelry in a large country house during the plague.[13] An urgently felt danger may enhance sex by adding a dimension of guilt, but one difference between the Black Death and today's problems is the plague's visibility as it killed one-fourth of Europe's population between 1348 and 1350. We become so little exercised about the less tangible problems of our day that one experienced discussion leader who talked to many groups of young people concluded that they respond to themes of war and death with ". . . always a shrug of the shoulders."[14]

Our comparative diffidence toward basic problems contrasts with the growing importance of sex in advertising and mass media, which probably drains off much libidinal energy that formerly found outlets in sexual activity. Paradoxically, our society's near-satiation with sex may lead to a decline in its direct expression, as in the classical example of the *Thousand and One Nights*. The Sultan Shahriyar had a policy of killing every woman with whom he spent a night of love, so that Scheherezade knew she was to die on the morning after her bridal night. But she told so interesting a story to the Sultan that he wanted her to finish it on the following night. She would always stop her tale at its most provocative moment. For a thousand nights, stories about love were so gratifying to the Sultan that he fell asleep every morning fully satisfied, but without having had intercourse. The Sultan's satiation gives the *Thousand and One Nights* a special relevance for the many American homes in which the condition of a television tube is often more important than the functioning of a fallopian tube.

Satiation can involve both the underlying drive and specific expressions of sexual appetites.[15] The underlying drive, which Freud regarded as constant and described as libido, is biological although its outlets are influenced by social and cultural factors. Several lines of evidence suggest that many young people who date early, go steady, make love during the dating years, and are subject to a continuing barrage of sexual stimuli from mass media, may lose interest in sex at a relatively early age. The Godiva Principle implies that persons who begin dating later, do not go steady as adolescents, eschew love-making on dates, and are uninvolved in popular culture, would maintain a very substantial level of sexual activity in later life. A careful study of the latter group concluded that its members actually do engage in a very high level of sexual activity as adults.[16]

Growing up in a repressive situation may, ironically enough, have contributed to interest in the opposite sex being sustained for longer than is likely under current conditions of sexual hyperstimulation of the young. As libido becomes more diffuse, any one source of its gratification tends to become less fulfilling. Traditional procedures for romantic courtship almost insured its taking place on an intense emotional level that helped to give its participants the energy to play their parts. It provided mystery and an atmosphere conducive to later sexual expression, as in a story told about Victor Hugo, who was addressing the French Senate in his eightieth year. "It is as difficult for a man of my years to address this august body as it is for me to make love three—no, four times in a single afternoon," he remarked. One reason Hugo could maintain such a high level of activity was his society, which was intensely committed to the romantic ethos of which the writer was such a splendid example.

It would be surprising if many young people growing up in today's America will become sexually active octogenarians. Our comparison with Denmark suggests that sexual activity is likely to start earlier and be more frequent when it has an oppositional quality, and in contemporary America it hardly possesses this dimension. One reason for the Kinsey finding that people who start young generally remain sexually active for long periods of time could be that his older interviewees had grown up in the relatively repressive America of the late nineteenth century.

It is likely that a number of the Kinsey interviewees had engaged in sexual activity because its connotations were enhanced by romantic ideology, but contemporary men and women find it comparatively difficult to respond to romance. When a sample of adult men and women was asked, "Who or what comes to mind when you think of romance?," 24 percent of the men and 21 percent of the women could not answer the question at all.[17] The largest single response was related to foreign locales. Alienation from others emerges clearly in our inability to project a romantic relationship on the screen of fantasy. One possible reason for selecting a place rather than a person is that a place cannot reject anybody, although a person can. Over one-fifth of the respondents, given an opportunity to write the script for a dream, could not even provide a cast of characters.

A country's level of sexual activity reflects externals of social life as well as attitudes toward romance, and the French could have developed their reputation for being great lovers because their living-room furniture was so uncomfortable. Perhaps we are making love less frequently because of our bedroom furniture, now that fewer Americans are likely to be sleeping in a double bed. Anything that facilitates a couple's spending time in bed is likely to encourage sexual intercourse. When Mussolini wanted to increase the birth rate of Italian colonists in Libya, he arranged for the central utilities office to switch off all electric lights early every evening—and the birth rate jumped. In several different communities, the introduction of central heating was uniformly followed by a decline both in sexual intercourse and the birth rate, because of the lesser proximity of husband and wife in bed.[18] The greatest number of conceptions during a year occur during winter and the fewest in summer. If we regard the average number of conceptions per month in the United States as 100, August would have the fewest (92.4) and January the most (108.6).[19]

We could expect the American shift from double to twin beds to lead to a decline in proximity and sexual contact. The change is revealing because of the bed's relationship to satisfaction of deep personality needs, although a person seldom becomes aware of the security and refuge provided by his bed until he experiences difficulty in relaxing when sleeping away from home.

During the early 1940's, 87 percent of American families had a double bed, but ten years later the proportion had dropped to 68 percent. The majority of people currently buying bedroom furniture select twin beds, although they are usually twice as expensive as one double bed.[20] If bedrooms were larger, even more people would buy twins, especially since the night table that separates them averages two feet in width. We do not know the proportion of husbands and wives in separate bedrooms, but there is reason to believe that their number has increased steadily over the last twenty years.

A bedroom smaller than 12' x 17' often has swing twin beds, consisting of two beds using the same headboard. Near-acrobatic agility is required to make up swing twins because each must be pulled away from the headboard. Another disadvantage is that they are more likely to clank and rattle than a double bed. A twin-bedded couple that wishes to be close to one another will almost inevitably end up in the space between the beds, with torn bedsheets and bruised bodies and sensibilities among the resulting inconveniences. The space between the swing twins often seems to function like the plank that separated bundling New England couples.

Lack of interest in being close to a spouse is a major reason for the growing popularity of the super-size double bed in the last decade.[21] Many couples have been abandoning the traditional 54″ width in favor of 60″ ("queen-size"), 78″ ("king-size"), and even 96″ ("sultan"). Consumer studies have concluded that over three-fifths of the super-sizes are bought because the increased space makes greater distance possible between husband and wife. *Noli me tangere* could be the motto of many a super-size purchaser.

Most of the other purchasers are responding to the high status connotation of the super-size. Although a number of actors and actresses have been photographed in poses connoting the sex-playground aspects of their big beds, they are not necessarily scenes of more or more varied sex than the traditional double bed. One handsome "bachelor" star relishes telling interviewers about his "sultan" bed but does not mention that the only erection associated with it is the hydraulic pump that raises the bed three feet above the ground.

A hotel's trappings of change and luxury would seem to make it one place where couples might enjoy a double bed. But a husband and wife will be given a room with twin beds unless they specifically ask for a double. It is understandable that hotels catering to conventions and businessmen have few doubles, but even motels and family hotels average one double to every four or five twin-bedded rooms. If customers asked for double beds, hotels would have them. The double's being less expensive than a twin-bedded room should provide an additional reason for it to be requested by hotel guests, but it has been steadily decreasing in popularity.

The Age
of Tiresias

One possible gain resulting from women's new leadership could be the ability of some to achieve more satisfying sexual response. The Indiana researchers concluded that peak frequency of orgasm was reached by late adolescence in males but did not occur in women until their thirties.[22] Society's acceleration of girls' interest in sex may help to bridge a gap that has been described as "nature's joke" by making the frequency and age of onset of women's orgasms more compatible with men's.

Any new similarity between the sexual behavior of men and women may reflect deep-rooted correspondences that had previously been masked by cultural stereotypes. The Indiana investigators found that both sexes can achieve orgasm in approximately the same time, and also that the female does not seem to be as slow as had been believed. Another myth punctured by their data was that post-orgasm excitement recedes more slowly in women than men. More recently, Masters and Johnson have suggested that the vaso-congestive and pelvic-genital contraction phenomena which constitute orgasm are quite similar in both men and women.[23]

Wide dissemination of such findings and greater acceptance of women's sexuality are modifying stereotypes about the need for men to initiate psychological and other sexual stimulation of the woman. Helene Deutsch's classic study assumed that "the awakening of the vagina to full sexual functioning is entirely dependent upon the man's activity."[24] Van der Velde cautioned the husband about how he played "this delicate human harp" and Balzac had earlier warned the man not to be an orangutang playing a violin. Balzac rhapsodically compared the man to an orchestra conductor who gradually elicits a response from otherwise muted instruments. Tender was the knight and non-responsive his lady.

Cross-cultural studies have amply demonstrated that the initiative in sexual intercourse is evenly distributed between the sexes.[25] Some popular folklore, however, still deals with the traditional passivity of American women, as in a once popular story. A Cannes policeman who came across a dead woman on the beach went to telephone for a physician. He returned to find a man making love to the woman. This was too much for even the sophisticated gendarme, and he angrily restrained the man. "Stop! That woman is dead!" "My God!" gasped the man, "I thought she was an American."

Such stories would not get a response in our time of Bedwomanship. Men are far less likely to read Balzac and Helene Deutsch than women are to study marriage manuals, which demonstrate remarkable ingenuity in suggesting quasi-military erotic maneuvers for the instruction of women. They are reminiscent of a remark of George Sand: "Last night I had Mérimée; there is not much to him."

Women readers of the manuals may ultimately help to reestablish Tiresias' evaluation of the relative pleasure that men and women derive from sex. On the basis of having been first a man and then a woman, Tiresias estimated that women got nine-tenths and men only one-tenth of love's pleasure. Women who diligently apply the manuals' wisdom may not do quite so well, but will receive instructions detailed enough to embolden the most Timid Wife. After all, a woman who is active and aggressive during the day can hardly be expected to rely on her husband's ministrations at night.

Psychoanalyst Ralph R. Greenson has commented that: "Today I rarely see a woman patient who accepts her frigidity. In fact, most of them demand orgasms and feel they are cheated by their sexual partners if they do not obtain them readily. . . . Today it is the women who complain that their husbands do not seem to be eager for sexual relations."[26] It is not the man but the woman who is increasingly urged toward a regime of cold showers and hard physical exercise.

Typical of many a wife's desire for the ecstasy without the agony are techniques like the "ice-spurred special."[27] The wife brings a plate of ice cubes to her night table for use if the husband responds Too Quickly. She cools his ardor with the ice cubes, and then presumably reestablishes a mood of romantic receptivity. Turning knobs and switching levers have replaced the poetic and rapturous effulgences of the *Kama Sutra* and D. H. Lawrence's warm mysticism.

Manuals also exist for the unmarried girl who needs instructions in how to remove her clothes while turning out lights, etc. Books and articles set forth instructions on how to trap the wary male, in a prose that has all the precision of a cookbook. The goose being cooked is the male, married or unmarried. Judge Woolsey permitted *Ulysses* into the United States in 1933 because, among other reasons, ". . . his locale was Celtic and his season Spring," but it is a Celtic Spring 365 days a year in the writings of our new female predators. Small wonder that a perfume which failed when it was called "Lady" became a success when its name was changed to "Hussy."

Another positive effect of the new climate is a decrease in hypocrisy. For her whole life prior to marriage, a young woman had been urged and exhorted to maintain a stainless-steel virginity, although she was expected to become a woman of passion overnight, through participation in a marriage ceremony. By exposing her to sexual stimulation and information from childhood, society is preparing her to be a better sexual partner, although not necessarily a more romantic wife. The audience of *Luv* laughs when the wife unrolls a chart that records how much sex she has been getting, but it is the nervous laughter of recognition.

"Pious pornography" is gradually overcoming some effects of the years during which such instructional material was regarded as inappropriate for the wife. American women were believed to be so asexual that the second line of Martin Luther's famous advice to married couples was often omitted when the verse was quoted: "A week two/Is the woman's due./Harms neither me nor you./Makes in a year twice fifty-two."

Young women were expected to define limits and specify the prohibitions surrounding their relationships with dates. A girl could hint that the future might bring a change of mind, but her answer was clearly "No!" On a date, American girls often implied that they were reluctantly preventing themselves from being overwhelmed by their attraction to the boys. Their young men would be confident that the urgency of their protestations would be met by equally strong objections from girls.[28]

American men's belief that their girls would reject ardor led to international misunderstanding during World War II. G.I.'s stationed in England who dated local girls often behaved as they had in America, where the girl remained chaste while chased. British girls' protective shyness may have been more appropriate in contacts with their traditionally phlegmatic countrymen than in dates with American servicemen, who expected to be met with words, gestures, and facial expressions communicating humor, regret, and aloofness. Unaware of the artificiality of G.I. aggressiveness, many a British girl who fell in love was tearful and confused when her man was transferred and did not make an effort to remain in contact with her. Since many such girls had become pregnant, the problem came to the attention of American authorities, who ordered a major educational campaign for their troops.[29]

Girls being dated by the sons of World War II veterans have more emancipated attitudes than their mothers.

Many could be taking cues from contemporary actresses
who have been forceful in matters of the heart. In an England recovering from the excesses of the Regency, Har-
riette Wilson had the courage not only to publish a book
about the men with whom she had been intimate but to
ask each one for two hundred pounds *not* to be mentioned
in it. But Zsa Zsa Gabor and Elizabeth Taylor cause little
stir when they publish books about the men who have
provided them with supreme moments.[30] Linda Christian's autobiography takes her from a convent to Errol
Flynn's attempt at seduction: ("We had to part now before it became too late. I hoped that Errol would bring
himself to understand.")[31] She reports on relationships
with stock manipulator Robert Schlesinger, industrialist
"Baby" Pignatari, racing driver Marquis Fon Portago,
and marriage to Tyrone Power and Edmund Purdom.

In our day we are almost more likely to expect buccaneering and candor about romance from a woman than a
man. We admire women who go directly where the heart
leads, regardless of consequence or convention. Julie
Christie spoke frankly to a reporter about a young painter: "He's much more than a mate. I can't really imagine
living without him. I just don't think marriage is compatible with modern living. . . . There's no reason why two
people in love can't live together without marrying and
getting all tied up in little knots." A few months later she
said, "I live . . . with two friends . . . a girl chum and
Don Bessant. . . . I can't understand why people are
offended. . . . If they're shocked, it's just too bad."[32]
Even ten years ago, we might have raised our eyebrows at
such remarks. Women, traditionally the first to condemn
unconventional behavior, seem to be solidly behind the
contemporary women of feeling who are the new playboys
of the western world.

Women's initiative in sex has been greatly enhanced by
the birth control pill and the intrauterine device. They

give the woman an initiative in contraception which had previously been the man's in the substantial proportion of cases where condoms were used.[33] We may speculate that one reason for the current success of women's dresses, coats, and boots of vinyl, in spite of the material's stiffness and non-porousness, could be that a woman in vinyl somewhat resembles a penis sheathed in a condom. The vinyled "shower curtain" or "wet look" woman may be reminding man, on a non-verbal level, that the decision-making power which he formerly had via the condom has shifted to her because of the pill and the IUD.

The pills also make a 60-day menstrual cycle possible and may have the capacity to postpone menopause and extend fertility into later years. A recent best-seller claims to document the thesis that "menopause is a hormone deficiency disease, curable and totally preventable. . . . Every woman . . . can safely live a fully-sexed life for her entire life."[34] Several independent investigations have confirmed the effectiveness of estrogen hormone replacement therapy in helping women to retain youthful skin, vitality, and figure. Such findings contribute to making Tiresias a prophet with honor in our day.

Sex
Nouveau

At the same time that many men are trying to respond to today's hard sell for orgasm, they may have more misgivings about their ability to do so than did their ancestors. Previous generations' attitudes are implicit in a story that originated during the 1930's, and concerned a middle-aged executive. One morning he arrived early at work and found a secretary going through his petty cash drawer. Shocked, he moved to the phone in order to call the police. She begged him not to do so: "Please don't. I'll do anything for you if you don't." "Anything?" he inquired. "Anything," she replied. "Very well. Take off your clothes and lie down on the couch in my office." He also stripped, and tried repeatedly but unsuccessfully to get an erection. After a half-hour he dressed and sighed: "Well, I'll have to call the police." Today the same executive would probably worriedly be consulting Dr. Greenson.

He might also consult a marriage manual, which could only intensify his anxiety. The manuals may embolden women readers, but are likely to make husbands aware of inadequacies in comparison with norms described in elaborate detail. Some men have undoubtedly reinforced paranoid or Puritan-linked fears of the Threatening Woman by reading what was expected of them in the marriage bed. American men's anxiety about sexual norms has surely become more acute since the early 1920's, when Scott Fitzgerald was sufficiently concerned about the inadequate size of his penis to seek reassurance from Ernest Hemingway.[35] Few men are lucky enough to have a thoughtful friend like Hemingway, who gave Fitzgerald confidence by a lecture on anatomy and techniques and took him to study nude statues at the Louvre.

In recent years, there has been great enthusiasm for humor which questions the size of American males' sex organs. A typical story deals with a midwestern contraceptive manufacturer who received a Russian order for one hundred million condoms, all to be twelve inches long. The manufacturer consulted a State Department official, who advised him: "You can fill their order, but let's use the situation for some psychological warfare. Label them all 'medium.' "

One way in which some husbands are coping with anxiety about their sex organs is suggested by the recent American popularity of several versions of a venerable English limerick:

A nancy boy once in Khartoum
Took a Lesbian up to his room.
As he switched off the light
She said "Let's get this right,
Who does what and with which and to whom?"

Many jokes have expressed the same theme, especially during the last ten years. The popularity of the theme reflects a great increase in the use of neuter organs—the mouth and anus—in sexual activity.

There are no comparative data that enable us to say with certainty that there is more anal and oral sex than in previous generations, but such a conclusion is suggested by several independent kinds of evidence. The most thorough early study of marital sex concluded that only eight percent of the husbands engaged in any oral activity, but nineteen years later, Kinsey reported mouth-genital contact in the sex history of three-fifths of his sample of men.[36]

Decreasing interest in coitus may find some echo in the changing demands of men who visit prostitutes. A quarter-century ago, the typical customer wanted coitus. Perhaps one or two percent wanted fellatio, and a brothel with twenty prostitutes might have one who performed fellatio or oral stimulation as a prelude to coitus ("half and half"). Today, however, approximately four-fifths of the customers want fellatio.[37] Even though we do not know the relationship between preferences of prostitutes' customers and other men, oragenital sex seems to be meeting needs of a substantial part of the population. Fellatio's new popularity suggests an increased passivity and fear of the vagina in many men. Their decreased forcefulness also emerges in the growing popularity of men's use of the fatalistically passive verb "to get laid" to describe sexual intercourse. A generation ago, the definitive dictionary of American sexual slang did not even mention the phrase, and men were far more likely to use an active verb.[38] Recent years have also witnessed enthusiasm for slang that conveys diminutive connotations for the penis (teenie-weenie; pin; peanut).

One of the most popular new dances of non-contact is the Gobble, which is a charade of oral sex. The man swings low, circles the woman's waist without touching her, and darts his tongue toward her hips. He leans back as she pushes her hips forward. She then bends low and it is her turn to move down toward him.

Difficulties in making the assertion represented by an erection and sustaining it in intercourse have probably been compounded in recent years by counter-Oedipal guilt. Little more than a decade ago, *Lolita* would have been a bizarre improbability, since May-December relationships were regarded as vaguely improper. Romance between aging Ezio Pinza and Mary Martin in *South Pacific* was probably somewhat acceptable because she was identified with "My Heart Belongs to Daddy." A man with a wife of forty or fifty who looks like a teen-ager may experience counter-Oedipal guilt which eases his acceptance of fellatio.

Relationships between youthful women and older men constitute themes of recent popular humor. One story deals with a seventeen-year-old girl in bed with a sixty-five-year-old man. As he reached for a condom, she said, "That won't be necessary. I take pills." The man replied, "I'll use it anyhow; the moisture is bad for my arthritis." The listener does not know if the girl is really using pills or thinks that the man is impotent. She is expressing age-graded expectations that are appropriate for her role in today's culture, and so is the man, but he displaces and denies his declining sexual powers by calling attention to the arthritis that is associated with old age. The two groups in the population that repeat the story most enthusiastically are teen-age girls and older men. Girls enjoy the aggressiveness and superiority of its heroine and men identify with defensiveness and passivity. Reversal of traditional sex roles, which is implicit in the story, could be one important reason for fellatio's appeal to both sexes.

Women as well as men are finding that oral sex meets their needs. Although oragenitality was known to only eleven percent of a sample of wives in the 1920's, by the 1940's, three-fifths of the younger generation had participated in it.[39] Many women prefer fellatio because it involves less personal commitment and physical contact than coitus. One California woman recently told an interviewer: "I prefer using my mouth on a man's penis to having to get undressed. It's quick, less messy, and it doesn't mean anything to me. If I really like the guy, I'll let him come to a climax. If I don't like him much, I'll stop before he comes." Fellatio appears to be regarded as a less intimate experience than even dorsal-ventral heterosexual intercourse.[40] The 1920's study found practically no anal activity, but one generation later perhaps half the population was finding some degree of erotic satisfaction through anal stimulation.[41]

All available evidence indicates a shift from the use of mouth and anus in forepleasure play to their replacing coitus for many persons. What is the emotional loading of such a change? Instead of being tributary to genital sexuality, the mouth and anus are used to bypass genitality, and replacement of coitus by the use of neutral organs may have profound effects. Coitus permits each sex to reflect complementary roles and use unique and reciprocal organs that are identical in both sexes. But in oral and anal sex, at least one partner has a genderless stimulus or response.

A partner may also experience a weaker orgasm than might occur from coitus. Mouth and anus are pregenital organs which play a part in the process of sexual arousal that heightens tension. This libidinal tension is pleasurable for a relatively short time and was traditionally succeeded by the exciting sensations of genital orgasm. Although individual differences are enormously important in the achievement of sexual satisfaction, the range of tension release achieved by oral and anal intercourse could be less than coitus makes possible.

One positive unanticipated consequence of increased use of neuter organs is an insight into the treatment of homosexuals. Some psychiatrists have been able to move homosexual patients toward heterosexuality by suggesting that they might engage in oral or anal sex with women if they have done so with men. The patient is reassured that the mouth and rectum are similar in men and women. Once the patient can begin to contemplate such activity with a woman, he may ultimately engage in coitus with her.[42] The new orality and anality also, of course, express our greater freedom, increased leisure, and greater regard for sex as play. The growing use of neuter organs, however, may be related to a blurring of feelings of personal identity. It is possible that devaluation of craftsmanship due to automation and the loss in significance of work are contributing to an erosion of personal identity that makes coitus too demanding for some people.

Current preferences for neuter organs are reflected in slang. A generation ago, two of the most ferocious insults possible were to call a person by slang terms suggesting that he engaged in either fellatio or cunnilingus. No western European language has a verbal equivalent for the American expressions, which were once likely to lead to a fight even when said in jest. Our former disapproving attitudes toward non-coital sex can be inferred from a story that used to elicit uneasy laughter from generations of first-year law students. A prosecutor had prepared an airtight case against a defendant accused of rape. After presenting a series of witnesses in an overwhelmingly convincing display of evidence, the judge acquitted the defendant. The outraged prosecutor spluttered, "Why, your honor, why?" "The two cases just before yours were for sodomy," the judge replied. "Your man at least was trying to do the right thing." We no longer share the judge's moralistic attitude, but can be concerned that oral and anal sex may reinforce feelings of neutering. Such consequences are independent of another possible interpretation of orality and anality that would stress their regressive elements.

Our interest in neuter organs may help to explain the results of one study of "popular" sex responses on the Rorschach ink blot test, which concluded that there was more agreement than disagreement in the way both sexes selected sex stimuli on the ink blots.[43] Men and women shared eleven "popular" sex responses, the men establishing thirteen and the women fifteen such responses.

Current trends toward neutering were predicted by poets like Wordsworth and e. e. cummings. Philosophers like Norman O. Brown have been optimistic about the effects of man's functioning at a non-repressed level of development and others have sung the virtues of a utopia without repressions and where there is freedom to be polymorphous perverse. The popularity of oral and anal sex suggests that this aspect of the millennium may have already arrived.

Our speculations on the effects of using neuter organs make no assumption about what is natural or normal in sex. Practically any variation in sex behavior is, of course, consistent with health and satisfaction. We also seek not to exaggerate the importance of sex, to impute feelings of guilt about any practices, or to return to the deliberate hypocrisies of Victoriana. As in a number of other effects of depolarization, the use of neuter organs could serve to reinforce as well as reflect underlying trends.

Pleasure versus
Propagation Sex

Advances in contraceptive techniques should be making it easier for men and women to combine the tender with the sensual and cope with the problems which arose from the separation of propagation from pleasure sex.[44] Some of our current difficulties still derive from the lack of a model for sexual activity that is conducted for non-procreative purposes.

It is possible that some Americans are also losing their model for procreative sex. Both the marriage rate and age composition of the female population are favorable to a higher level of fertility than actually exists.[45] Our birth rate has declined continuously for ten years. The 3,767,-000 births in 1965 represented the smallest annual total since 1951, and a 24 percent decline since 1957. Although predicting the birth rate with complete confidence is impossible, one of the most thorough investigations of American fertility patterns has seen a downward trend for the next twenty years.[46]

Dr. René DuBos has suggested that Americans will soon be seeking values to substitute for those previously provided by offspring. A second car may take the place of a third or fourth child in many homes. The proportion of Americans regarding four or more children as the "ideal" number declined from 49 percent in 1945 to 35 percent in 1966, according to a Gallup poll. The drop in our birth rate also involves the draft, unemployment among young people, and a growing demand for higher education, which may discourage early marriage and childbearing. A population shift from rural to urban areas and from large, stable families to smaller, movable families is also a factor along with greater acceptability of birth control. But another reason may be that asserting one's sex role, implicit in the decision to have a child, is more difficult when so much of the personal and social environment reflects depolarization and neuterization.

The decision to have fewer children may represent one way in which some people respond to confused sex roles. Others may run away into a reaction formation, i.e., an excess of sexual activity. Relatively few are likely to move toward homosexuality, which is not likely to be fostered by our society's blurred sexual identification. Societies with little or no homosexuality, like the Arapesh, Lepcha, and Mundugumor, have blurred goals of masculinity and femininity.

Even though homosexuality is not a single clinical entity but a symptom with different meanings, there would seem to be less occasion for it when masculinity and femininity are not idealized values. Children whose parents' gender is ambiguous will probably demonstrate decreased identification with the parent of the same sex and lesser likelihood of becoming homosexuals.[47] Homosexuality resulting from rebellion against the repressions of an antisexual society is also less likely to be found in our libidinized America.

Homosexuals really may be fewer at the very time that they seem to be becoming more numerous. What could be the illusion of numbers may reflect more tolerant attitudes which encourage many homosexuals to identify themselves, increased sympathy of mass media, and the missionary activity of homophile organizations. The Indiana researchers estimated that about 4 percent of men and 2 percent of women are exclusively homosexual, but these proportions may actually have dwindled somewhat over the last twenty years.

Homosexuality could also be declining because of the mannish aspects of women's appearance. A fashionable woman of today could sport a hard, boyish Vidal Sassoon haircut and a crash helmet, with a chin-strap framing her colorless face. Her pants suit would minimize the display of breasts and buttocks. A relationship with such a woman could displace or sublimate homosexual impulses, especially now that oral and anal sex are achieving heterosexual popularity.

And with the hand on a rotating hip the starting position for the frug, some of the more flamboyant gestures of the male homosexual are being taken from him. At just about the same time, the gaiety and genital and hip display of modern men's clothes and their use of perfume have provided additional avenues of homosexual sublimation for the "straight" man. Heterosexual and homosexual represent a far less differentiated choice than they did a generation ago.

Another response to ambiguous sexual identification may be an acting out of a depolarized sex by persons who engage in both heterosexual and homosexual activity. There is reason to suspect an increase in the amount of bisexuality or "switch-hitting" or "AC-DC" sex, with an estimated 14 to 16 percent of American men now responding to either males or females.[48] We can only hope that men and women of the future will have the sangfroid of Joe E. Brown in *Some Like It Hot*. When told that the woman he loves is really a man, he unabashedly replies, "Well, nobody's perfect."

The Prudent
Amorists

One reason for the thread of neutering that runs through the fabric of our time is the dissociation among mind, body, and emotions in response to sex. One pre-jet but still current American story deals with the man and woman who met in the club car of a transcontinental train, had a few drinks, and retired to the man's compartment. By the time he awoke on the following morning, the woman had gone. The man went to the dining car for breakfast and was delighted to see his companion of the previous night. "Hello, honey," he said as he slid into the seat opposite her. She indignantly snapped, "I beg your pardon, but since when does sexual intercourse constitute a formal introduction?" Such separation of emotional closeness from physical gratification suggests one way in which sex can be compartmentalized. For some new Puritans, sex is a duty and an injunction to be lived up to; for others it is prudent.

One reflection of our sexual fractionation is the enormous popularity of the two magazines most directly concerned with impersonal sex: *Confidential* and *Playboy*. In its heyday, *Confidential* dealt primarily with the sexual activities of the famous and did less to provide a sexual catharsis for readers than to deplete and enervate them. *Confidential*'s documentation of mindless and emotionless sex attracted many Americans who were confused about their sexual identity.

The magazine presented gossip about sex; a reader learned something other people didn't know. If he felt somehow dissatisfied with his sexual identity, what could better reinforce such dissatisfaction than having inside information on the confused sexual identity of the famous?[49] Stories about celebrities in ambiguous sex situations showed readers that their own fantasies might be less unworthy. Impressive documentation of *Confidential*'s broad appeal is provided by its having become the most successful magazine ever published in this country in terms of newsstand sales.

Another reason for its success was the public's desire to think less of contemporary heroes, in response to the same needs that led to the hero's disappearance from the arts. A reader who read about a celebrity's unbuttoned private life in *Confidential* had a leash on him, in revenge for his *hubris.* "I know what you're doing but you're not getting away with it—I know all about your feet of clay."

Although the editors of *Playboy* seem to have some awareness of differences in gender, they present sex as an aspect of leisure to be handled with detachment. The magazine straddles the dichotomy by making sex a pleasant consumption item and the Playmate a servant who represents an infantile ego boost. Probably the only feature differentiating *Playboy* from innumerable similar magazines is its presentation of a fully clothed Playmate who is shown nude on the next page, so that the reader can strip her just by turning a page.

The Playmate's very nudity is non-sexual because her whorish pose is in sharp contrast to the demure, fully clothed appearance at her regular job, e.g., graduate student of Sanskrit. Even though the Playmate looks as if she ought to be available, she turns out to be a pearl unattainable at any price. Readers' fantasies about her are likely to be non-genital and are conveyed by the quip that many young men subscribe to *Playboy* in order to keep abreast of the times. The magazine epitomizes the prudery and thrill-seeking of our time and the guilt with which the latter is spiced because of the former. Almost every issue carries editorials and philosophical musings that try to reassure the reader.

Confidential and *Playboy* represent impressive tributes to the appeal of voyeuristic and uninvolving sex and an archeologist of the future would get more insight into the New People from such modern graffiti than from the official documents that are usually included in time capsules. Any impressions suggested by the magazines would be strengthened by books that ask *What Are You Doing After the Orgy?*[50]

The magazines' popularity is hardly surprising in a country that made burlesque more popular than it ever has been elsewhere. Before World War II, every large city

in America had one or more burlesque theatres, patron-
ized primarily by lower- and middle-class men who came
alone.[51] Other cultures have produced erotically stimulating spectacles that were preludes to more solid pleasures,
but burlesque is unique in providing a visual satisfaction
complete in itself. The frozen-faced strippers would
alternate with comedians whose jokes had the dual theme
of women rejecting men and the probability that something would always interfere with consummation.

Burlesque has made a successful comeback in our frug-
ging and voyeuristic age, and there are now about sixty
theatres devoted to it and many more that show burlesque
and other public stag films. Americans' desire to look
without touching also expresses itself in the popularity of
topless waitresses. There is probably no other country
where such waitresses could go about their business,
confident that men would not even try to touch them.

American homes have proportionately more windows to
space than in any other country with comparable climate.
Our desire to look finds other outlets in the picture windows which began staring out at suburban streets in the
1940's, and led to the glass cages inside which go-go girls
"shake it out" at discotheques.

Peep magazines have flourished during a decade that
saw new popularity for voyeuristic jokes. A representative
story concerns an attractive woman who had been prepared for surgery and was lying nude under a sheet in a
hospital corridor. Three men walked by within a few minutes of one another. Each raised the sheet, looked, and
nodded to the woman. When the fourth man similarly
lifted the sheet, she asked him: "Doctor, when will they
operate on me?" The man replied, "I don't know, lady.
We're only the painters."

Such detached voyeurism leads to anti-sentimentality
and avoiding strong emotions, even in greeting cards.
Greetings that communicate a pleasant if frequently sop-

py sentiment are giving way to clever cards that minimize rather than celebrate an occasion. A sharp reminder of the change is provided by the holiday, birthday, and anniversary "studio cards" which now account for over two-fifths of all greeting-card sales and convey an unconventional, frequently hostile greeting. A typical card to be sent to a sick friend shows a frog on its outer jacket. Above the frog is the legend "Don't tell me." The person receiving and opening the card will find the rest of the legend, "You're gonna croak?"

The boom in studio cards suggests that the simple communication of warmth toward a relative or friend may be as difficult to express in writing as in direct contact. Similar impulses have made the wisecrack a uniquely American form of humor. Wisecracks are often cruel and deny gentleness and feeling, in contrast to the softer, flickering, and subtle wit of other countries.

Our acceptance of psychoanalysis has undoubtedly contributed to the climate. Once we could dissect and explain love in terms of its constituents, we began to think in terms of relationships and defense mechanisms. Falling in love becomes much less spontaneous when people are more evaluative about their own feelings. A person who might once have been embraced with feeling may now be studied at fingertip length.

In a country that finds it so difficult to express emotion, playwrights who seem to have it may develop large followings. Lack of passion in the theatre led to overpraise of an O'Neill who appeared to have it and may be responsible for our overestimation of Archibald MacLeish and Arthur Miller. Even the rhetoric and fustian of *J.B.* and *After the Fall* were hailed extravagantly.

The importance of passion in drama can be seen in the special eminence occupied by the overemphatic and operatic direction of Elia Kazan. His unerring eye for the violently melodramatic, hysterical, and sentimental makes him the last nineteenth-century director. Kazan's heavy emotional theatrical effects and unshaded performances came at just the right time for a theatre starved for passion and the presentation of people confronting one another.

Playwrights who try to present people involved with one another seem unable to achieve this happy end. Their characters, like those in Miller's *Incident at Vichy,* usually emerge not as people but as ambulatory attitudes. Writers' inability to create characters who relate to each other has led to the popularity, by default, of dramatists whose theme is the difficulty of significant involvements. Albee's key subject is not only that the desire for a relationship with someone else is better than not having such an impulse, but also that a connection based on love is not possible. His splendid theatricality, brilliant dialogue, and stage excitement make his themes more palatable to audiences that might otherwise have winced at what he is saying. Tennessee Williams' craft fascinates as it presents characters who, at least once in each play, make tender advances that are doomed.

Although emotional barrenness has characterized the theatre for so long, the situation may be changing. Harold Pinter's *The Lover* and *The Caretaker* suggest the possibility of people making contact with one another, even though they do not succeed. *The Homecoming* appears to be concerned with a prototypical family searching for love and responding to it. Pinter's modification of Albee's basic theme suggests a growing audience interest in emotion, especially since the increasing recognition of Pinter as England's leading playwright. Pinter's "We won't but we might" represents only a small advance from the "We can't" of Albee, but it is a step forward.

Playwrights have stressed how sexual intercourse that draws on mind, body, and emotions and expresses passion is bound up with psychological gratifications. Sex with a

prostitute and as part of an involving emotional relationship is differentiated in connotations and satisfactions
by the thoughts, fantasies, and feelings surrounding the
sex act itself. A pianist who presses the same black note on
the piano with similar pressure to make both G sharp
and A flat reads each of the two notes differently and his
audience also hears the difference. It results from melody,
rhythm, and timbre, from what precedes and follows the
note, and other notes included in a chord.

Any meanings of the sex act similarly depend on its
connotations. Where nothing precedes, accompanies, or
follows the sex act, it will have no significance beyond itself, just as G sharp and A flat are indistinguishable if
each note is not related to any other. Different meanings
may be relevant at different times and not every sex act
needs the tidal-wave qualities celebrated by D. H. Lawrence. As Roger in *Prater Violet* pointed out, ". . . the best
things in my life" have been "good, unexpected lays."[52]

Roger's observation suggests the irrelevance of the
meanings that sex had, when passion reflected its origin in
the Latin verb for suffering. Troubadour passion involved
a state of being in love which was suffered or undergone.
Victorian fantasies about passion were obsessively based
on man's alienation from his body and were accompanied
by grave sexual problems.

George Bernard Shaw summarized the whole Victorian
sexual ethos in his observation that he could not understand how a man and woman could do *that* to each other
in the dark and then face each other in the sunlight over
the breakfast table. We have moved sex into the sunlight,
so that passion can involve a mutual encountering of personalities and constructive identification of the self with
some aspects of the loved one, rather than masochistic
renunciation, suffering, and non-fulfillment. To today's
young people, society's earlier attempts to suppress sex
seem irrational and dishonest. As sex has lost its sacred

character, it has retained few compulsions from the past and is less constrained by promises of the future.[53]

Living is most worth its cost when it includes the enlargement of experience and joyfulness in which each sex explores the other and simultaneously discovers new depths in the self. A genuine I-Thou encounter between a man and woman involves a communion, an exchange, giving and taking. It is a unifying and sharing experience, evocative of creative depths. Awareness of such meanings can help to bridge the gap between sex and passion and lead to relationships in which sex is an authentic and vital experience between human beings.

Patterns of love and sex in America vary not only within a community but on the same street, and even in adjacent apartments in the same building. There is also considerable intra-person variation, and the situation is compounded by the lack of established symbols for the expression of passion. A modern concept of love may build on connotations and fantasies related to meanings that are relevant today. How distant some of these meanings are from romance can be seen in the guidance which many marriage manuals offer the husband suffering from premature ejaculation, who is often advised to develop fantasies about an unpleasant experience, while making love to his wife.

As the husband recalls a disagreeable experience, it is likely that the fantasies of his wife will not be overly romantic. An American woman might well be the contemporary hero of a story told about Gustave Flaubert, who won a bet that he could achieve orgasm in intercourse without disturbing the ash on a cigar he was smoking. Flaubert's detachment may be congenial to the modern wife who studies technocratic prescriptions in the manuals and for whom sex is as lyrically rapturous as assembling an Erector set.

Truly personal and meaningful connotations and fantasies could help reestablish polarization of the sexes. Extensive new knowledge of the self has led to many associations that are humanistic and not based on fear or sanctions. They stem from the unique appositeness of each sex, deal with the present, build on the past, point to the future, and include the many-meaninged irrationality that is part of being human.

Some effects of our lack of passion may be inferred from many incidents in which people saw and heard women being raped and murdered and did not even phone the police. In March 1964 in New York City, Kitty Genovese's screams while being murdered were heard by 38 people, not one of whom responded. Their extraordinary non-response is usually attributed to a desire not to get involved. Why don't people want to be involved with each other? Without the connotations of romantic love, passion has declined. When passion is so unimportant, it is less possible to reach out to another person. As one result of our incapacity for identifying with even one person, there is a lack of compassion for others. Historically, it has not necessarily been true that compassion exists where passion flourishes. But history has amply demonstrated that where there is no passion, there can be no compassion.

Another dimension in the non-response of many citizens to murder and rape reflects the "delighted eye" that is so important to the success of *Confidential, Playboy,* and the frug. It seems easy today for many people to derive pleasurable voyeuristic excitation from identification with the aggressor or victim of an assault, or with both. The excitation interferes with their ability to behave in a socially responsible way and summon law-enforcement authorities, just as voyeurism may complicate their ability to express passion in a relationship with another person.

For many young people, drug use has replaced the ideology that characterized earlier youth revolts, and represents a statement about the kind of world the user would like to see come into being. Along with such utopian goals and the Rosicrucian dimension of tapping hidden powers, some youngsters seek to embrace rather than escape reality by drug use. For them, it is a positive effort to get into a major stream of the reality of adolescent life.[54]

However, there are other young people whose difficulties in relating to others represent one reason for their interest in LSD, amphetamines, marijuana, and barbiturates.[55] Drugs provide temporary relief from the prison of aloneness for many youngsters who feel uncomfortable with their status as latent human beings. Unable to develop meaningful ways of relating to others, a youth may modify his relationship with himself by the use of chemicals. Another youth may use drugs to displace sexual fantasies because, as one New York teenie-bopper explained, "When you're high, you see beauty and beauty is independent of male and female. . . ."

The depersonalization and flattening of sex roles experienced by some of today's young people can be so threatening that they defend themselves by contracting their life-space and withdrawing from active participation to the trippy world of inner experience provided by drugs.[56] Many young people who have lost moorings to femininity or masculinity in our society anchor upon the self and employ drugs as an ultimate prosthetic. Chemicals provide an additional appeal in the ritual of ingestion, which, like the be-in or love-in, is often a tragically fragmented caricature of the religious and secular rites that have largely disappeared from modern life. Drug use also represents one of the few ways in which young people who were brought up to be individuals can still differentiate themselves from an adult society which does not appear to be very sympathetic.

The disengagement which is sometimes fostered by drugs and has become an important motif for many of today's New People succeeded the self-centered and anti-middle class Beat movement of the 1950's as well as the enthusiastic altruism of the early 1960's, which had expressed itself in civil rights, student protests, and the New Frontier. During the last few years, growing numbers of activist youths became disenchanted over their inability to achieve significant changes in American life and drifted away from political goals. In contrast, young people of the 1930's who were involved with society had tended to throw themselves into efforts on behalf of the New Deal and against Fascism. World War II provided an opportunity to focus on a visible enemy and a chance for a better world, but dreams began turning into nightmares a few years after the war's end, coinciding with the onset of our current epidemic of drug abuse and the beginning of the real Age of Neutrality.

It is possible to regard the Age as really having begun in the 1920's, but to have been interrupted by the Depression. Perhaps the unifying experience provided by our efforts to cope with the 1930's facilitated each sex's resumption of more traditional roles. By the end of World War II, America was again ready to plunge into depolarization. Novels, plays, humor, and leisure activities of the 1920's were as thematically similar to those of the 1960's as they differed from underlying emphases of the 1930's.[57]

Our times include the new and threatening atmosphere of the atomic bomb, which invades all discussions of the future like a cold wind in a drafty house. We know that people are seldom able to voice their anxieties about the bomb.[58] So monstrous yet impersonal is this brutal symbol of the universe's indifference that the true moral feelings it should evoke have been banished to the unconscious. We simply cannot accept unthinkable events as part of our daily lives.

The bomb is so frightening that it hardly ever emerges in the form of dreams, which deal with material with which we are ready to cope. We can only speculate about attitudes toward the bomb, some of which are reflected in one oft-repeated story about a school air-raid drill. When the teacher instructed the students to sit on the floor and put their heads between their knees, one boy asked his neighbor the reason for the instruction. "Because," was the reply, "when the bomb comes, you better kiss your penis good-bye." The complete nihilism possible in our age of overkill is similarly perceived by many people as a castration, an attack at the roots of their very existence.

The bomb's capacity to wipe out men and women is completely beyond our control; it cannot be propitiated and becomes a metaphor of the silence of the gods and of our total rejection by the world. The bomb, in the algebra of the unconscious, is an ultimate instrument for a crude but final resolution of all our guilts, anxieties, challenges, and fears. Many of us expect it to separate the sinners from ourselves and purge our sins in ultimate fire. In a world that is so threatening, where any attempt to improve our situation could be as unreal as an Eleventh Crusade, many people feel that there is little incentive for each sex to express its unique qualifications. What any one person can do seems pitifully insufficient in the face of this ultimate symbol of man's alienation from himself and his powers to build and bring forth the fruits of his sacred human promise.

Such concerns make the bomb a most conspicuous and convenient example of a technology which has outstripped our ability to manage it. In 1938, insecurity similarly predisposed people to accept the possibility of uncontrollable catastrophic events which were based on new scientific developments, as in their response to Orson Welles' radio invasion from Mars.[59]

The hopelessness latent in a large proportion of the population seems to have found one outlet in the considerable emotional distress uncovered by interview studies during the winter of 1956–1957, when New York City was in a state of vigilance because of a Mad Bomber who had left a number of bombs in public places. Substantial numbers of New Yorkers regarded the Bomber as a paradigm of the world—"always about to explode . . . every day the news is worse . . . I knew something bad would happen . . . it's a shriek against everybody" and, ominously, "he'll never be caught. . . ."[60] The Bomber provided a general social threat in which people could probe with the grappling hooks of their uneasiness and fears, already so prevalent that every third person in a large Manhattan sample was found to have symptoms of psychological disorder.[61]

A more intensely disconcerting source of worry was the November 1965 northeast power failure, which represented a sharp reminder of vulnerability for many Americans. Post-blackout interviews identified a goodly number who believed that similar failures would occur again and be more devastating. Similarly numbing anxiety and apathy could be observed in New York City when the subways greeted the arrival of 1966 by not running. Interviews conducted during the strike revealed a wearied resignation and a fatalistic feeling that it was another insult to be endured by people who regard such problems as a part of daily living. It was only one in a long list of reminders that the large city is less the centerpiece of civilization than an ecological regression, perhaps the least humane physical environment in history.[62] Many a city seems to be acting out E. M. Forster's story, "The Machine Stops," in which the mechanism controlling the world sputters to a halt.

The strike was a vivid reminder of how dependent we are on externals that fail us and of our powerlessness to influence events. "I feel like a kid who has been forcing himself to eat unappetizing food because there was no choice, and now even that food has been taken away from me," said one middle-aged man about the strike. "It's lucky I don't think about it or I'd be paralyzed."

Paralysis is not too strong a word for the behavior of many New Yorkers during the blackout. Although lights went out at 5:27 p.m., thousands of passengers were still standing in stalled subway trains and had made no effort to do anything as late as 9 and 10 p.m. One train stopped at a station platform, but two and a half hours later not even the conductor had made a move to tell the hundreds of stranded people that they could leave the train. The astonishing and Kafka-esque torpor uncovered by postblackout interviews suggests the deadly *acidia* of many city dwellers.[63]

Blackouts and strikes are unusual events, but our emotional energy is continually drained by the daily and deadly physical environment. The sixty tons of soot that fall on a city square mile each month and contribute to the smog umbrella over many urban areas, the urban noise and congestion depressing our level of functioning, even infiltrate our fantasies and reinforce feelings of depression and misgivings—life slips away without having been lived.

In so many other ways, the environment is grinding people and slowly but cumulatively sapping their ability to cope. Droughts plague the cities. Our ability to meet food requirements has been seriously questioned. Such problems seem remote, but must subtly undermine confidence and self-esteem, and indirectly influence sex and every element of feeling and action. Fertility rates among city dwellers have consistently been lower than those of nearby rural populations as the stresses of crowded city life curtail the ability and desire to have sexual intercourse. The feelings of self-mastery and satisfaction which a person must develop are major determinants of his sexual behavior. Events which call such feelings into question so persistently have a direct impact on male-female relationships.

The confidence and optimism about America which traditionally drew immigrants to this country have given way to more modest expectations about the future. International events have surely contributed to feelings of confusion about personal identity, and many Americans have replaced dreams of a new world by more pragmatic goals. Some have found it hard to realize that countries seldom act on the basis of principle but tend to respond to their own interests. One end product of the seeming permanence of the state of tension that we call the cold war is a feeling of resignation, which gives way to hopelessness at times of crisis. After twenty years of constant vigilance, we have learned to accept the unlikelihood of any resolution of the cold war.

Most recently, a substantial part of the population has exhibited the response of *atonie,* or apathy and lack of resonance with reality.[64] Such "tuned out" persons are likely to have an inadequate sense of self, a dim view of the future, and faulted masculinity and femininity. Removing the seventh veil from this considerable number of disconnected people is likely to reveal a flattened sexuality that differs in degree but not in kind from many other Americans' feelings of gender.

10

the way of the neuter

The unique capacities of each sex are especially significant these days, when at least some quantitative aspects of a Great Society seem within reach. "Nothing but the best, the richest and fullest experience possible is good enough for man," said John Dewey. We believe that our citizens should be able to achieve a maximum in both quantity and quality of experience, but what is attainable by men and women in our day of the neuter is hardly rich and full.

Even though history should not be used as a warehouse from which to cull samples that support a particular theory, one approach to understanding our situation is by examination of the fate of earlier cultures that reflected similar confusion. Difficulties in coping with the contemporary era of in-between may be eased by lessons of the past. Man may propose and God dispose, but history still imposes. Perhaps a comparison with classical Athens and Rome may suggest some possible outcomes for current American patterns. The two classical societies which gave birth to much of our culture and many of our institutions could also foreshadow some implications of America's current way of life.

The Past
as Prologue

Even though our industrial society could hardly be
more different from early Athens and Rome, they provide
examples of what is almost "history in the flesh," since
sexual attitudes and behavior seem to have been deeply
involved in the fate of both civilizations. Just as our analysis of the New People has been based on the kind of information that would interest a hypothetical archeologist,
our knowledge of classical society largely derives from
sometimes trivial records of the lives of patricians, whose
way of life had reverberations on other socioeconomic
groups.

In what was probably the first non-fiction novel, Thu-
cydides has given the classic account of the Peloponnesian
War, and one that suggests some possible parallels between early Athens and contemporary America. We know
that power shifted from Athens to the south and, not too
much later, to the north after the surrender of Athens to
Sparta in 404 B.C. By the end of the fourth century, B.C.,
the Athenian city-state had ceased to be a creative force
and a once-vital idea was trapped in the silence of its
monuments.

Athens' decline from an extraordinarily seminal and
powerful state with the world's greatest concentration of
genius to a quiet university center is usually attributed to
a series of military defeats and political blunders. But
such defeats and blunders may have resulted, at least partially, from the changing patterns of relationships between
men and women. The shift in male-female roles that
seems most relevant to contemporary America occurred
during the hundred years commencing around 450 B.C. It
can be seen in the kinds of leaders who emerged in

Athens, the shape of sex, and changes in women's role and in philosophy, art, and architecture. No contemporary writer had set himself the task of presenting a picture of Athenian civilization before and even during the Golden Age, so that we can only infer its interpersonal relations.

Alcibiades is one of the Athenians whose erratic leadership helped to hasten the twilight. The attitudes represented by such a pivotal leader appear to have been intertwined with society's acceptance of new relationships between the sexes. Plutarch described Alcibiades' "effeminacy in dress—he would trail long purple robes through the agora." Alcibiades was implicated in mutilation of the phallus of several statues of Hermes, just before leading the Athenian fleet against Sicily in 415 B.C. One widely accepted version of the manner of Alcibiades' death is that he was killed after visiting the courtesan Timandra, in whose robes he was buried. He is said to have dreamed that she was dressing him in women's clothing and painting his face.

Although sexuality figures prominently in Homer's poems, they do not record any erotic relationship between men. Achilles became livid when he lost his favorite slave girl, and Homer implicitly denies any homosexual relationship between Achilles and Patroclus.[1] Heterosexual relationships are dominant in Homer and a century later in Hesiod's *Theogony*. Prior to the second half of the sixth century B.C., strict codes governed family life and marriage was indissoluble.

By the fifth century, a number of writers were praising pederasty and homosexuality was so acceptable that Aristides and Themistocles became estranged over young Stesilaos. Although Hippocrates had said that a woman whose womb was not regularly stimulated by a man's semen could get restless and develop what he called "hysteria," orality and anality were very common in fourth-century Athens. Bisexuality was frequent and Demosthenes could say that "we have wives for childbearing, hetairae for pleasure, and concubines for daily needs."

In Periclean Athens, women could not attend the Assembly, own property, or hold office. In his famous speech in honor of the Peloponnesian War's casualties, Pericles suggested that the best reputation a woman could have was "not to be spoken of among men either for good or evil." Women left their homes only under surveillance and Xenophon recommended bolts and bars for the entrance to their part of the house.[2] Partly as a result of women's restlessness from being left at home during the long war between Athens and Sparta, the move toward equality had begun by the last quarter of the fifth century. Many Athenian women participated in the orgiastic dances of the Eleusinian Mysteries. The only surviving satyr-play, Euripides' *Cyclops,* was first produced around 425 B.C., and the audiences for it and similar scabrous plays appear to have included women.

Although no women seem to have been permitted to attend the great schools of philosophy in the fifth century B.C., they were accepted at Epicurus' school when it moved to Athens early in the fourth century. A woman gymnasiarch in Athens conducted programs of physical training and girls participated in races and other formal athletic competition.[3] By the Hellenistic period, women had become much more active in community life, and a strong line of fiery women from Arsinoë to Cleopatra exerted great influence on politics and symbolized their power and freedom.

Depolarization between men and women took place at the same time as an attrition of extremes in philosophy. Early Greek philosophers stood for a fairly rigid morality and emphasized self-restraint. Socrates and Plato provided an unassailable logical foundation for Virtue. Later philosophers criticized traditional morality and Protagoras stressed the relativity of truth. In the fourth century, the Cyrenaic philosophers were Hedonists who believed that wisdom consisted in the right choice of pleasures.

In art, as in life, the ideal mode became less important as idealized masculinity and femininity dwindled. The change can be seen in the contrast between the heroic grandeur of Olympia's universalized pedimental sculpture and the almost photographic old women in Tanagra figurines. Athenian sculptors also expressed the blurring of differences between men and women in their presentation of the genderless human body.[4] The Korai on the Acropolis can barely be distinguished as female figures and the sex of other figures can often only be determined by hair or clothes. Hermes and Aphrodite have the same boyishly slender body, girlishly fine arms, and sexually undifferentiated expression. A robed Apollo carrying his lyre and leading a chorus of Muses does not seem significantly more masculine than the members of his female train. The later Athenians believed there was no difference of principle or dividing line between men and women and that nothing was exclusively attractive to one sex or repellent to the other.

Women were presented in the nude in sculpture only after they had begun to assume greater prominence in community affairs. There was a change from the fully-clothed female figure, peplum folds exactly in place, to nudes like "Aphrodite Rising from the Sea" at Rhodes and "Venus de Milo." Earlier rejection of the female nude could be seen in an experience of Praxiteles. When the Athenians commissioned him to execute an Aphrodite, he made one clothed statue and a nude that represented the first female figure sculptured without drapery. The Athenians chose the conventional draped statue, which became known as the "Aphrodite of Cnidus" and was one of the most admired works of antiquity.

Changes in architecture mirrored the same impulses

that helped to make the female nude commonplace by the late fourth century B.C. The strength, solidity, and force of the fifth century's masculine Doric column, with its simple channeled shaft tapering slightly toward the top, began to become less popular than the Ionic column during the fourth century. Femininity in the Ionic is conveyed by a richly molded base, many flutings, and an ornamented scroll gracefully dipping across the top of the column. The upward reach of the Doric column began to become less popular almost simultaneously with Athens' decreasing ability to reach outward.

Rome, which provides perhaps the most tantalizing example in history of a rigid and polarized culture that became more sexually blurred, experienced the same kind of changes in sex roles that appear to have contributed to the fading of Athens. Many historians have speculated about the decline of Rome ever since Gibbon stressed the role of morality in the triumph of religion and barbarism.[5] We can speculate that sexual crisscrossing could have contributed somewhat to each of the conditions identified in the various post-Gibbon theories. Although no single cause can adequately explain the decline of Rome, the blurring of sex roles might have facilitated a multiplicity of developments that changed the quality of life from what it was in the best days of the republic to what it had become under Elagabalus.

Cato the Elder personified the polarization and moral rigor that characterized Rome from its beginning to the end of the second century B.C. One example of very early morality is provided by Tarquinius Superbus, the seventh and last king of Rome. At the peak of Tarquinius' reign, his son Sextus raped Lucretia, who subsequently killed herself. Rape was regarded as so outrageous a crime, even on the part of royalty, that the king and his family were deposed and banished. Such punishment could be imposed by the early Romans because their society's cohesion depended on sexual rectitude and strict observance of established male-female roles.

Life began to become less rigorous in the first century B.C., as one result of Roman soldiers' contact with foreign countries. The soldiers had been accustomed to the relative unapproachability of their own women and were pleasantly surprised to discover greater accessibility in other countries. Slave girls' ready availability further encouraged sexual expression.

Just preceding the empire, sex expression became much more free, and male-female differences blurred. Julius Caesar was sometimes described as every man's wife and every woman's husband. His ambivalent sexual preferences became the subject of a marching song of his favorite legion. Antony's harem of both men and women and Domitian's bisexuality were matters of common knowledge. Although Suetonius is not always reliable, his description of Nero's marriage to a castrated male is convincing. Nero's excellence as a provincial administrator could have been less important than the example he set by his sexual proclivities. Several later emperors were bisexual, and Elagabalus and others made public appearances in women's clothes. The feminism that was found during the early Imperial period had reappeared by the third century.

Martial wrote love lyrics to both men and women, just like some contemporary beat poets. Petronius, Tibullus, and Propertius were among the writers who frequently alluded to the sexual ambiguity of their times. Juvenal's satires present an unforgettable picture of sexual ambivalence, and his denunciations of feminized perfumed dandies were often posted publicly. Poetry was a public profession and frequently disseminated sexual gossip, especially in the early years of the empire. Some events during Augustus' reign could even have been as widely discussed as the celebrities' errancies chronicled in *Confidential*.

It could be merely an extraordinary coincidence that any description of Augustus' career has so many similarities to that of President Johnson. Augustus was a comparatively obscure youngster when he left Illyria for Italy, but soon displayed great political and administrative skills.[6] He took over in Rome after the assassination of a charismatic leader. Some of Augustus' subsequent problems arose because of opposition from Mark Antony, who had been Julius Caesar's closest associate. Antony might have succeeded Julius Caesar as head of state, had the latter not been assassinated.

Augustus was so sensitive to public opinion that he was accused of manipulating it. Although questions had been raised about the tactics he used to win power, he became mellow in later years and preferred to be known as the *princeps* or senior statesman of the republic. Augustus reestablished forgotten ceremonies, effected reforms, facilitated free elections, sought the consensus of all classes, and developed an army large enough for the demands of the empire.

Although Augustus relied heavily on a few loyal friends, he made some exceptional appointments to high office. He closely supervised international relations, was a stickler for detail, and stimulated the arts. His wife, Livia, was a strong person and their marriage was very close and satisfying. Augustus' personality and official conduct not only resembled Mr. Johnson's in many other ways, but surviving statues suggest that his physical appearance was also similar.

Were it not for the substantial resemblances between Roman and American life, the similarities in political role and personality between Augustus and Lyndon B. Johnson, at such a great time interval, would merely be curiosa. As our environment becomes more neutral in tone, it may become easier for us to escape from freedom of assertion and move voluntarily toward the Caesaristic leadership and concentration of power that seems to characterize every forceful modern western democracy.[7]

The post-Augustus crisscross of sex roles and the general level of social behavior between the first and third century A.D. reached a level that can be analogized to contemporary America. Rome's enormous power in the middle to late third century was somewhat illusory and its leaders displayed considerable brusqueness at their decreasing ability to control other nations. Any speculative analogy of the United States with Rome must take account of the enormous acceleration of social change that characterizes our time. In twentieth-century America, the events occurring between Augustus and the third century could be compressed into a generation.

It is ironic that Athens and Rome laughed at joke representations of hermaphrodites, because hindsight enables us to perceive that changes in the fortunes of both societies could have partially stemmed from their increasing androgyny. The change did not necessarily reflect sexual license, although some scholars have claimed that the relaxation of sexual restraint in a civilization is likely to lead to its downfall.[8] Even if this be the case, there is no necessary relationship between promiscuity and blurring of sex roles. Any attempt to speculate about the classical civilizations must be mindful of the many hazards of generalizations based on limited evidence, of problems in comparison of different cultures and evaluation of change and unique events, and of the differences between analogy and identity. Yet the similarities between contemporary America and the classical civilizations are almost as pronounced as the pre-revolutionary parallelism between France and Russia to which Trotsky called attention. As he noted, some circumstances uniquely clarify the interrelationships between personality and more objective factors.[9]

Such speculations must also consider differences between immediate and underlying causes. Changes in relations between men and women represent underlying causes that may reflect shifts in leadership and ultimately express themselves in the ability of a state to cope with challenges. Our hypothesis is that its citizens' capacity to adapt to the demands of reality could be related to clarity of sex-role differentiation and of identification with models of the same sex. Loss of clarity of masculine identification seems to be influential in the decline of ability to cope with new problems.

Role differentiation is only one variable in the dynamics of social change. A full consideration of the conditions and factors producing change would include political, economic, technological, cultural, and demographic dimensions as well as rates of invention, acculturation, cultural diffusion, crisis, and resistance to change. The dimension of role is relevant to many of these aspects of change and can contribute to our understanding of the process without recourse to schematizing that tries to fit the gritty events of history into a grand design. Role ambiguity is especially likely in contemporary America, where uncertainty extends to age-graded as well as sex roles, and the multiplicity of stimuli and complexity of life contribute to fuzziness of behavior models.

Multivalent, amorphous, and depolarized roles might theoretically lead to increased flexibility and options in behavior, but in actuality may tend to invoke uncertainty. Some tolerance of ambiguity is desirable for a healthy personality, but today's environment and culture are ambiguous enough to tax the adaptability of even the healthiest personalities.[10] The other extreme is represented by the completely polarized sex roles that we associate with the reactionary ideology of totalitarianism.

There is no evidence that any one kind of family structure is inherently healthier than any other and history seems to suggest that almost any male-female role structure is viable, so long as there is clear division of labor and responsibilities. An equally important lesson of the past is that overly explicit roles can be pathogenic, because they do not permit the expression of individual differences or of a personal style. It is most disquieting to contemplate the bizarre possibility that the ambiguity of sex roles in our open society might ultimately prove to be almost as hazardous as the rigidities of Fascism.

Adam and Eve and the Fruit

There should be some wry consolation in the realization that thousands of years have brought us full circle to where we were In The Beginning. Adam and Eve were not aware of nudity or sex differences until eating fruit from the tree of knowledge of good and evil made them realize their nakedness. Although modern civilization has resulted from knowledge acquired since they left the Garden of Eden, our awareness of the differences between men and women has been sapped of its vitality. The farther we go from the wisdom obtained from the fruit, the more we are likely to forget the lesson of Adam and Eve.

When a basic category like masculine-feminine has become stripped of much of its meaning, there may be more utility in defining roles operationally. If, in order to replace outworn stereotypes, we define masculinity as what men do, and femininity as what women do, traditional attributes like aggressiveness and independence in men and passivity and dependence in women have less relevance. True, the sexes may still differ in terms of other behavior that they initiate, persist in, or discontinue.[11] But such differences are becoming narrower as our society makes it less necessary for Professor Henry Higgins to ask, "Why can't a woman be more like a man?"

At a time when the environment is flattening masculinity and femininity, the very reason for sex differences is becoming less important, as science brings about a growing separation between the phenomena associated with sexual attraction and those involving reproduction.[12] Experiments in obtaining and storing human sperm and ova for future use appear likely to perfect the process within a few years, so that "marriages" across generations can occur with human reproductive cells that have been "banked." The University of Michigan Medical Center has reported routinely successful impregnation of women with sperm that had been frozen for several years. The children show no defects traceable to the frozen sperm.[13]

An unfertilized egg cell from a woman's ovaries has been removed from her body, normally fertilized by a human sperm in a laboratory flask, and the resulting embryo has been kept alive for 59 days. Production of human embryos in the laboratory would make it possible for a woman to have babies by proxy, in accordance with principles of selective breeding. The egg cell could be fertilized in a test tube by sperm and nurtured in the body of another woman until birth, as has already been successfully accomplished with sheep and rabbits. The mind boggles at the implications of genetic engineering and deliberately controlled alterations in human inheritance that follow the models established by animal husbandry. What might happen if some popular singers, in their declining years, decided to sell quantities of their frozen sperm?

In an age of disposable outer furnishings, it is inevitable that science and technology will soon perfect not only the morning-after pill but other techniques for disposable sex and even children. Mary Quant, who has already proved to be a pace-setter in other aspects of modern life, has suggested two directions: "Gestation is so slow, so out of date. I really don't see why it can't be speeded up. . . . Why not transplant both the male and female bit into someone who adores having babies?"[14] Some keen observers of the

American family have pointed to the possibility that marriage of the future may become a totally nonsexual situation.[15]

Complete plants have been grown in a laboratory from a single cell, without seed or pollination, and effectively bypassing sex. The major federal science agencies have concurred in a recommendation by the American Chemical Society that the synthetic creation of life be made a national goal. When asked whether the program might ultimately include the creation of new organisms as complicated as human beings, president Charles C. Price of the Society said: "I couldn't imagine this would not happen. . . . We may be no further today from at least partial synthesis of living organisms than we were in the nineteen-twenties from the release of nuclear energy or in the nineteen-forties from a man in space."[16]

In 1929, James Thurber and E. B. White humorously asked, *Is Sex Necessary?* In a few years, the same question could elicit hollow laughter in a world where sexual intercourse may not be necessary to create life and in which neutering has metastasized. We New People are earning obsolescence as men and women by acquiescing in the process. Because the atom bomb was developed in wartime secrecy, we cannot hold ourselves responsible for its genesis. But there has been no clandestine attempt to promote neuterization. We must accept responsibility for the shift away from masculinity and femininity, which could finally be as important as the bomb. Most of us have been cooperating in the drift by everyday choices that have cumulated in the short-circuiting of the electric spark that used to leap between the two terminals.

The pervasive nature of depolarization has made it a routine feature of the cultural landscape that we take for granted, and our casualness about it may have led us to unwitting acceptance of a near-revolution in social life. When we try to explain how America moves forward in spite of the prevalence of neutering, Gibbon's observation could be significant: "Instead of inquiring why the Roman Empire was destroyed, we should rather be surprised that it had subsisted so long."[17] It does not require a technological determinism to raise questions about how long America can sustain itself in the face of the seeming contradiction of its shared emotional language with some basic necessities of human nature.

One Plus One
Equals Zero

Our abandonment of polarized sex roles and of the mystery that once surrounded sex may help to explain the attractiveness of systems of philosophy, psychology, and social thought that are concerned with death. Existentialism is the first philosophy to attract the American public, and one reason for the system's great popularity since Sartre's visit in 1946 could be its identification of death as the ultimate mystery to be embraced by everyone. Sex could be yielding to death in its ability to excite, incite, and help in achieving insight.

Our times may ultimately be remembered for having substantially replaced enthusiasm for the activity most closely linked to the creation of new life—sex—with extensive consideration of the end of life.[18] Death is now a subject for popular books (*The American Way of Death*), motion pictures (*The Loved One*), and has provided a major motif for women's makeup, in the pallor that is today's most fashionable non-look.

We appreciate dark because we respond to light, and we hear noise through our knowledge of quiet. But when femaleness and maleness become blurred, the differences between them can hardly help one to enrich the other. Each sex can best find itself if the other provides a balance.[19] One sex can achieve fruition only by tapping those aspects of the opposite sex that it also encompasses. Such fulfillment is still far away, and a more realistic goal may be for each sex to accept inter-dependency and help the other express itself complementarily. One reason for depolarization may be men's being forced to express more femininity as women become less able to relate them to the feminine side of themselves, and vice versa.

We know enough about our society to see the irrelevance of antipodal views of sex differences. The eighteenth-century Enlightenment thinkers who contended that there were really no differences between men and women, and the nineteenth-century Romantic philosophers who believed in total sex differences, were both taking positions that are not meaningful for us. Otto Weininger pointed out that masculine and feminine are only rough terms that define the presence of a preponderance of characteristics, and both are present in varying proportions in each person.[20] Following Weininger's insight, masculinity and femininity may be regarded as two dimensions, each of which is present in every person to some extent, rather than representing the extreme of a single continuum.

In spite of the plasticity and lability of our roles today, and general acceptance of the thesis that neither sex should be locked into one pattern of behavior, men and women still experience themselves and the world in ways that reflect the two great modalities of paternal and maternal. The emancipation of women and their greater equality and participation in the affairs of society were long overdue. But equality does not mean equivalence, and a difference is not deficiency. It is not inherently good or bad.[21] Proponents of both male and female chauvinism ought to abandon special pleading and realize that we cannot go back to the good old days. "Life can only be understood backward," Kierkegaard reminds us, "but it must be lived forward." Neither sex is a "better half" in an America which needs both daring women and men who are sensitive to the feelings of others.

The Vaertings concluded that traditionally masculine qualities are those we ascribe to the sex that is dominant in work and wooing.[22] For perhaps the first time in history, the dimension of dominance-subordination has become almost irrelevant. In America today, the strong man who takes the initiative is becoming as historical as the submissive protected woman. For some men, the incompatibility between the role they are playing and the one they want to assume has had very serious consequences. Their difficulties may be reflected in America's showing the greatest post-1930 increase in the male over the female death rate of any country.[23]

For almost four centuries, it has been known that women live longer than men, but this difference between the sexes has been increasing rapidly in recent years in this country. We can speculate that the diseases contributing to the jump in our male death rate are often related to a man's conflict between his desire to be dependent and an antithetical urge to be assertive and independent. As the energy available for functioning and maintenance of his total organism is drained by the conflict, the man could become more susceptible to illness, disease, and, ultimately, an earlier death.

Such pathological outcomes of role conflict may result from living by ideals that are no longer workable. Many Americans continue a highly emotional involvement in myths about femininity and masculinity, in spite of compelling evidence to the contrary. If we take the traditional definition of a role as a position in the social system which has normative expectations associated with it, our society must be said to have blurred sex roles almost hopelessly. It is fortunate that for many young people, new awareness of the relationship between family and society, work and worth, morality and social role is helping them to seek adulthood in ways different from their parents.

There is little that can weaken a cause so effectively as to embrace everything that seems to go in the same direction. Our stressing depolarization does not preclude the possibility of movement in the opposite direction. But there are so few areas of modern life in which masculinity and femininity assert themselves that only a very brave soul would seriously suggest that polarization of the sexes is likely to increase significantly. Even though the strength of the sex drive itself may place some limit on the situation, there is little evidence to suggest much movement away from our latitude zero of gender.

Depolarization may be one of those evils that would be less evil if it were more evil, because our progress in other areas of national life may help to mask each sex's loss of uniqueness. Some Americans, like Norman Mailer, have reacted to depolarization by seeking salvation through primitivistic sex, which is a form of one-stop shopping for many emotional and social needs and a panacea for the basic problems of human existence. For such persons, sex is an object of almost religious devotion and a vision of the future. What do most Americans think of our drift to neutering? To paraphrase Kuprin, the horror of it is that there is no horror. Other Americans who have experienced a sense of drift and confusion and remarked on the deterioration in the quality of American life may have been responding to its depolarization.[24]

One metaphor of response to neutering is provided by the final scene of *Red Desert*, Antonioni's brilliant film about the effects of industrialization. A six-year-old boy notices birds flying very near several huge smokestacks that are belching forth fire and smoke. When he asks his mother what happens to birds that fly too close to the fire, she says that they must learn not to go so close.

Throughout the film, the smokestacks have symbolized homogenized mass society. Like the chimney swift, we New People must learn to live near or even in the smokestack and not be swallowed up by the flames.

Mathematics suggests an analogy.[25] An algebraic system widely used in modern mathematics and computer technology is the "group of integers modulo 2." In this method of addition, one plus one equals zero. If our age of electronics and computers continues to drift toward depolarization of sex, there is indeed a possibility that men and women will ultimately be able to produce nothing together and each will become a less appropriate audience for the distinctive performance of the other.

We can appreciate the prescience of Freud in his observation that the future of sexuality would give the answer to and be the measure of the future of mankind. Long before, Plato in the *Phaedrus* pointed out that a person's attitude toward love is a necessary precursor of his attitude toward life. In fine, let us hope that the intense ferment in so many different aspects of sexual identity and social role today is less the increased brightness of the light bulb before it burns out, than a glow that presages an awakening.

acknowledgments

Many friends and colleagues have given most generously of their time, patience, and expertise in helping me to a better understanding of the matters discussed in this book. Among them are: Paul Ackerman, Phillip Akre, William Attaway, Leo Baer, Arnold Bernstein, Leon Brill, Jack Collozuol, Alvin Eisenman, Murray Friedman, Leyna Gabriele, Constantine Georgiou, Harold D. Gilmore, Richard J. Goldman, Stanley Green, Harold Greenwald, Gerard R. Guteri, Dr. Thorstein Guthe, Mitchell Habeeb, Penny Hills, Dr. Herbert Holt, Timothy J. Horan, Henry Jacobson, Edward Jaffe, Asya L. Kadis, Alan Kapelner, Dr. Joel Katz, Herbert Krugman, Gershon Legman, Morris C. Leikind, George Loukides, Howard Mandel, Renée Miller, Marcel Mommers, Charles Mosler, Eleanor Nagler, Dr. Marie Nyswander, Iver M. Olsen, Nathan Perlmutter, Anthony Pezzello, Wardell B. Pomeroy, James Pozoli, John Putnam, Jean Rich, Philip Roddman, Bernard Rosenberg, Frederick M. J. Ruf, Richard Runes, Arthur A. Rupprecht, David Schendler, Herman Schoenfeld, Rosina Singer, Gene Sosin, Edith Stephen, William D. Stevens, Irving W. Stone, Mark Strage, Carl Watson, Ralph Wehrenberg, David M. White, William Willey, Dr. Martin Winick, Elliott Winick, and Benjamin Wolstein.

Among the organizations that have been very helpful in providing information are the Brewers Association, Children's Book Council, Fairchild Publications, Gaines Dog Research Center, Harvard Club of New York, Hilton Hotels, National

Shoe Manufacturers Association, Toy Information Bureau, and the World Health Organization.

A number of persons have been kind enough to read and comment on sections of the manuscript. For their many valuable suggestions I am most grateful to James Becker, Robert A. Bernstein, William Cole, Robert E. Cowart, Frederick Edell, Jacob Goldstein, Marie Hauser, Nat Hentoff, Emil Lang, Louis H. Levy, Charles MacPhee, Edward Madnick, Allan Morrison, Douglass D. Paige, Martin Samit, Larissa B. Warren, and Herbert J. Wolf. I am fortunate in having been able to tap Sam Tomlin's encyclopedic recollection of film history. An earlier version of "Have Chum, Will Travel," was written in collaboration with Elliot Horne and Joseph Rosner permitted me to call on his unique knowledge of the history of the arts. My wife, Mariann A. Winick, contributed many imaginative ideas, keen insights, and helpful editorial suggestions.

Most of the references to jokes derive from the panel for collecting orally communicated jokes that is described in my article on "A Content Analysis of Orally Communicated Jokes," *American Imago,* 20, 1963, pp. 271–291. I have drawn on a number of my other publications and am grateful to the editors of the *Antioch Review, Arts and Sciences,* and the *Journal of Broadcasting* for permitting me to quote extensively from "Dear Sir or Madam, As the Case May Be," "Matinee Idols, Hail and Farewell. . . ." and "Fan Mail to Liberace," respectively.

Only I am responsible for the use and interpretations made of the work of others and for any errors of omission or commission.

Charles Winick

notes

Chapter 1

1 For this and a number of other insights into discotheques and their development, I am greatly indebted to James O. Wade, who also read and commented critically on the whole manuscript.

2 Anatole Broyard, "Mambo," *Neurotica* #6, 1950, pp. 29–30.

3 Interviewed on *Wild World of Discotheque*, WABC-TV, New York, December 30, 1964.

4 Leonard Lyons, "The Lyons Den," *New York Post*, July 18, 1965, p. 27.

5 Charles Winick, "Teenagers, Satire, and *Mad*," *Merrill Palmer Quarterly*, 8, 1962, pp. 183–203. The meanings are so well established that the radio and television version of the lyrics for "St. Louis Blues" replaces the sexual activity implicit in the line ". . . like a Kentucky colonel loves his rock an' rye" with "like a Kentucky colonel loves his mint and rye." Copyright © 1924 (renewed 1942) by W. C. Handy.

6 Normand Poirier, "The Discotheques," *New York Post*, July 14, 1965, p. 39.

7 Charles Winick and Herbert Holt, "Some Uses of Music in Group Therapy," *Group Psychotherapy*, 13, 1960, pp. 76–86.

8 *The Cash Box*, April 20, 1957, p. 44.

9 Roger Pryor Dodge, "Throwback," *Jazz Review*, May 1959, p. 7.

10 Elaine Dundy, "The Image in the Marketplace," *Esquire*, July 1965, p. 114.

11 An analysis was conducted of the content of popular song lyrics of the first years of rock-and-roll (1949–1955) and compared with those of 1925–1931. The two six-year periods studied were roughly similar in terms of economic condition and both followed a major war. The songs of the two periods were compared by establishing thirteen thematic categories and assigning each song to one of them.

The categories were: narcissistic over-evaluation, connubial bliss, nostalgic yearning, phallic playfulness, euphoria, pseudo-masochism, infidelity, rejection, yearning, protestation, seductiveness, inconstancy, and a miscellaneous category for songs that did not belong in any other grouping. See Alvin Scodel, "Changes in Song Lyrics and Some Speculations on National Character," *Merrill Palmer Quarterly,* 7, 1961, pp. 39–47.

12 Richard Goldstein, " 'Strawberry Fields'—Enter Phase Four," *World Journal Tribune, New York,* March 12, 1967, p. 23.

13 These lyrics originated in the Berkeley area. See James T. Carey, *Bohemian Life Styles.* Berkeley: University of California School of Criminology, 1967, p. 42.

14 Annabel Farjeon, "Russian Ballet Schools," *New Statesman,* March 20, 1964, pp. 462–463.

15 Lord Snowden, "Nureyev," *Life,* November 27, 1964, p. 105.

16 Gershon Legman, *Love and Death.* New York: Breaking Point, 1948.

17 Max Nordau, *Degeneration.* New York: D. Appleton, 1895.

18 Charles Winick, "Good Modern Art Replaces Gow," *Denver Post,* Paperback Book Supplement, March 13, 1960.

19 Leo Gurko, *Heroes, Highbrows, and the Popular Mind.* Indianapolis: Bobbs Merrill, 1953, pp. 185–192, has been a basic source for this discussion.

20 Peter Smith, "Mary McCarthy," *Vogue,* October 15, 1963, pp. 98–99; Mary McCarthy, *The Humanist in the Bathtub.* New York: New American Library, 1964, pp. 195–216.

21 Eugene Goodheart, "The New Apocalypse," *The Nation,* 100th Anniversary Issue, 1965, pp. 207–211.

22 Charles Winick, "The Remora Syndrome: Sick Characteristics in Search of an Author," *Business Horizons,* 6, 1963, pp. 63–72.

23 O. Johnson and R. H. Knapp, "Sex Differences in Aesthetic Preferences," *Journal of Social Psychology,* 61, 1963, pp. 279–301.

24 Ken Lessler, "Culture and Freudian Dimensions of Sexual Symbols," *Journal of Consulting Psychology,* 28, 1964, pp. 46–53; Levon Melikian, "Sexual Symbolism: A Cross Cultural Study," *International Journal of Social Psychiatry,* 11, 1965, pp. 226–229.

25 Lionel Goitein, *Art and the Unconscious.* New York: United Book Guild, 1948.

26 Germain Seligman, *Merchants of Art.* New York: Appleton Century Crofts, 1961, p. 221.

27 During 1964, the Louvre exhibit of the work of both painters made such a comparison very graphic.

28 Fernand Hazan, *Dictionary of Modern Painting.* New York: Paris Book Center, 1958, pp. 178–184.

29 Paul Klee, *The Diaries of Paul Klee.* Berkeley: University of California Press, 1964.

30 Wilhelm Worringer, *Abstraction and Empathy.* New York: International Universities Press, 1953.

31   Frank Getlein, "The Long Run," *Jubilee*, April 1961, pp. 52–54.
32   Brian O'Doherty, "The New Nihilism: Art Versus Feeling," *New York Times*, February 16, 1964, p. 15; "Vanity Fair: The New York Art Scene," *Newsweek*, January 4, 1965, pp. 54–59.

Chapter 2

1   M. O. Lee, "A Bas Lohengrin," *Saturday Review*, February 29, 1964, pp. 63–64.
2   Columbia SL-101. Transposing down is almost always a sign of inadequate vocal power. Mary Garden could easily take a high C in her World War I recording of "Sempre libera." But by 1926, near the end of her career, she had the aria transposed down from G to F so that its climax is a high A instead of B.
3   E. Herbert-Caesari, *The Voice of the Mind*. London: Robert Hale, 1951, p. 241.
4   "This Week," *Opera News*, 27 (18), 1963, p. 2.
5   Paul Gardner, "3 of Stage's First Ladies Salute Actors Equity on 50th Birthday," *New York Times*, May 6, 1963.
6   Eric Bentley, "Theatre," *New Republic*, April 19, 1954.
7   Charles Winick, in "Sign This, Please," *Cue*, March 31, 1956, p. 14.
8   Jess Stearn, "Broadway's Switch to Women," *New York Daily News*, December 20, 1955, p. 3.
9   Henry F. May, *The End of American Innocence*. New York: Knopf, 1959.
10   Walter Kerr, "The Handbook, Updated," *New York Herald Tribune*, December 1, 1963, p. 31.
11   John D. Mitchell, "Applied Psychoanalysis in the Drama," *American Imago*, 14, 1957, pp. 263–280; "Contemporary American Theatre," *Natya*, 4, 1960, pp. 1–10.
12   Robert A. Bernstein was kind enough to read and comment on this section.
13   Ezra Goodman, *The Fifty Year Decline and Fall of Hollywood*. New York: Simon and Schuster, 1961, p. 366.
14   Parker Tyler, *The Three Faces of the Film*. New York: Thomas Yoseloff, 1960, p. 85.
15   The newspapers, fan magazines, and trade papers of the silent period are unequivocal in pointing to the male stars as far more potent at the box office than the period's actresses.
16   Observations on and descriptions of the characteristics of movie actors since 1955 are based on panel and interview studies conducted by the author with moviegoers. The characteristics imparted to stars from the beginning of talkies to 1955 represent summaries of contemporary discussions in fan magazines, trade papers, and marketing research studies. Generalizations about the comparative importance of men and women, in the case of silent as well as talking

pictures, are also based on a content analysis of the comparative importance of the sexes in the billing of stars, e.g., the performers whose names precede the title of a picture.

17   Catherine De La Roche, "That 'Feminine Angle,'" *Penguin Film Review,* 8, pp. 25–34.

18   Richard Warren Lewis, "Hollywood's New Breed of Soft Young Men," *Saturday Evening Post,* December 1, 1962, pp. 73–76.

19   Eugenia Sheppard, "Socialite in the Window," *New York Herald Tribune,* June 12, 1964, p. 15.

20   Thanks are due David T. Bazelon for permitting the author to read an unpublished manuscript in which this point is made.

21   Max Lerner, "Return of the Femme Fatale," *Ladies' Home Journal,* June 1963, pp. 80–81.

22   Gerold Frank has suggested this interpretation.

23   Hedda Hopper, *The Whole Truth and Nothing But.* New York: Pyramid Books, 1963, pp. 282–283.

24   Peter Bart, "Holden: All-American Boy?" *New York Times,* December 12, 1965, Section X, p. 11.

25   Herbert Gans, "The Rise of the Problem Film," *Social Problems,* 11, 1964, pp. 327–335.

26   Charles Winick, "The Face Was Familiar," *Films and Filming,* 11 (4), 1965, pp. 12–17; "Matinee Idols, Hail and Farewell," *Arts and Sciences,* 2, 1964–1965, pp. 16–20.

27   Jim Henaghen helped to clarify the sequence of these changes.

28   Ernest Callenbach, "Temple of the Seventh Art," *Sight and Sound,* 35 (1), 1966, pp. 12–17.

29   "Theatres Adapt to Suburban Life," *New York Times,* January 19, 1964, pp. 1, 5.

30   An extended discussion of Liberace can be found in Charles Winick, "Fan Mail to Liberace," *Journal of Broadcasting,* 6, 1962, pp. 129–142. The quotations are from this article.

31   An Ohio widower moved his children to Kansas in *The Road West.* Brother Frank had a strong role in *The Legend of Jesse James. The Rifleman, Bat Masterson,* and *Maverick* worked with relatives and Barbara Stanwyck and her brood rode the *Big Valley.*

32   Jess and Slim in *Laramie* were inseparable and *The Law Man* worked with a young protégé. The archetypical *Virginian,* a lone fighter for honor in four previous movie versions, metamorphosed so radically that the villain of the original became one of three heroes of the television version. *Wyatt Earp* got help from a tubercular dentist who had come to the bullet-spattered frontier for reasons of health. *The Tall Man* and *Yancy Derringer* had cohorts and *Marshal Dillon* could hardly go into action without having some of Chester's morning coffee. Clint Walker was part of a near-regiment of ethical gun-slingers that attacked evil on a mass basis in *Cheyenne. Bronco* and even *Daniel Boone* were always flanked by colleagues.

33   Cattle trail boss Faber in *Rawhide* needed help from two assistants,

two colleagues rode the *Wagon Train*, and three Texas Rangers shared responsibilities and laughs in *Laredo.*

34 *The Loner* had the advantage of excellent production values, a well known star (Lloyd Bridges), and television's best known writer (Rod Serling). It dealt with a disillusioned Civil War veteran who moves from town to town, helping its residents to cope with their problems. *The Loner* was a prototypical pre-group western, but its purity of form was largely responsible for its inability to survive one season. *Branded*'s solo hero Jason McCord, who preferred anonymity and galloping away from the scene of his good deeds, could not attract an audience. The several other attempts to build a program around a lone hero uniformly failed to attract viewers.

35 Alfred Towne, "The Myth of the Western Hero," *Neurotica,* #7, 1950, pp. 3-7.

36 Charles Winick, *Taste and the Censor in Television.* New York: Fund for the Republic, 1959, p. 7.

37 John G. Cawelti, "Prolegomena to the Western," *Studies in Public Communication,* 4, 1962, pp. 57-70.

38 An ironic commentary on the domesticity now associated with westerns was a statement from the producer of *Empire,* a television western with a contemporary setting. He announced that he was dismissing Terry Moore and Anne Seymour because viewers erroneously believed that *Empire* dealt with the Old West, as a result of the domestic atmosphere provided by the two actresses! See " 'Where Are We, Mommy?' Asked Boom-Boom," *TV Guide,* April 13, 1963, pp. 15-18.

39 Bosley Crowther, " 'A Fistful of Dollars' Opens," *New York Times,* February 2, 1967.

40 Russell Baker, "Lament for Old Rogues," *New York Times,* October 17, 1963.

41 The program's audience vanished after a casting change that left hero Stu Bailey on a solo caper without associates Edd Byrnes, Roger Smith, and Louis Quinn.

42 A trio of investigators appeared in *Surfside 6, Bourbon Street Beat, Checkmate,* and *Follow the Sun.* Two sleuths worked together in *Hawaiian Eye, King of Diamonds,* and *Target, the Corrupters.* Peter Gunn had an associate, as did Rod Taylor in *Hong Kong.*

43 Charles Winick, "The Psychiatrist in Fiction," *Journal of Nervous and Mental Disease,* 136, 1963, p. 46.

44 Earl Wilson, *New York Post,* June 4, 1964, p. 16.

45 James Stewart-Gordon, "007—The Spy with the Golden Touch," *Reader's Digest,* October 1965, pp. 113-117.

46 *New York Times,* August 20, 1965, p. 35.

47 Fleming's sympathetic biographer, John Pearson, has suggested that Fleming was a kind of Walter Mitty who projected his fantasies into Bond. Pearson notes that the character of Admiral M. was suggested by Fleming's mother, whom he used to call "M." See

"Rough Rise of a Dream Hero," *Life,* October 14, 1966, pp. 113–128.

48 Charles Winick, "Censor and Sensibility: A Content Analysis of the Television Censor's Comments," *Journal of Broadcasting,* 5, 1961, pp. 117–135.

49 Richard Lattimore, Introduction to the *Oresteia,* in David Grene and Richard Lattimore, editors, *Aeschylus.* Chicago: University of Chicago Press, 1959, pp. 6–7.

50 Emanuel K. Schwartz, "The Fear of Violence," *Bulletin of the Postgraduate Center for Psychotherapy,* October 1960, pp. 1–3.

51 *Variety,* March 8, 1967, p. 28.

52 This chapter has been substantially improved by the probing questions and comments of students in a Colloquium at the University of Pennsylvania's Annenberg School of Communications, where I presented its substance, in September 1966. I am grateful to Dean George Gerbner and Professor Robert Louis Shayon for the opportunity of speaking to the Colloquium. Comments by Lila S. Roisman and Alan Soffin were particularly valuable.

53 Joseph Rosner, *The Hater's Handbook.* New York: Delacorte, 1965, pp. 121–122.

54 Charles Winick, "The Public Image of the Museum in America," *Curator,* 5, 1962, pp. 45–52.

55 Harold Mendelsohn, "Socio-Psychological Perspectives on the Mass Media and Public Anxiety," *Journalism Quarterly,* 40, 1963, pp. 511–516; Charles Winick, "Children's Television Fan Mail," *Television Quarterly,* 3, 1964, pp. 57–71.

56 *Honor Blackman's Book of Self Defense.* New York: Macmillan, 1966. Quotation is from the publisher's catalog.

57 *Newsweek,* April 4, 1966, p. 94.

Chapter 3

1 Walter Carlson, "Woman's Pocketbook Domain," *New York Times,* August 8, 1965, p. F12.

2 Professor Martin Samit has been most helpful in the preparation of this section.

3 For example, Bloomingdale's in New York used to carry AA widths in regular stock in its Briolett line but now only gets them on a special order basis.

4 Joyce A. Perbix, "Relationship Between Somatotype and Motor Fitness in Women," *Research Quarterly of the American Association for Health and Physical Education,* 25, 1954, pp. 84–90.

5 *National Recreation Survey:* A Report to the Outdoor Recreation Resources Review Committee, ORRRC Study Report, 19. Washington: Government Printing Office, 1962. Other figures on outdoor recreational activity cited in the chapter derive from this report.

6 John Del Torto, "On Gambling," *Neurotica,* #6, 1950, pp. 11–22.

7 Bureau of Advertising, *A Study of the Opportunity for Exposure to National Newspaper Advertising.* New York: The Bureau, 1965, p. 9.

8 Sid Ross and Neal Ashby, "Rah, Rah, Girls, Fight! Fight! Fight!", *Parade,* February 23, 1964, pp. 6–7.

9 James A. Knight, "Motivation in Skiing," *Western Journal of Surgery, Obstetrics, and Gynecology,* 69, 1961, pp. 395–398.

10 Joshua Slocum, *Sailing Alone Around the World.* New York: Sheridan House, 1954.

11 "Mates Outrank Skippers on Deep Mauve Seas," *New York Times,* January 19, 1964, p. 8.

12 "Horsemanship Becomes a Middle-Class Sport," *New York Times,* October 25, 1965, p. 44.

13 "What's New at the Net?" *New York Herald Tribune,* June 12, 1964, p. 14.

14 Austrian Association of Professional Ski Teachers, *The New Official Austrian Ski System.* New York: A. S. Barnes, 1958.

15 *Time,* January 6, 1967, p. 62.

16 John Weitz, *Sports Clothes for Your Sports Car.* New York: Sports Car Press, 1958.

17 J. Campbell Bruch, "Queen of Cues," *New York Times Magazine,* March 23, 1952, pp. 38–39.

18 "The Inquiring Photographer," *New York Daily News,* February 8, 1964, p. 15.

19 Ralph R. Greenson, "On Gambling," *American Imago,* 4, 1947, pp. 61–77. See *America's No. 1 Participant Sport* (Association of Playing Card Manufacturers, New York: 1960) for details of card game preferences by sex.

20 F. Scott Fitzgerald, "Winter Dreams," in *All the Sad Young Men.* New York: Scribner, 1926, pp. 57–90.

21 Cleveland Amory, *Who Killed Society?* New York: Harper, 1960, pp. 195–246.

22 Ann Geracimos, "Sorry No Ladies Allowed But—." *New York Herald Tribune,* January 20, 1964.

23 Anthony Sampson, "The Mystique of British Clubs," *Harper's,* November 1962, pp. 40–47.

24 Murray Hausknecht, *The Joiners.* New York: Bedminster Press, 1962, p. 31.

25 Last year, Americans spent $705,000,000 on pet food and $493,000,000 on baby food.

26 Interview with Dr. Dean White, Institute for Human-Animal Relationships, WOR, New York, November 11, 1964. The Pet Food Institute has estimated that there are 26 million cats and 25 million dogs.

27 This conclusion derives from 1,500 interviews with pet owners that were conducted by the author in 1957 and 1958. Thanks are due the R. T. French Company for its original encouragement of studies in pet trends.

28   William Cole and Tomi Ungerer, *A Cat Hater's Handbook* (New York: Dial, 1963) has been extremely helpful in the preparation of this section.

29   Frances and Richard Lockridge, "The Cat's Behavior in Two Worlds," in Brandt Aymar, editor, *The Personality of the Cat.* New York: Bonanza Books, 1958, pp. 170–176; Agnes Repplier, "Agrippina," in *ibid.,* pp. 219–220.

30   H. H. Miller, *Speaking of Pets.* New York: Fleet Publishing Company, 1958, p. 3.

31   Charles Winick, "Leisure, the Problem That Isn't," *Leisure,* 1, 1960, pp. 25–27.

Chapter 4

1   Leo Baer has suggested this phrase.

2   Peter Bart, "Women Emancipated in Liquor Campaign," *New York Times,* October 18, 1963; Clementine Paddleford, "The Lighter Whiskeys—A Womanly Touch," *New York Herald Tribune,* November 13, 1963.

3   Bureau of Advertising, American Newspaper Publishers Association, *The Vodka Consumer,* September 1962.

4   *Nationwide Survey of Beer and Ale Consumption,* 1954; other survey findings mentioned in this chapter are from this report.

5   *The Brewers' Almanac,* 1963, pp. 33, 36.

6   "The Peanut Butter Battle," *New York Post,* October 27, 1965, p. 35.

7   *Time,* August 28, 1964.

8   George Christy, "The Lifetime Diet, White House Style," *Town and Country,* November 1965, pp. 146–147, has been the major source for this discussion. It might be noted that although mineral oil is the only no-calorie fat, some authorities feel it should not be used in food because it interferes with absorption of vitamin A, and possibly vitamins E, D, and K. Government regulations ban the use of mineral oil in any commercially prepared foods.

9   *New York Post,* November 18, 1965, p. 5.

10   "Glow in Stogies," *Barron's,* November 25, 1957, p. 1; "The Mellow Cigar," *Barron's,* September 5, 1960, pp. 1–3; "A Good Five Cent Cigar," *Barron's,* November 11, 1963, pp. 3, 10.

11   Eugenia Sheppard, "A Cool Smoke," *New York Herald Tribune,* December 9, 1963.

Chapter 5

1   *Harper's Bazaar,* April 1965, p. 214.

2   Lois Long, "Feminine Fashions," *The New Yorker,* September 25, 1965, pp. 170–175.

3   Jo Ann Sargent, "The Eyelash: Fur or Hair," *Atlantic Monthly,* June 1965, pp. 120–122.

4   Charles Winick and Herbert Holt, "Eye and Face Movements as Nonverbal Communication in Group Therapy," *Journal of Hillside Hospital,* 11, 1962, pp. 67–69.

5   Wassily Kandinsky, *Concerning the Spiritual in Art.* New York: George Wittenborn, 1947, p. 63.

6   Malcolm Cowley, "Exploring a World of Nightmares," *New York Times Book Review,* March 27, 1960, p. 20.

7   "Hair Curling Survey Shows Manly Approval," UPI Release. Chicago: September 8, 1964.

8   "A Beautiful Abundance of Riches," *The Givaudanian,* October 1964, p. 8.

9   Marylin Bender, "Style Counts with Women in Business," *New York Times,* December 12, 1964, p. 24.

10   "News and Notes," *American Home,* September 1965, p. 96.

11   Charles Winick and Herbert Holt, "Some External Modalities of Group Psychotherapy and Their Dynamic Significance," *American Journal of Psychotherapy,* 15, 1961, pp. 56–62.

12   Charles Winick, "Taboo and Disapproved Colors and Symbols in Foreign Countries," *Journal of Social Psychology,* 59, 1963, pp. 361–368.

13   Russell Lynes, *The Domesticated Americans.* New York: Harper and Row, 1963, pp. 245–285.

14   "Report on the Twelfth Annual Case Goods Furniture Survey," *Home Furnishings Daily,* 1960.

15   "Seventh Annual Furniture Survey," *Retailing Daily,* October 17, 1955.

16   *Retailing Daily,* October 8, 1956.

17   *Retailing Daily,* 1955, *op. cit.*

18   Siegfried Giedion, *Mechanization Takes Command.* New York: Oxford University Press, 1948, p. 498. The classical chaise longue must be distinguished from today's "chaise lounge," an inexpensive aluminum folding chair with webbing and widely used in outdoor situations. Its use is not, of course, restricted to women.

19   Herbert Collins, "The Sedentary Society," *Scientific Monthly,* 79, 1954, pp. 285–292; Charles Winick and Herbert Holt, "Seating Position as Nonverbal Communication," *Psychiatry,* 24, 1961, pp. 171–182.

20   Barbara Plumb, "They Coined 'Modern' More Than 30 Years Ago," *New York Times Magazine,* April 3, 1966, p. 78.

21   Rita Reif, "A New Age of Metals," *New York Times Magazine,* August 8, 1965, p. 55.

22   Milton R. Sapirstein, *Paradoxes of Everyday Life.* New York: Random House, 1955, pp. 120–145.

23 "Furniture: Durable But Different," *Federal Reserve Board of Philadelphia Bulletin,* November 1960, pp. 7–19.

24 Elaine Kendall, "A Man's Office Is His Castle," *New York Times,* March 15, 1964, pp. 52–59.

25 Harold D. Eberlein and Abbot McClure, *The Practical Book of Period Furniture.* Philadelphia: J. B. Lippincott, 1914; Joseph Aronson, *The Book of Furniture and Decoration, Period and Modern.* New York: Crown, 1941.

26 Ada Louise Huxtable, "Pop Architecture: Here to Stay," *New York Times,* October 4, 1964.

27 William Snaith, *The Irresponsible Arts.* New York: Atheneum, 1964, p. 125.

28 Vincent J. Scully on "Death of a Street," WNDT, New York, January 8, 1965.

29 George Nelson, "Architecture for the New Itinerants," *Saturday Review,* April 22, 1967, p. 66.

30 Robert Woods Kennedy, *The House and the Art of Its Design* (New York: Reinhold, 1953, pp. 508–520) has been very helpful.

31 Siegfried Giedion, *Architecture, You and Me.* Cambridge: Harvard University Press, 1958, pp. 145–146.

32 Ada L. Huxtable, "Dutch Planning: Cities in a Box," *New York Times,* December 12, 1965, p. X20.

33 Walter Abell, *The Collective Dream in Art.* Cambridge: Harvard University Press, 1957; Wylie Sypher, *Four Stages of Renaissance Style.* New York: Doubleday Anchor, 1955, p. 15.

34 James M. Fitch, *Architecture and the Esthetics of Plenty.* New York: Columbia University Press, 1961, pp. 261–264.

Chapter 6

1 Eugene Field, "Jest 'Fore Christmas," in *The Writings in Prose and Verse of Eugene Field.* Vol. 4, Poems of Childhood. New York: Scribner's, 1894.

2 March 6, 1964, on the Jack Paar program.

3 Daniel Adelson, "Attitudes toward First Names," *International Journal of Social Psychiatry,* Special Edition I, Section A, 1964, pp. 81–86; William F. Murphy, "A Note on the Significance of Names," *Psychoanalytic Quarterly,* 26, 1957, pp. 91–106.

4 B. M. Savage and F. L. Wells, "A Note on Singularity in Given Names," *Journal of Social Psychology,* 27, 1948, pp. 271–272.

5 Albert Ellis and R. M. Beechley, "Emotional Disturbance in Children with Peculiar Given Names," *Journal of Genetic Psychology,* 85, 1954, pp. 337–339.

6 It was hypothesized that the names given to children would reflect our culture's tendency toward depolarization of sex. Birth an-

nouncements between the current and preceding generations appearing in *The New York Times* over a fifteen-year period (1948–1963) were analyzed, in terms of a comparison between names of the children and their parents.

A listing was made of every third one of the 43,337 children whose births were announced during this period. The frequency of occurrence of each name found among the 14,446 newborn, along with the incidence of the names of their parents, was tabulated. There were 816 different given names in the 14,446 that were sampled.

It was possible to prepare a table consisting of five columns, with the first containing the name, the second the number of fathers with the name, and the third column the number of mothers who had the name. The fourth column represented the number of boy children who had the name, and the fifth the number of girl children with the same name.

With a frequency count in each of the five columns it was possible to use a chi-square test in order to compare the distribution of parents' versus children's names to see whether they were significantly different, with the 5% level representing significance of difference. All differences cited in the text were significant at the 5% level or better. The chi-square test was used because it is nonparametric and makes no assumptions about the existence of a normal or Gaussian distribution pattern in the universe of names published in the newspaper.

The same kind of analysis was conducted to measure the extent to which the names were sex-linked. It was assumed that the expected distribution for a name is to have it ascribed only to persons of one sex, with no persons of the opposite sex possessing it. This would be true if names had a unimodal distribution by sex. To the extent that the statistical analysis indicated significant differences from such a distribution, such differences would suggest that the names are being assigned to boys and girls on a basis other than the 100–0% ratio.

7   Jo Hubbard Chamberlin, "I'm Tender About Gender," *Coronet,* February 1960, pp. 55–57; the woman's name, of course, precedes the man's.

8   Ezra Goodman, *The Fifty Year Decline and Fall of Hollywood.* New York: Simon and Schuster, 1961, p. 281.

9   James Agee, *Agee on Film.* New York: McDowell Obolensky, 1958, p. 29.

10   G. Jahoda, "A Note on Ashanti Names and Their Relationship to Personality," *British Journal of Psychology,* 45, 1954, pp. 192–195.

11   H. L. Mencken, *The American Language:* Supplement II. New York: Alfred A. Knopf, 1956, p. 472; L. Allen, V. Brown, L. Dickinson, and K. C. Pratt, "The Relation of First Name Preferences to Their Frequency in the Culture," *Journal of Social Psychology,* 14, 1941, pp. 279–293.

12 Alfred I. Kolatch, *These Are the Names.* New York: Jonathan David Co., 1948.

13 Bureau of Records and Statistics, New York City Health Department, Report on Preferred Names for 1928, 1948, and 1964, dated April 28, 1965.

14 John G. Fuller, "Trade Winds," *Saturday Review,* October 19, 1963, p. 8.

15 It proved possible to conduct interviews with a probability sample of adults between the ages of 17 and 50 about the connotations of these names. The sample, interviewed in connection with a larger study, consisted of 983 women and 957 men in the metropolitan New York area. In order to avoid any influence of the positioning of the ambiguous names in the total list, their sequence in the list was systematically rotated. The subject was handed a card on which the name had been typed and asked, "Could you please describe the kind of person that someone with this first name is likely to be?" He was encouraged to respond until he commented on both the sex as well as the personality characteristics of the name. He was then shown the next card in the series, until he had responded to all six cards.

16 Michael Young and Peter Willmott, *Family and Kinship in East London.* London: Routledge and Kegan Paul, 1957, p. 10.

17 Manuel Prenner, "Ora Jones Married Ora Jones," *American Speech,* 17, 1942, pp. 84–88. It is possible that such attitudes are especially important in large cities and may be less significant in rural areas. Dr. Earle H. MacCannell of Portland State College was able to identify the sex of 99% of the children born in Chelan County in 1954 (a rural area in the state of Washington) by their given names (personal communication).

18 Intersexual first names represent the most obvious use of names to express crisscrossing of sex roles. A subtler approach is found in retention of a clearly sex-linked name like John or Mary, but selecting it from an ancestor related to the opposite sex. A study of middle-class Chicago families in the 1950's concluded that their sons were more apt to be named for maternal grandparents and maternal collateral kin and less likely to be named for paternal relatives than in the 1920's. Girls were more likely to be named for paternal grandparents and paternal collateral kin and less apt to derive names from maternal grandparents and aunts than in the 1920's. Such a tendency, like the popularity of neutral names, could become even more conspicuous as our culture sidesteps toward depolarization. See Alice S. Rossi, "Naming Children in Middle Class Families," *American Sociological Review,* 30, 1965, pp. 499–513.

19 A. Caswell Ellis and G. Stanley Hall, "A Study of Dolls," in Hall, *Aspects of Child Life and Education.* New York: D. Appleton, 1921, pp. 157–204.

20 Mariann A. Winick, "Little Girls and Their Dolls." Unpublished manuscript.

21 "A Psychiatrist in Toyland," KMPC, Los Angeles, February 27, 1966.

22 Dr. Jacob Goldstein, personal communication.

23 Erik H. Erikson, *Childhood and Society.* New York: Norton, 1950, pp. 182, 194, 202, 209.

24 Gordon F. Ekholm, "Wheeled Toys in Mexico," *American Antiquity,* 11, 1946, pp. 222–228.

25 Karl Bühler, *The Mental Development of the Child.* New York: Harcourt, Brace, 1930, pp. 96–106.

26 Elizabeth Janeway, "Young Reader's Companions," *New York Times,* November 10, 1963, Section VII, Part 2, p. 1; Julius E. Heuscher, *A Psychiatric Study of Fairy Tales.* Springfield: Charles C. Thomas, 1963.

27 Charles Winick, "The World of the Young Viewers," in Ralph Garry, F. B. Rainsberry, and Charles Winick, *For the Young Viewer.* New York: McGraw-Hill, 1962, pp. 143–173.

28 Theodor Reik, *Psychology of Sex Relations.* New York: Rinehart, 1945, p. 117.

29 George Norvell, *What Boys and Girls Like to Read* (New York: Silver Burdett, 1958, p. 39) reported on the reading habits of 1,576 boys and girls in the third through sixth grades and concluded that fairy tales ranked last of the eight categories of their reading, in average interest score. Another national study concluded that fairy tales were the least popular of seventeen categories of children's reading, even in the 6–9 age group. See National Broadcasting Company, *Young People, Their Activities and Interests,* 1962, p. 47.

30 Eleanor M. Johnson, "What Is Happening to Children's Story-Books?" *Reading Teacher,* 17, 1963, pp. 178–181.

31 Anne T. Eaton, *Reading with Children.* New York: Viking Press, 1949, p. 66.

32 Leonard Baskin, "The Black Rainbow," *New York Herald Tribune,* Book Week Spring Children's Festival, May 10, 1964, pp. 28–29.

33 *Help Them to Grow Every Day,* Catalog of Creative Playthings, 1964, p. 27.

34 Hilde T. Himmelweit, A. N. Oppenheim, and Pamela Vince, *Television and the Child.* New York: Oxford University Press, 1958; Leonard M. Lansky, Vaughn T. Crandall, and Jerome Kagan, "Sex Differences in Aggression and Its Correlates in Middle Class Adolescents," *Child Development,* 32, 1961, pp. 45–58. Eleanor E. Maccoby et al., *The Development of Sex Differences* (Stanford: Stanford University Press, 1966) provides the most thorough coverage of this subject.

35 Talcott Parsons, "Age and Sex in the Social Structure," *American Sociological Review,* 7, 1942, pp. 604–616.

36 Judith Kranes, "What About Children's Allowances?," *Understanding the Child*, 26, 1957, pp. 13–17.

37 "Report on Children's Wear," *New York Times*, August 11, 1963, Section 6, Part 2.

38 Dick Schaap, "Tomorrow the World," *New York Herald Tribune*, August 6, 1965.

39 *New York Times*, August 11, 1963, *op. cit.*

40 Reik, *op. cit.*, p. 117.

41 Study conducted by the author in the metropolitan New York area in 1956 with 1,203 high school students. The questions were put to young people who were being interviewed as part of a larger study. See Charles Winick, "Tendency Systems and the Effects of a Movie Dealing with a Social Problem," *Journal of General Psychology*, 68, 1963, pp. 289–305.

Chapter 7

1 James Laver, *Style in Costume*. London: Oxford University Press, 1949.

2 Nan Ickeringill, "And the Bride Wore Pants," *New York Times*, February 16, 1966, p. 38.

3 "Shirts for Women Show Rise in Sales," *New York Times*, May 31, 1964, Section 3, p. 1, 7.

4 *New Statesman*, December 10, 1965, p. 944.

5 Marylin Bender, "They Agree on Who Wears the Pants: Everybody," *New York Times*, February 15, 1966, p. 29.

6 Russell Baker, *New York Times*, September 2, 1965.

7 Eugenia Sheppard, "Especially for Saturday," *New York Herald Tribune*, December 14, 1964, p. 12.

8 John Weitz, personal communication.

9 *Aubrey's Brief Lives*. Ann Arbor: University of Michigan Press, 1957, pp. 212–214.

10 "Sequins for Him, by Scott," *New York World Journal Tribune*, January 16, 1967, p. 9.

11 "A Transvestite Gets Legal Help," *New York Times*, October 13, 1964, p. 45.

12 George Auerbach, "If Men's Styles Never Change, Where Have Shoulders Gone?" *New York Times*, February 28, 1960, Section 3, p. 1.

13 "Leonardo Strassi," *New York Times Report on Men's Wear*, September 15, 1963, pp. 79–81.

14 Bureau of Applied Social Research, *A Conceptual Analysis of Motivation in Men's Clothing Behavior*, New York: The Bureau, 1949.

15 *New York Times*, October 24, 1965, p. F11.

16 Dan Jenkins, "Sporting Look," *Sports Illustrated*, April 25, 1966, p. 87.

17 Sal Nuccio, "Advertising: The Clothes-Conscious Man," *New York Times,* August 9, 1964, Section F, p. 14.

18 "New Look for a Man in Revolt," *New York Times,* March 4, 1966, p. 20.

19 E. R. Van Liew, "Fragrance and the American Male," *The Givaudanian,* May 1960, pp. 3–5.

20 "Fragrances Gain Favor Among Men," *New York Times,* December 6, 1963, p. 31.

21 Max Weber, *The Protestant Ethic and the Spirit of Capitalism.* New York: Scribner's, 1958, pp. 170–171.

22 Chris Welles, "Big Boom in Men's Beauty Aids: Not By Soap Alone," *Life,* August 13, 1965, pp. 39–40.

23 Mary Burt Baldwin, "Toiletries Catching on with Men, Stores Find," *New York Times,* December 6, 1962.

24 Russell Baker, "Smelling Like a New Man," *New York Times,* December 2, 1965, p. 40.

25 A study of men by the Crane Company, "Shower or Bath?," June 24, 1964, concluded that 63 percent showered, 25 percent took both baths and showers, and 12 percent took only baths. A study of women's bathing preferences conducted by the author in 1961 concluded that 36 percent showered, 41 percent took baths and showers, and 23 percent took only baths.

26 Vic Scher, "Sixty Million Men," *Beauty Fashion,* April 1965, pp. 40–41.

27 "The Young at Zero Cool," *Harper's Bazaar,* April 1965, p. 151.

28 Russell Baker, "Observer," *New York Times,* September 16, 1965.

29 "A Stylist Even Cuts a Man's Hair," *New York Times,* October 26, 1965, p. 37.

30 Norton Mockridge, *New York World Telegram and Sun,* January 24, 1966, p. 19.

31 *New York World Telegram and Sun,* November 26, 1965, p. 2.

32 Charles Winick, "The Folklore of Shoes," *Boot and Shoe Recorder,* 156, October 15, 1959, pp. 98–99, 190–194; "Women and Their Shoes," *Boot and Shoe Recorder,* 156, October 15, 1959, pp. 102–103, 178–182; "Status, Shoes, and the Life Cycle," *Boot and Shoe Recorder,* 156, October 15, 1959, pp. 100–101, 199–203; "Men and Their Shoes," *Boot and Shoe Recorder,* 157, January 15, 1960, pp. 42–58.

33 Mrs. Jane S. Droutman, of the Quaker Committee on Social Rehabilitation in New York, first called the author's attention to this attitude.

34 Weston La Barre, "Obscenity: An Anthropological Appraisal," *Law and Contemporary Problems,* 20, 1955, p. 541.

35 Eugenia Sheppard, "The Well-Decorated Leg," *New York Herald Tribune,* January 17, 1964.

36 "Remedy for Dumpling Knees," *New York Herald Tribune,* February 13, 1966, Section 2, p. 4.

37 "Total Market for Over-the-foot Footwear," News Release from National Shoe Manufacturers Association, March 16, 1964.

38 "Men Following in Women's Footsteps," *New York Times,* June 5, 1962.

39 M. R. Reed, "The Masculinity-Femininity Dimension in Normal and Psychotic Subjects," *Journal of Abnormal and Social Psychology,* 55, 1957, pp. 289–294.

40 John Weitz, "The Shape of Our Morality." Unpublished manuscript.

41 Several Columns by Eugenia Sheppard in the *New York Herald Tribune* dealt with this theme.

42 William James, *Psychology.* New York: Henry Holt, 1892, pp. 177–178.

43 Wardell B. Pomeroy, "An Analysis of Questions on Sex," *Psychological Record,* 10, 1960, pp. 191–201.

44 Gregory P. Stone, "Appearance and the Self," in Arnold M. Rose, editor, *Human Behavior and Social Processes: An Interactionist Approach.* Boston: Houghton Mifflin, 1962, pp. 86–118.

Chapter 8

1 John Herbers, "For Instance, Can She Pitch for Mets?" *New York Times,* August 20, 1965, p. 1.

2 Donald N. Michael, "Some Speculations on the Social Impact of Technology," in Dean Morse and Aaron Warner, *Technological Innovation and Society.* New York: Columbia University Press, 1966.

3 "De-Sexing the Job Market," *New York Times,* August 21, 1965, p. 20.

4 This discussion is primarily concerned with the middle-class family; "working-class" families, even in a suburban community like Levittown, New York, still have much conjugal segregation of roles. See William Dobriner, *Class in Suburbia.* New York: Prentice-Hall, 1963, pp. 85–126.

5 Lester Rand, Youth Research Institute, personal communication, December 16, 1964.

6 David B. Lynn, "Divergent Feedback and Sex-Role Identification in Boys and Men," *Merrill-Palmer Quarterly,* 10, 1964, pp. 17–23.

7 Urie Bronfenbrenner, "The Changing American Child—A Speculative Analysis," *Merrill-Palmer Quarterly,* 7, 1961, pp. 73–84.

8 Charles Winick and Herbert Holt, "Differential Recall of the Dream as a Function of Audience Perception," *Psychoanalysis and the Psychoanalytic Review,* 49, 1962, pp. 53–62.

9 Calvin Hall and B. Domhoff, "A Ubiquitous Sex Difference in Dreams," *Journal of Abnormal and Social Psychology,* 66, 1963, pp. 278–280.

10 Otto Ehrenberg, "Concepts of Masculinity, a Study of Discrepancies

Between Men's Self-Concepts and Two Different Ideal Concepts and Their Relationship to Mental Health," doctoral dissertation, New York University, 1960. There is a vast literature on the sociology of sex roles. Some representative studies are in Talcott Parsons, *Essays in Sociological Theory.* New York: Free Press, 1954, pp. 298–322; Mirra Komarovsky, "Functional Analysis of Sex Roles," *American Sociological Review,* 15, 1950, pp. 508–516; Philip Slater, "Parental Role Differentiation," *American Journal of Sociology,* 67, 1961, pp. 296–311; Rose Laub Coser, "Authority and Structural Ambivalence in the Middle Class Family," in Coser, editor, *The Family, Its Structure and Functions.* New York: St. Martin's, 1964, pp. 370–383.

11 Margaret Mead, "Cultural Determinants of Sexual Behavior," in W. C. Young, editor, *Sex and Internal Secretions.* Baltimore: Williams and Wilkins, 1961, pp. 1433–1479.

12 Mary C. Kohler and Andre Fontaine, "Are You Cheating Your Children Out of a Living?," *Good Housekeeping,* September 1963, pp. 76, 128.

13 Charles Richard Dolan, "An Investigation of the Authoritarian Figures in the Lives of Adolescents as Measured by a Forced-Choice Instrument," doctoral dissertation, Boston University, 1960.

14 John E. Kysar and Misha S. Zaks, "The War-Born Children Twenty Years Later," paper presented to the First International Congress of Social Psychiatry, London, August, 1964.

15 G. R. Bach, "Father Fantasies and Father-Typing in Father-Separated Children," *Child Development,* 17, 1946, pp. 63–80; Pauline T. Sears, "Doll Play Aggression in Normal Children: Influence of Sex, Age, Sibling Status, Father's Absence," *Psychological Monographs,* 65 (6), 1951; Lois M. Stolz, *Father Relations of Warborn Children.* Palo Alto: Stanford University Press, 1951.

16 Herbert Holt and Charles Winick, "Some Psychodynamics in Divorce and Separation, *Mental Hygiene,* 49, 1965, pp. 443–452.

17 J. Richard Udry, "Complementarity in Mate Selection: A Perceptual Approach," *Marriage and Family Living,* 25, 1963, pp. 281–289; see also M. F. Ashley Montagu, "Marriage: A Cultural Perspective," in V. W. Eisenstein, editor, *Neurotic Interaction in Marriage.* New York: Basic Books, 1956, pp. 57–64.

18 Alice Taylor Day, "Divorce Down Under," *Columbia University Forum,* 7, 1964, pp. 19–22.

19 Mary Ellen Leary, "Our 'New Women' No Glamor Gal, says Johnson Aide," *New York World Telegram,* February 10, 1964.

20 Christie Rieuf, "Praying Mantises," *Atlas,* April 1961, pp. 40–45.

21 Thanks are due Professor David Riesman for calling this to the author's attention.

22 Carl F. Sulzberger, "Psychoanalysis and the Future of Sexuality," in Benjamin Nelson, editor, *Psychoanalysis and the Future.* New York: National Psychological Association for Psychoanalysis, 1959, pp. 107–116.

23 "Cigarette Sales Are Rebounding," *New York Times*, Section 3, March 15, 1964, pp. 1, 14.

24 Charles Winick, Statement on S. 559 and S. 547, 89th Congress, U.S. Senate Hearings, March 22–30, 1965, Serial 89-S, pp. 953–956.

25 Fred Astaire, *Steps in Time*. New York: Harper, 1959, pp. 233–234.

26 Ruth Benedict, "Continuities and Discontinuities in Cultural Conditioning," *Psychiatry*, 1, 1938, pp. 161–167, called attention to discontinuities at crucial points in the life cycle.

27 Eugenia Sheppard, "Better Dressed Than Mother," *New York Herald Tribune*, April 17, 1963; "Mother Is a Pre-Teen," *New York Herald Tribune*, December 16, 1964.

28 "Is Childhood Old-Fashioned?" *New York Sunday News*, January 12, 1964, pp. 80–81.

29 *New York Times*, January 10, 1967, p. 47.

30 Leo Lowenthal, *Literature, Popular Culture, and Society*. New York: Prentice-Hall, 1961, p. 121.

31 Irene M. Josselyn, *Psychosocial Development of Children*. New York: Family Service Association of America, 1956, pp. 75–92; Otto Fenichel, *Psychoanalytic Theory of Neurosis*. New York: Norton, 1945, pp. 62, 110.

32 J. D. Unwin, *Sexual Regulation and Human Behavior*. London: Williams and Norgate, 1933.

33 *Look*, May 17, 1966, p. 58.

34 *New York Sunday News*, January 12, 1964, pp. 80–81.

35 Charles Winick, "Maturing Out of Narcotic Addiction," *U.N. Bulletin on Narcotics*, 14, 1962, pp. 1–7; "Epidemiology of Narcotics Use," in D. M. Wilner and G. G. Kassebaum, *Narcotics*. New York: McGraw-Hill, 1965, pp. 3–18.

36 The quotations are from Thomas Mann, *Stories of Three Decades*. New York: Modern Library, 1936, p. 432.

Chapter 9

1 C. Van Emde Boas, "Sex Life in Europe," in A. Ellis and A. Abarbanel, editors, *The Encyclopedia of Sexual Behavior*, Vol. I. New York: Hawthorne, 1961, pp. 373–383.

2 R. T. Anderson and G. Anderson, "Sexual Behavior and Urbanization in a Danish Village," *Southwestern Journal of Anthropology*, 16, 1960, pp. 93–103; H. Hoffmeyer, "Anti-conception," *Ugeskrift for Laeger*, 113, 1951, pp. 569 ff.

3 G. Jonsson, "Sexual vanor has avensk ungdom," *In Ungdomen Moter Samhället*. Ungdomsvardskommittens sluthekankarde. Stockholm: 1951; C. Melbye, *Studentmoral*. Oslo: Universitas, No. 7–8, 1946; K. Svalastoga, "The Family Life in Scandinavia," *Marriage and Family Living*, 16, 1954, pp. 374–380.

4 The scale was a ten-point Guttman type; see H. T. Christensen

and G. R. Carpenter, "Value Discrepancies Regarding Premarital Coitus in Three Western Cultures," *American Sociological Review,* 27, 1962, pp. 66–74; and "Timing Patterns in Premarital Sexual Intimacy, an attitudinal report on three modern western societies," *Marriage and Family Living,* 24, 1962, pp. 30–35.

5 Alfred C. Kinsey, W. B. Pomeroy, C. E. Martin, and P. H. Gebhard, *Sexual Behavior in the Human Female.* Philadelphia: Saunders, 1953, pp. 288–307; Kirsten Auken, *Undersogeleer over Unge Kvinders Sexualle Adfaerd.* Kebenhaun: Rosenkilde og bagger; Oslo: Olaf Norlis Bokhandel; Stockholm: Almguist and Wiksell, 1953. The subsample consisted of 235 women between 20 and 35, with a mean age of 26.

6 The 1920's average of 335 cases of gonorrhea per 100,000 dropped in the 1930's to 262, and in the mid-1950's to 174 per 100,000. Comparable figures for syphilis are 70 per 100,000 in the 1920's, 21 in the 1930's, and 5 per 100,000 in the 1950's. See *Medical Report for the Kingdom of Denmark, 1960.* Copenhagen: National Health Service of Denmark, 1963, pp. 51–53.

7 Wardell B. Pomeroy, *New York Mattachine Newsletter,* 9 (4), 1964, pp. 3–4.

8 Lillian B. Redcay, "Adolescent Reactions to a Film Regarding Premarital Sex Experiences," doctoral dissertation, Pennsylvania State University, 1964.

9 *New York Times,* March 14, 1964; *Columbia Spectator,* November 22, 1963, p. 1.

10 Mervin B. Freedman, "The Sexual Behavior of American College Women: An Empirical Study and An Historical Survey," *Merrill-Palmer Quarterly,* 11, 1965, pp. 33–48.

11 The 1938–1957 percentages applied in all three basic indicators of illegitimacy: number, ratio, and rate. Number indicates the total volume; ratio is the number of illegitimate births per 1,000 live births; rate is the number of illegitimate births per 1,000 unmarried females of childbearing age and is the most reliable measure because it considers the total number of unmarried females in each age group. The 1957–1963 change applied to ratio and rate. During this six-year period, the increase in the number of illegitimate births to teen-agers reflected an increase in teen-age females in the population as a result of the 1945–1947 baby boom. See Clark E. Vincent, "Teen-Age Unwed Mothers in American Society," *Journal of Social Issues,* 22, 1966, pp. 22–33.

12 Stanton Wheeler, "Sex Offenses: A Sociological Critique," *Law and Contemporary Problems,* 25, 1960, pp. 267–268; Alfred C. Kinsey, Wardell B. Pomeroy, and Clyde E. Martin, *Sexual Behavior in the Human Male.* Philadelphia: Saunders, 1948, p. 354; J. Dreyfus-Moreau, "A Propos de Quelques Facteurs Favorisant l'Impuissance," *L'Evolution Psychiatrique,* 29, 1964, pp. 437–458.

13 William L. Langer, "The Black Death," *Scientific American,* 210, February 1964, pp. 114–121.

14   Udo Derbolowsky, "Two Years of Discussion Groups." Paper presented to First International Congress on Social Psychiatry, London, August 1964.

15   A. Margoshes and S. Litt, "Sexual Appetite and Sexual Drive," *Psychological Reports,* 16, 1965, pp. 713–719.

16   F. Rigney and D. Smith, *The Real Bohemia.* New York: Basic Books, 1961.

17   Study conducted by the author in 1960, with a national probability sample of 1,800 adults.

18   Charles Winick, "Anthropology's Contribution to Marketing," *Journal of Marketing,* 25, 1961, pp. 53–60.

19   Alan F. Guttmacher, *Pregnancy and Birth.* New York: Signet, 1956, p. 130; see also "Seasonal Variations of Births, United States, 1933–63," *Public Health Service Publication No. 1000,* Series 21, No. 9, 1966.

20   Eric J. Dingwall, *The American Woman.* New York: Signet, 1958, p. 225; Reginald Reynolds, *Beds.* New York: Doubleday, 1951, p. 193.

21   The major mattress manufacturer reports that one-third of the sales of his line of double beds are represented by super-size.

22   Kinsey, 1953, *op. cit.,* pp. 257–258, 587; Kinsey, 1948, *op. cit.,* 176–187.

23   William S. Masters and Virginia E. Johnson, *Human Sexual Response.* Boston: Little Brown, 1966.

24   Helene Deutsch, *Psychology of Women.* New York: Grune and Stratton, 1944, Vol. I, p. 233.

25   Clellan S. Ford and Frank A. Beach, *Patterns of Sexual Behavior.* New York: Harper, 1951, p. 105.

26   *Medical Tribune,* October 18, 1965, pp. 1, 8.

27   John E. Eichenlaub, *The Marriage Art.* New York: Dell, 1962, pp. 107–108.

28   Clifford Kirkpatrick and E. Kanin, "Male Sex Aggression on a University Campus," *American Sociological Review,* 20, 1957, pp. 52–58.

29   Margaret Mead, "The Study of National Character," in Daniel Lerner and Harold D. Lasswell, editors, *The Policy Sciences.* Stanford: Stanford University Press, 1951, p. 83.

30   Zsa Zsa Gabor, *My Story.* Cleveland: World, 1960; Elizabeth Taylor, *Elizabeth Taylor, An Informal Memoir.* New York: Harper and Row, 1965.

31   Linda Christian, *Linda, My Own Story.* New York: Crown, 1962, p. 47.

32   Jean Antel, "Julie Christie: I Am Not 'Darling,' " *New York Times,* November 21, 1965, p. X11; May Okon, "Movies' Voom Girl," *New York Sunday News,* March 13, 1966, p. 8.

33   Lee Rainwater, *Family Design* (Chicago: Aldine, 1965, pp. 209–210) suggests that the condom is still the best known contraceptive procedure.

34   From the dust jacket of Robert A. Wilson, *Feminine Forever.* New

York: M. Evans and Co., 1966. The Food and Drug Administration, however, has raised questions about some of the claims made for birth-control pills in preventing menopause. See *New York Times*, November 17, 1966, p. 30.

35 Ernest Hemingway, "A Matter of Measurements," in *A Moveable Feast*. New York: Scribner, 1964, pp. 189–193.

36 G. V. Hamilton, *A Research in Marriage*. New York: Albert and Charles Boni, 1929, pp. 174–179; Kinsey, 1948, *op. cit.*, pp. 368–373.

37 These figures derive from interviews conducted since 1961 with prostitutes in over 100 American cities, to be reported in a forthcoming paper by Charles Winick and Paul M. Kinsie. See also Charles Winick, "Prostitutes' Clients' Perception of the Prostitutes and of Themselves," *International Journal of Social Psychiatry*, 8, 1963, pp. 289–297.

38 Josephine H. Ross, "A Cultural Change As Reflected in Verbalizations Dealing with Sex," *Psychoanalysis*, 4, 1955, pp. 3–11; "Justinian," *Americana Sexualis*. Chicago: The Author, 1939. The descriptiveness of sexual slang has been documented more recently in the cross-cultural studies conducted by Dr. Bernard Lander of Hunter College. In the North Kenmore area of Chicago, "cutting" is used for coitus, which is usually associated with violence and weekend binges. On East 100th Street in New York, where it is called "scheming," coitus is a manipulative, planned activity.

39 Hamilton, *op. cit.;* Kinsey, 1953, *op. cit.*, p. 371.

40 John P. Brady and Eugene E. Levitt, "The Scalability of Sexual Preferences," *Psychological Record*, 15, 1965, pp. 275–279.

41 Alfred C. Kinsey, Wardell B. Pomeroy, Clyde E. Martin, and Paul H. Gebhard, "Concepts of Normality and Abnormality in Social Behavior," in *Psychosexual Development in Health and Disease*. New York: Grune and Stratton, 1949, pp. 11–32.

42 Dr. Herbert Holt first called this approach to the author's attention.

43 Barrie Shaw, "Sex Populars in the Rorschach," doctoral dissertation, University of Kentucky, 1949.

44 Dr. Meyer Maskin suggested this terminology.

45 Joseph A. Loftus, "Postwar Population Leap Is Dwindling to a Brisk Hop," *New York Times*, January 17, 1966.

46 The crude birth rate goes from 24.7 per 1,000 in 1955–60 to 22.3 in 1980–85, in the projections reported in Pascal K. Whelpton, Arthur A. Campbell, and John E. Patterson, *Fertility and Family Planning in the United States*. Princeton: Princeton University Press, 1966, p. 401. No discussion of fertility can ignore changes in socio-economic status: see Ronald Freedman, "The Sociology of Human Fertility," *Current Sociology*, 10, 1961, pp. 53–59.

47 Charles Winick, "Dear Sir or Madam, As the Case May Be," *Antioch Review*, 23, 1963, pp. 35–49.

48 Bruce Ogilvie, "The Social Setting of Homosexuality," California

Health Department Venereal Disease Control Informational Report #8, 1964, p. 8.

49 Charles Winick, "Celebrities' Errancy as a Subject for Journalism: A Study of *Confidential*," *Gazette*, 7, 1962, pp. 329–334; "Thoughts and Feelings of the General Population as Expressed in Free Association Typing," *American Imago*, 19, 1962, pp. 67–84.

50 By Henny and Jim Backus. New York: Prentice-Hall, 1962.

51 Goeffrey Gorer, *Hot Strip Tease*. London: Cresset Press, 1937.

52 Christopher Isherwood, *Prater Violet*. New York: Random House, 1945, p. 92.

53 Nelson N. Foote, "Masculinity and Femininity," paper presented to Conference of Sex Information and Education Council of U.S., Washington, D.C., December 2, 1966; J. L. Simmons and Barry Winograd, *It's Happening*. Santa Barbara: Marc-Laird, 1966, p. 106.

54 Herbert Blumer et al, *The World of Youthful Drug Use*. Berkeley: University of California School of Criminology, 1967, p. 59.

55 Charles Winick, "Marihuana Use By Young People," in Ernest Harms, editor, *Drug Addiction in Youth*. New York: Pergamon Press, 1965, pp. 19–35; "Narcotics Addiction and Its Treatment," *Law and Contemporary Problems*, 22, 1957, pp. 9–33.

56 Nathan Adler, "LSD and Campus Culture," paper presented to the California Psychological Association, San Francisco, January 28, 1966.

57 Charles Winick, "The Remora Syndrome: Sick Characteristics in Search of an Author," *Business Horizons*, 6, 1963, pp. 63–72.

58 Samuel A. Stouffer, *Communism, Conformity, and Civil Liberties*. New York: Doubleday, 1955.

59 Hadley Cantril, *The Invasion from Mars*. Princeton: Princeton University Press, 1940, pp. 155–158.

60 Charles Winick, "How People Perceived 'The Mad Bomber,'" *Public Opinion Quarterly*, 25, 1961, pp. 25–38.

61 Leo Srole et al., *Mental Health in the Metropolis*. New York: McGraw-Hill, 1962.

62 Ian L. McHarg, "Man and Environment," in Leonard J. Duhl, editor, *The Urban Condition*. New York: Basic Books, 1963, pp. 44–58.

63 Arthur and Norma Sue Woodstone, "In the Blackout and Transit Strike, How Did New Yorkers Really Act?" *Herald Tribune*, New York, February 20, 1966, pp. 7–10.

64 Charles Winick, "Atonie: The Unemployed and the Marginal Worker," in George Fisk, editor, *The Frontiers of Management*. New York: Harper and Row, 1964, pp. 269–286.

Chapter 10

1 C. M. Bowra, *The Greek Experience*. Cleveland: World, 1957, p. 28.

2   H. D. F. Kitto, *The Greeks.* Harmondsworth: Penguin, 1951, pp. 152–170.

3   H. A. Harris, *Greek Athletes and Athletics.* London: Hutchinson, 1964, pp. 182–184.

4   Richard Lewinsohn, *A History of Sexual Customs.* New York: Fawcett, 1961, pp. 43 et seq.

5   Reasons suggested to explain the decline include ineffectiveness of the elite (Seeck), physical degeneration (Kaphen), racial decline (Frank), the diminution of slavery (Weber), class struggle (Rostovtzeff), the failure of response to a challenge at a time of moral crisis (Toynbee), and barbarian invasion (Piganiol). See M. C. D'Arcy, *The Meaning and Matter of History.* New York: Meridian, 1961.

6   Ronald Syme, *The Roman Revolution.* Oxford: Oxford University Press, 1939.

7   C. L. Sulzberger, "Caesarism in Democracy," *New York Times,* March 2, 1966, p. 40.

8   David Mace, *Does Sex Morality Matter?* London: Rich and Cowan, 1943.

9   Lev Trotsky, *History of the Russian Revolution.* New York: Simon and Schuster, 1932, Vol. 1, pp. 91–95.

10   T. W. Adorno, E. Frenkel-Brunswik, D. J. Levinson, R. Nevitt Sanford, *The Authoritarian Personality.* New York: Harper, 1950, pp. 480–481.

11   John Money, "Developmental Differentiation of Femininity and Masculinity Compared," in Seymour M. Farber and Roger H. L. Wilson, editors, *The Potential of Women.* New York: McGraw-Hill, 1963, pp. 62–63.

12   Robert S. Morison, "Where Is Biology Taking Us?" *Science,* January 27, 1967, pp. 429–433.

13   *New York Herald Tribune,* April 7, 1966, p. 3; Jane E. Brody, "Egg Fertilized Outside the Body; Aid to Infertile Women Foreseen," *New York Times,* March 4, 1966, p. 21.

14   Maureen Cleave, "Mary Quant, Limited—Kinky Success Story," *New York Times Magazine,* March 19, 1967, p. 70.

15   Don D. Jackson, "Family Rules: Marital Quid Pro Quo," *Archives of General Psychiatry,* 12, 1965, p. 589.

16   John A. Osmundsen, "U.S. Scientists Are Urged to Recreate Life," *New York Times,* September 14, 1965.

17   Edward Gibbon, *Decline and Fall of the Roman Empire.* New York: Harcourt, Brace, 1960, p. 525.

18   Herbert Holt and Charles Winick, "The Consention Approach to Dreams," *Journal of Existential Psychiatry,* 1, 1960, pp. 219–232.

19   Asya L. Kadis and Charles Winick, "The Role of the Deviant in the Therapy Group," *International Journal of Social Psychiatry,* 6, 1960, pp. 277–287; Florida Scott-Maxwell, *Women and Sometimes Men.* New York: Alfred A. Knopf, 1957.

20 Otto Weininger, *Geschlecht und Charakter.* Wien: W. Braumüller, 1905.

21 Erich Fromm, "Sex and Character," in *The Dogma of Christ.* New York: Holt, Rinehart, and Winston, 1963, pp. 107–130.

22 Mathilde and Mathias Vaerting, *The Dominant Sex.* New York: Doran, 1923.

23 The most thorough review of the literature on differences between the male and female death rate is Wilson T. Sowder et al., *Man to Man Talk About Women and Men.* Jacksonville: Florida State Board of Health, 1966, Monograph No. 10.

24 "What's Happening to America?," *Partisan Review,* Winter 1967, pp. 1–20.

25 The group of integers modulo 2 is a set consisting of two elements 0 and 1 together with a rule of addition as follows: $1 + 1 = 0$; $1 + 0 = 1$; $0 + 0 = 0$. It forms an algebraic group and is similar to the ordinary set of integers, i.e., $0, \pm 1, \pm 2, \pm 3 \ldots$, in that the familiar laws of addition are still valid: the associative law $[(a + b) + c = a + (b + c)]$, the commutative law $[a + b = b + a]$, the zero law $[a + 0 = a]$, and the inverse law [for every number a there is a number b such that $a + b = 0$].

DATE DUE

APR 17 '74			
MAY 8 '74			
MAY 8 '74			
GAYLORD			PRINTED IN U.S.A.